Law and Philosophy Library

Volume 146

The Law and Philosophy Library, which has been in existence since 1985, aims to publish cutting edge works in the philosophy of law, and has a special history of publishing books that focus on legal reasoning and argumentation, including those that may involve somewhat formal methodologies. The series has published numerous important books on law and logic, law and artificial intelligence, law and language, and law and rhetoric. While continuing to stress these areas, the series has more recently expanded to include books on the intersection between law and the Continental philosophical tradition, consistent with the traditional openness of the series to books in the Continental jurisprudential tradition. The series is proud of the geographic diversity of its authors, and many have come from Latin America, Spain, Italy, the Netherlands, Germany, and Eastern Europe, as well, more obviously for an English-language series, from the United Kingdom, the United States, Australia and Canada.

Deryck Beyleveld • Stefano Bertea
Editors

Theories of Legal Obligation

Springer

Editors
Deryck Beyleveld
Durham Law School
Durham University
Durham, UK

Stefano Bertea
Department of Law
University of Messina
Messina, Italy

ISSN 1572-4395 ISSN 2215-0315 (electronic)
Law and Philosophy Library
ISBN 978-3-031-54066-0 ISBN 978-3-031-54067-7 (eBook)
https://doi.org/10.1007/978-3-031-54067-7

This Springer imprint is published by the registered company Springer Nature Switzerland AG
The registered company address is: Gewerbestrasse 11, 6330 Cham, Switzerland

Paper in this product is recyclable.

Contents

Introduction

Deryck Beyleveld and Stefano Bertea

This volume collects six original essays on different dimensions of the concept of legal obligation. Earlier versions of these essays were first presented at the Workshop on 'Legal Obligation' held at the Law School of Durham University on 16 February 2022. This event was made possible by a generous contribution from the Institute of Advanced Study, Durham University. We are grateful to the Directors of the Institute—Alexander Easton, Nayanika Mookherjee, and Patrick Zuk—for their encouragement, stimuli, and support.

The discussion carried out at the workshop and further developed during the preparation of this collection of essays had three main directions. First, some of the contributors addressed the question, 'What is a Legal Obligation?', viewed as an ontological question, to which two distinct yet broadly coherent answers are given.

Lorenz Kaehler claims that we can grasp the real nature of legal obligation by reflecting on reasons that support the conventional understanding of the kind of obligation engendered by the law. He argues that such a reason-based approach, which contrasts both with linguistic analyses and conceptual analyses of legal obligation, has the potential to unlock the necessary and sufficient traits of a legal obligation. He claims that there are four such traits: ontological ideality, reference to an action, reference to a person who is capable of acting, and normativity. He further argues that the existence of an obligee and the issuance of a sanction for the breach of an obligation are not necessary components of a legal obligation.

Stefano Bertea agrees with Kaehler that reference to linguistic usage and local conventions are ill suited to give us insight into the ontology of legal obligation. He also agrees that existence in thought (hence immateriality) is an essential dimension

D. Beyleveld
Durham University, Durham Law School, Durham, UK
e-mail: deryck.beyleveld@durham.ac.uk

S. Bertea (✉)
University of Messina, Department of Law, Messina, Italy

D. Beyleveld, S. Bertea (eds.), *Theories of Legal Obligation*, Law and Philosophy Library 146, https://doi.org/10.1007/978-3-031-54067-7_1

of what is legally obligatory. From these premises, he develops an account that differs in part from Kaehler's in depicting legal obligation as an abstract, collective and created object that exists in time whilst lacking any distinctive spatial dimension.

The second part of this volume is devoted to two non-positivist theories of legal obligation.

Deryck Beyleveld criticises the positivist attempt to offer a morally neutral understanding of legal obligation. He disputes any idea that a legal obligation just is what an obligation-asserting rule of law requires. Compliance with an obligation-asserting rule of a legal system is, in his view, an obligation only if there is a moral obligation to obey the rule, and a specifically legal obligation arises only if the legal system is morally authorised to promulgate it. His essay systematically defends this two-pronged claim by arguing (by synthesising the arguments of Immanuel Kant and Alan Gewirth for the existence of a categorical imperative, which he claims employ the same methodology) that positivists depict law as a system of hypothetical imperatives without realising that hypothetical imperatives cannot be understood in isolation from the concept of a categorical imperative and that merely understanding the concept of a categorical imperative together with the idea that it can be thought requires assent to its existence as a specific moral principle, Gewirth's Principle of Generic Consistency.

Martin Borowski explores Gustav Radbruch's alternative non-positivist approach to legal obligation. After explaining the reasons why Radbruch's legal thought has not been discussed to a greater extent in the Anglo-American literature, he introduces Radbruch's conception of legal obligation as an a priori normative concept rather than an empirical one according to which a legal obligation exists only insofar as one has an objective justificatory reason for moving from a conditioning fact to a conditioned consequence. Radbruch argues that this objective justification can only come from morality, which he claims can only bind in conscience. As a consequence, his theory of legal obligation associates a non-positivist account of law with evaluative, or axiological, relativism. Borowski finds this problematic because it results in a split, or dual, account of legal obligation. In this account, there may be a mismatch between the legal obligations that are acknowledged by legal officials and those that are recognised by legal subjects. For legal officials, a legal obligation exists if a legal statement has been authoritatively issued and is socially efficacious. By contrast, a legal subject recognises as legal obligatory only those statements of law that, in addition to being authoritatively issued and socially efficacious, can be considered non-iniquitous from the standpoint of the legal subject's own conscience.

In the third part and final part of this volume, Diego M. Papayannis and Noam Gur connect debates about legal obligation with closely connected discussions, respectively those about the existence of an obligation (or duty) to care in tort law and the notion of legal authority.

Papayannis embraces a rule-based view that combines elements of H.L.A. Hart's and Josef Raz's theories of legal obligation. On this view, a legal obligation is a rule of law that sets out what is *prima facie* socially right to do. As such, the existence of an obligation-stating rule gives legal subjects an independent justificatory reason to do what the law requires by excluding other considerations that may direct legal subjects to act otherwise. On this premise, Papayannis criticises existing arguments against the existence of a duty (or obligation) not to harm in tort law and offers an original argument to show that the legal duty not to harm others is a cornerstone of tort law in general, which enables him to critically assess the most influential general theories of tort law currently on offer.

Lastly, Gur's contribution is concerned with the idea of authority, which is conceptually bound up with the idea of legal obligation on the standard view that the existence of an obligation to obey the law presupposes the possibility of justifying the authority of law. Gur critically evaluates Raz's response to the paradox of authority claimed by philosophical anarchism (with particular reference to the work of Robert P. Wolff) and argues that Raz's stance does not completely vindicate the compatibility of moral autonomy and legal authority. Autonomy and authority *are* in tension and partially incompatible when a key dimension of the former, the subject's decision-making powers in the present, are at stake. While Raz's theory of authority is compatible with the recognition of a subject's capacity to devise future-oriented, or forward-looking, decision-making strategies, deference to legal authority (as Raz understands it) prevents us from independently setting our present courses of conduct.

Part I
What a Legal Obligation Is

Towards a Minimal Concept of Legal Obligation

Lorenz Kaehler

1 A Reason-Based Construction of Legal Obligation

In order to understand a legal obligation, it is important to find the properties that are necessary and sufficient for it to exist. Only then can one determine whether one bears an obligation or duty[1] and whether particular properties, such as sanctions, are necessary conditions for all obligations or only for some of them. There are three approaches that may be used to try to ascertain these properties, all of which face their own specific challenges. The first approach is to ask what the word 'obligation' means in a certain language, answering which requires one to investigate what competent speakers intend when they use this word and what role it plays in ordinary language.

Although this approach can reveal the underlying rationale of a linguistic practice, the analysis is confined to language usage. In discovering what is understood as an obligation, the question of what an obligation actually is remains open because obligations could have properties that have, to date, gone unnoticed and so not become part of their definition within a certain language. For instance, it could emerge that every obligation corresponds to a specific right without this being implied by the use of the word 'obligation'. Thus, a full understanding of the concept of obligation cannot be reached through a linguistic analysis alone. Legal theory is, after all, not confined to lexicography (Hart 1953, p. 21; Finnis 1980, p. 4).

[1] Both concepts will be used interchangeably in what follows.

L. Kaehler (✉)
University Bremen, Law faculty, Bremen, Germany
e-mail: lkaehler@uni-bremen.de

D. Beyleveld, S. Bertea (eds.), *Theories of Legal Obligation*, Law and Philosophy Library 146, https://doi.org/10.1007/978-3-031-54067-7_2

A second approach is to analyse the concept of an obligation within a certain legal system. In this case, one needs to investigate the obligations of a particular legal system and find out whether they have properties in common. This can be revealing because a legal system usually contains so many different obligations that the discovery of common properties can provide an insight into their general nature. Common properties throughout a multiplicity of obligations are hardly an accident.

However, if the analysis is confined to a single legal system, one could not be sure whether these features are only prevalent within this particular legal system or are also present within any other legal system. Also, without further argument, one could not tell whether the features of the investigated obligations are necessary or whether they just happen to be present in all of them. Conversely, a feature that all the obligations of a particular legal system lack might nevertheless be present in future cases so that one cannot deduce from its current absence that an obligation cannot have it as a matter of principle. Similarly, a legal system might prescribe only certain kinds of obligations and omit—for pragmatic reasons—other kinds for reasons that have nothing to do with the concept of an obligation. For instance, it might be the case that obligations in a certain legal system are always sanctioned in some way even though they would still be obligations if there were no sanctions for their breach. Consequently, legal theory cannot confine itself to the contingent features of one legal system alone and needs to be more than a dogmatic study of such a system.

But if neither language nor a legal system is a sufficient basis for an understanding of an obligation, what does suffice to explain it? What is an adequate basis upon which to ascertain the concept of a legal obligation? The third approach tries to avoid the previously mentioned difficulties by proposing an inquiry into the nature of an obligation on the basis that there is a natural concept of an obligation that is valid at all times, places, and in all legal systems.

However, such an approach is excessively demanding. It presupposes that there is only one natural concept of obligation and not a plurality of concepts between which different languages and legal systems can select. This presupposition is difficult to prove because one can, at the very least, imagine various concepts of obligations, such as narrow and broad ones. It seems unclear upon what basis one can choose from among them and decide which one is the right or natural one once particular languages and legal systems do not play a role in this. How can one be sure that a certain concept is valid throughout all times and places?

Fortunately, the choice between a concept of an obligation that is confined to a particular legal system, and a natural concept valid for all times and places, is not exhaustive. This is because it is possible to use current legal systems and their languages as a starting-point and to proceed by asking against this background which general concept of an obligation is the most plausible. Such a concept can not only build upon a developed concept but can also diverge from it if there are convincing reasons to do so. In this way, it is reasons—not contingent facts about a particular legal system or a particular language—that are ultimately decisive.

The point is that, in such an approach, the usages, understandings, and the distinctions of a particular language or legal system *can* be used unless there are convincing reasons not to do so. Experiences of both law and everyday practice might thus help to construct a general concept of a legal obligation without constituting its limits. The foundation of such a general concept lies in generally applicable reasons for finding it the most convincing. Because of their generality, these reasons do not depend upon one particular legal system or language but must still be informed by them. For, if a concept does not cover a norm that is commonly perceived as an obligation, either the concept must be changed or it must be proved that the perception of this norm is wrong.

Such a reason-based construction will be undertaken here. Against the background of modern legal systems, this chapter looks for properties that can, reasonably, be assumed to be necessary and sufficient for an obligation. This approach differs from conceptual analysis, at least as this is commonly understood (see Marmor and Sarch 2019) because it does not presuppose that there is an already established concept that merely needs to be analysed. Instead, a reason-based construction is open for the development of a new concept if there are reasons that support it. The most convincing concept of an obligation, hence, does not need to be conventional in nature.

Because the crucial question about any concept is, 'What are the necessary or sufficient properties for it to exist?', the chapter proceeds as follows. First, it investigates four necessary properties of a legal obligation. These are its ontological ideality, reference to an action, reference to a person who is capable of acting, and its required normativity. Secondly, in order to check whether these properties are sufficient, it looks at various additional properties that are sometimes thought to be necessary for a legal obligation. Among these properties are the existence of an obligee and of a sanction for the breach of an obligation. Thirdly, it argues that these additional properties, while widespread, are not necessary, so that the developed concept is comparatively minimal in its demands. This has the advantage that the core idea of an obligation is captured and not blurred by practices, which, for understandable reasons, merely use some, but not all kinds of, obligations.

To repeat, the aim of a reason-based construction is not merely to obtain a definition for its own sake but to illuminate the reasons that are decisive for it. Because these reasons help to answer controversial questions about obligations, they are what is ultimately of primary importance.

2 Necessary Properties

2.1 Ontological Ideality

In order to understand the nature of an obligation, it is first necessary to determine what kind of entity it is. It makes a difference whether one conceives of an obligation as a kind of social practice or, instead, as an abstract object. In this regard, it is interesting that one can impose an obligation on a person without any physical connection to him or her, or to the situation in which he or she is situated. For example, a statute might provide that employers as such have certain obligations towards their personnel. They are obligated, no matter how distant they are from the legislator or whether they have any physical link to the place of legislation. Even future employers can, thereby, already be obligated. That an obligation is in total or in part constituted by a physical link to the regulated situation is thus excluded.

This independence from the physical world is one of the reasons why legal obligations must be thought of as immaterial, even if they arise from legislative acts that are based upon material facts. Obligations cannot be confined to the physical world as it currently is. They must apply to states of affairs that might arise in the future. In this regard, they resemble other legal entities, such as rights and norms. All of them are immaterial and can refer to states of affairs that might or might not arise. If this were not the case, the possibility of regulating behaviour would be severely hampered. For example, duties towards future generations would, in principle, be excluded because of the lack of a physical link to them.

The immaterial character of obligations derives from the fact that they have propositional content, part of which is a reference to a required action or omission. Although this act or omission is regularly physical in nature, reference to it is nonetheless immaterial. Although expressed in a certain language it consists of a proposition that is independent of it and could also be formulated in another language. This is why obligations themselves must consist of propositional content. It is irrelevant whether or not the state of affairs to which an obligation refers holds. For this reason, an obligation can exist even though the obligated act has not been carried out or will never be carried out. It is the very purpose of obligations to refer to states of affairs that have to be brought about or realised, and do not exist at the moment.

Although the reference to the required act is not part of the physical world, its formulation is regularly materially instantiated in at least one place. This might be a stone on which an obligation is written or a computer screen on which it is displayed. The obligation, for instance, to drive at not more than 50 kmph inside a city is, in many places, written on paper and shown on a screen or on road signs. But it is not the paper nor the ink nor any other material object in which the obligation lies, but the meaning that is attributed to the words written on these material objects. It is this meaning, which is different from the material means by which it is expressed, that constitutes the propositional content that is the obligation.

Once obligations have arisen, their continued existence does not depend on any particular physical object with the help of which they are formulated. Legal obligations remain in force even if the words with which they were uttered have faded away. If the paper on which a contract is written gets lost, the agreed upon obligations thereon still remain. Similarly, burning legal treatises does not destroy the law or its obligations, although it might become more difficult to implement them. This is only possible because obligations consist of physically indestructible propositional content and not in the material object by which this content is expressed.

Given this, one might be tempted to understand obligations as abstract objects (cf. Rosen et al. 2021). Although the concept 'abstract object' enjoys some popularity among legal theorists (Mackor 2016, pp. 127–149; Himma 2019, p. 124), this designation is, at least for legal entities such as obligations, questionable because there are no concrete objects from which obligations can be abstracted. For example, the obligation not to drive faster than 50 kmph inside a city does not stand in a relation of abstraction to the various cars that do not drive at more than 50 kmph. Even if they drove more quickly, or if there were no cars driving through cities at all, the speed-limit would remain. The obligation is not part of their driving, but, amongst other things, part of the motivation of why drivers do not go faster. And even this motivation is not the basis from which an obligation can be abstracted, but merely a possible instantiation of its propositional content.

In this regard, obligations differ from abstract objects such as colours or numbers, for which it is, at least *prima facie,* plausible that they can be abstracted from concrete objects. One might understand the colour red as an abstraction from all red things or the number three as an abstraction of all sets of entities with three elements. Abstract properties, such as red, are instantiated in concrete objects and correspond to them. But, in the case of legal obligations, as for law in general, no such correspondence is visible (cf. Hart 1953, p. 25). Obligations do not stand in the same relationship to behaviour they regulate as red stands to red things. They are not part of a physical event, but state, instead, what is to happen in it.

The concept of an 'abstract object', which is frequently used for physical theories, can thus not—without serious adaptation—be applied to normative phenomena such as obligations. It seems more appropriate to conceive of them as 'ontologically ideal' or 'ideational'. But their ontological ideality is different from aesthetic or normative ideality because no optimal content or form is required for it. Even cruel or bureaucratically formulated norms are ontologically ideal because they are equally immaterial as other norms, and, like them, have propositional content. It is thus important to distinguish between being morally or aesthetically ideal from being ontologically ideal, which corresponds to the distinction between ideal and ideational in many languages.[2]

The ontological ideality of obligations also helps us to understand whether, and if so, in what sense obligations are thought-independent. One might call obligations, in the terminology of Frege, 'thoughts'. But then one has, like him, not only to distinguish them from physical objects, but also from psychological imaginations (Frege 1918, p. 69). 'Thoughts' are, in this terminology, not actual sensations or imaginations in the brain, but the propositional content that might or might not be instantiated in them. The difference between physical and ideational thoughts is quite important for legal obligations because their normative force would decrease considerably if they were to depend upon a manifestation in the brain of one or several persons. Parents, for instance, owe their children a duty of care, even if neither they, nor the children, nor anyone else, is aware of this.

Similarly, a claim for damages due to the breach of an obligation is not refuted simply because, at the time of this breach, no one thought about the obligation. On the contrary, lack of awareness of it might be part of the reason why the obligation was breached. Obligations as 'thoughts' in Frege's terminology consist in a certain

---

[2] 'Idéelle' and 'idéal' in French, 'ideell' and 'ideal' in German or 'идеа́льный' and 'иде́йный' in Russian.

propositional content that is not necessarily the actual thought of a particular person. The same holds for numbers and other ideal objects. For instance, the number three does not disappear only because no one thinks about it. As far as the actual existence is concerned, obligations are thus thought-independent.

Against this thought-independence, one might argue that, at least at the time when the obligation was created, someone had to be aware of it. An obligation of which no one is ever aware could not have a practical impact and thus not fulfil the law's function of governing behaviour. However, the pertinent question is not about the conditions under which an obligation arises. It is about what properties it necessarily has once it has arisen. Even if every obligation needs a conscious act of creation, obligations can exist without the awareness of anyone because a once created obligation might persist independently of whether people think about it. One has to distinguish the creation of an obligation and the obligation as its product (Kelsen 1960, p. 2). Although the obligation-creating act requires materiality and, arguably, consciousness, none of these are properties of an obligation and the normative power of obligations is partially due to this independence from material objects. Unlike them, they cannot be destroyed by physical force. *Cum grano salis*, one might say in Williams[3] words 'only an obligation can beat an obligation' (Williams 1985, p. 187).

Obligations frequently figure in ordinary language as objects to which one can refer and which one can possess. For example, one might say that someone has an obligation, and characterise this obligation further by its particular content. At first glance, this resembles the possible characterisation of material objects such as cars or trees, which one can also possess and characterise by further properties, such as being red. In this perspective, to have an obligation is similar to having a car or to possessing another physical object. In each case, it appears as an object that can be further characterised.

However, this understanding of obligations as objects can be misleading because it neglects that obligations are neither material objects nor a substance that can be conceived independently of its properties. To have an obligation is nothing other than being obligated. To say that one carries a certain obligation φ is equivalent to saying that one ought to φ. Instead of saying 'one has an obligation', one might simply say that that one is obligated. No information is lost by this re-formulation because no propositional content is added by using the noun rather than the verb or *vice versa*. There is no such thing as an 'obligation' that would remain if one took away the very property of being obligated.

All of this does not make discourse about obligations wrong. One might refer to them as ontologically ideal objects, characterise them by their properties, such as being sanctioned, but should not be misled by this language into the assumption that there must be an ontologically ideal 'thing' that one can possess in a similar way that one might possess material things. It might be a useful shorthand to refer to the fact that someone is obligated as an obligation that he or she has. But such an abbreviation, as well as its linguistic role within a certain sentence, does not confer upon it an ontological status as an object. It might be preferable, like Carnap (1956,

[3] Williams himself rejects this statement.

p. 205), to use the concept of an 'abstract entity' instead, because this avoids the suggestion that there is any object apart from or above a certain property.

However, obligations are objects under the definition of an object as a 'potential referent of a singular term' (Berto and Plebani 2015, p. 142). Such usage is possible because legal obligations can be characterised by singular terms, such as sections of a particular statute which function as proper names. So, one might refer to Section 433 para. 2 BGB in order to state that, by German law, a buyer has to pay the agreed upon price. Similarly, one might refer to an obligation in singular terms if one uses, for this purpose, the time and place of its creation. For instance, one can refer to the obligation to pay a certain amount of money due to the contract made on the 2 November between A and B in London. These examples show that obligations can be the referents of singular terms. This should not come as a surprise, because most, if not all, legal norms were created at a particular time and place and can, hence, be referred to by singular terms that state these circumstances.

This possibility is less obvious for obligations that were not created by a positive act, but which are instead either the result of (supposed) eternal norms of natural law or presupposed by every legal system. For instance, a general duty to obey the law can hardly be identified by a singular term because such a duty was not created at a certain place and time and does not bear a proper name. At this point, it is not important whether such a duty is valid and part of a particular legal system or even of all law. It suffices that one can discuss the existence of such a duty on the presupposition that it can be identified. Even those who deny its validity have to refer to it and cannot use singular terms for this purpose.

This seemingly leads to the conundrum that some obligations can be referred to by singular terms and are, according to the proposed definition, objects, whereas other obligations cannot be referred to by singular terms and are therefore, according to this definition, not objects. But this is an unattractive position because the characterisation as an object is so fundamental for an entity that it cannot vary with its other properties and has hence to be constant. That is, it has to hold for each and every of its instantiations or none of them. It would be weird if a certain entity was, in some cases, an object, and, in other cases, not. Being an object does not seem to be a property akin to having a certain colour which can change over time without a change of the entity's identity. This suggests that either the definition of an object must be revised in order to accommodate general obligations which are not identifiable by singular terms, or that being an object is not an essential property for an obligation.

Be that as it may, if one knows that somebody is obligated, no information is gained by knowing that he has an obligation. In contrast to the case of material objects, one cannot conclude from the fact that an entity is an ontologically ideal object that it has a certain weight and occupies a certain place during a certain time. This again shows how important it is to understand that obligations are, due to their propositional content, immaterial and hence ontologically ideal. They are so fundamentally different from material objects that it is more confusing than illuminating to include them under the same concept of an object. As far as their ontological status is concerned, it suffices to note that obligations are ontologically ideal, as are numbers, stories, or other ideas.

2.2 *Reference to an Action*

Once it is clear that obligations consist of a certain propositional content, the crucial question becomes, 'What, precisely is this content?' A minimal requirement for obligations is that something must be done or omitted. This includes, first of all, reference to an action that must either be undertaken or omitted. It is central to the idea of obligations in law and morality that they guide behaviour by prescribing certain actions or their omissions. For example, the obligation to pay a certain amount of money has—at its core—the payment to which the obligation refers.

The 'referred-to action' does not have to be an actual action, i.e., an action that is currently taking place or will take place in the future. It is sufficient that it is *supposed* to take place. An obligation can arise even if the obligated person dies before he or she can fulfil it. This shows that both the obligation as the referring entity and the obligated act as the 'referred-to' entity are not necessarily existing empirical facts but merely possible ones. This is no accident. It is the very purpose of obligations to require acts that have not taken place yet and, thereby, to bring about changes. Nevertheless, the action that is referred to is, in contrast to the obligation, supposed to be an empirical event. It does not merely consist of propositional content but must be materialised. If A owes B money, it is not sufficient that A 'imagines' paying B. A has to do it in order to carry out the obligation. Thus, the fulfilment of obligations regularly requires empirical facts that constitute the obligated actions, and it is important to distinguish between the reference to actions and the 'referred-to' actions. The former exclusively consist of propositional content, the latter supposedly of empirical facts.

These facts might even be impossible to bring about, as when one promises to deliver an amount of gold that does not in fact exist. In this case, it is merely a matter of positive law whether such obligations are void ('*impossibilium nulla est obligatio*')[4] or recognised as valid law. In both cases, there is a reference to an action so that, at least, this property of an obligation is given. Consequently, the question of whether impossible obligations are still obligations, despite its ontological flavour, does not depend on philosophical considerations, but on positive law.

Nevertheless, it is interesting to note, first, that even an impossible obligation can be classified as an obligation (although, possibly, a void one). This should not come as a surprise, because even an impossible action can be referred to and hence become the subject matter of an obligation. Because of its ontological ideality, this reference has no physical limitations. The obligation might refer to possible or impossible, trivial or significant, conceivable or inconceivable actions.

[4] Corpus Iuris Civilis, D.50.17.185.

Secondly, there is a crucial difference between the 'referred-to' action being impossible and the reference not concerning an action at all, although, in both cases, no implementation of the statement is possible. Only in the first case does one deal with an obligation. In the second case, there is no obligation at all. For example, the promise to build a rocket that is faster than the speed of light, despite its impossibility, generates an obligation. On the other hand, mere reference to a rocket that can travel faster than the speed of light cannot be an obligation because it lacks reference to an action. A mere description of an object or of a state of affairs lacks reference to an action.

This reference to an action might be direct or indirect. Reference is direct when the action is named or described in the obligation (as in 'Build a rocket!'). Reference is indirect when the obligation does not name or describe the obligated action but refers instead to a state of affairs to be maintained or brought about. In this case, all actions must be carried out that are necessary for the state of affairs to be maintained or brought about. For example, a tenant might take on an obligation to keep the street clean. This does not explicitly include obligations to shovel snow or to pick up waste from the street. Nevertheless, such obligations follow from the obligation to keep the street clean because it cannot be fulfilled without these actions. The reference to the action might thus be done indirectly by describing a state of affairs that needs to be maintained or brought about.

Given that nothing can restrict the reference of an obligation to actions, their content can vary considerably. As far as the concept of obligation is concerned, there is almost nothing that cannot become its object. It is at least conceivable to have an obligation even for past states of affairs or to agree to obligations that can only be carried out in remote places of the universe. Equally, as far as the concept of an obligation is concerned, it is immaterial whether the required action is advantageous or disadvantageous to the obligated person. Usually, obligations are a burden for him or her because he or she is required to do something. But the required action might be in total harmony with the wishes of the obligated person. For instance, one might be obligated to leave the workplace at a certain time when one wants to do so anyway.

The only unavoidable burden connected to every obligation is the limitation of autonomy of the obligated person. Once an obligation exists, one is inevitably in a situation in which some of one's possible actions will infringe it. One cannot avoid one's actions having these consequences. The choices that one has to make once an obligation exists are, hence, different from the ones that one may make without it. But this limitation concerns the *decisions* that the obligated person may make and not the *content* of the obligation.

This content can vary as long as the actions can be the object of thought. It is a matter for the legislator to decide which obligations to foresee and which ones to exclude. The ontology of an obligation does not restrict him or her but helps, instead, to understand the huge range of possibilities that he or she has.

2.3 *Reference to a Person*

Actions presuppose a being who performs them. This is why obligations not only refer to an action, but also to a person who is supposed to be performing the action. Most of the time, the obligation mentions these persons explicitly, be it the buyer or the seller, the driver or the pedestrian, the state or the citizen. But the reference to the person might also be indirect if there is no doubt as to who will carry out the obligated action. For example, a traffic-sign that states the maximum speed is directed at all drivers so that it does not have to specify the addressee. Instead, it suffices that it states the speed-limit and thereby indirectly refers to those who are to respect it.

The obligated person does not have to be a human being but can also be a juridical person, such as a corporation or the state. It suffices that it is perceived as capable of acting. Otherwise, the reference to the action would remain incomplete because it would remain open who should perform it. The person who is referred to in the obligation does not even have to exist. For example, the legislator can state obligations for large corporations that do not exist yet, because, to date, none has reached the defined size. Such obligations for not existing persons might be pragmatically irrelevant if no one's behaviour was, or would be, influenced by them. Nevertheless, obligations of this kind can, for example, be introduced, in order to prevent such corporations from emerging.

Equally, it is immaterial for the existence of the obligation whether or not the 'referred-to' person is capable of acting. An obligation can be made upon the wrong assumption that the obligated person can act. A corporation, for instance, might, due to a failure in its foundation, have no one who is currently authorised to act on its behalf and thus be incapable of action. An archaic legal system could, similarly, obligate animals, if it assumes that they are capable of performing the obligations.

The reason for this openness is, once again, the ontological ideality of the obligation because it is not bound to the current empirical reality. It is sufficient that the obligation is built upon the assumption that there is an obligated person who is capable of acting. If this assumption is lacking, i.e., if there is, even in the perspective of law, no reference to a person, there is no obligation at all. At best, there is a wish that something should happen. For example, the statement that the sun will shine all day remains a pure wish as long it neither directly nor indirectly refers to a person who is supposed to make it shine all day. Equally, the statement that a person P deserves money is also not an obligation because this statement does not specify anyone who is to pay him or her. The reference to a person is, hence, an essential element of an obligation.

This reference to a person implies recognition that this person is capable of acting. Because obligations usually carry with them a burden by which the autonomy of the obligated person is limited, this recognition frequently goes unnoticed. It is, nevertheless, important. This is because it remains a crucial difference whether a person is merely impacted by the implementation of a norm or whether he or she is addressed by it. For example, there is a difference between the state confiscating an object, and the state obliging someone to transfer it to the state. Only in the latter case is a human action of fulfilling an obligation involved. In the former case, the norm is fulfilled without the involvement of the addressee. Having a legal obligation signifies that one is, from the perspective of the law, not a mere object impacted by the law's decisions, but someone who is to be addressed as a person. The capacity to have obligations involves, at least, a recognition of the capacity to act, which is as fundamental as the much-discussed capacity to have rights (e.g., Raz 1984, p. 199; Raz 1986, p. 176).

Also, this reference to a person who is perceived as capable of acting does not necessarily involve further characteristics. It is, in particular, not required that the obligated person knows about his or her obligation. This is because it is possible to refer to people without them being aware of it. The law might—as a matter of convenience—make it a condition that certain obligations arise only if the obligated person knows about it. But this is only a prudential decision that applies to some kinds of obligations and not a reason why unknown obligations could—in principle—not exist. Law's regulatory potential would be considerably hampered if it were otherwise.

2.4 Normative Requirement

The final element without which no legal obligation can exist is the normative requirement that the referred-to action, as a matter of law, ought to be carried out. This is because obligations are not descriptions of what could happen or what *will* happen in fact but concern the normative question of what *should* happen. Therefore, obligations contain deontic operators such as 'shall' or 'ought', which turn a reference to a state of affairs into a normative requirement. This is the reason why obligations were even sometimes equated 'with the concept of ought in a narrow sense' (Bierling 1894, p. 169).[5] This succinctly expresses that, at their core, there is a normative requirement and that this requirement specifies what is most important for an obligation. That a person P is obligated to φ means hence that P shall φ and not that there are certain empirical facts about P. Legal obligations differ from other obligations merely in so far as the normative requirement is a legal one. In their case it is the law that requires a person P to φ.

Despite their normative character, legal obligations almost always rest on positive acts, such as the adoption of a statute or the conclusion of a contract. These acts might formulate an obligation but are, due to their empirical character, nonetheless different from them. They merely concern the process of norm creation and not the obligation as its result. It cannot be otherwise because no description of the empirical reality suffices to prove that there is a certain obligation. The *utterance* 'A shall φ!', which is an empirical fact, is to be distinguished from the *proposition* 'A shall

[5] My translation.

φ!', as only the former's occurrence is restricted to a certain time and a certain place. The norm-creating act merely maintains that there is a certain obligation. But this is very different from the state of affairs in which there is indeed such an obligation. A claim that someone is obligated might fail just like any other claim. Therefore, in order for an obligation to exist, one needs not only empirical facts such as speech acts in which a normative requirement is formulated, but, in addition, reasons explaining why a normative requirement holds for them. Only then is a person obligated and not just said to be so.

With the help of the normative requirement, one can, pace Hart, also distinguish the situation in which someone is obligated from the situation that someone is obliged without using the notion of a system of rules as Hart proposed it (Hart 1958, p. 98). In the case of an obligation, there is the normative requirement according to which the referred-to action must be carried out by the obligated person. When someone is obliged, no such requirement exists. Instead, there are merely factual circumstances due to which it is imprudent not to carry out the action (for example, because physical force will otherwise be applied). Although both situations can be combined so that one is not only obligated but also obliged, they do not necessarily go hand in hand. One might be obliged, due to natural forces, to undertake certain actions (for example, to wear warm clothes in winter) but can, from a normative point of view, remain free not to do so. In this case, one does not have an obligation.

The normative requirement might be a real requirement or a false one depending on whether the obligation is valid or invalid. A valid legal obligation usually rests on the normative power of the institution enacting the obligation. Interestingly, the lack of the power to enact an obligation might merely prevent the enacted obligation from becoming valid but does not prevent the obligation from coming into existence. Even an invalid obligation is an obligation and not no obligation at all. This is because an invalid obligation contains at least a claimed requirement that a certain person is to carry out an action, even if this requirement is invalid because the enacting institution is incapable of creating such a requirement or because some other condition of validity is or has been infringed. Therefore, it is not only important to ask whether there is an obligation but also whether this obligation is valid, i.e., whether it should indeed be carried out.

As an illustration, take the much-discussed example of a gunman shouting, 'Your money or your life!' The debate as to whether there is an obligation in this situation (Hart 1961, p. 80; Marmor 2011, p. 70) is mainly due to the incompleteness of such a statement. If, 'Your money or your life!', means that the victim shall hand the money to the gunman and will be sanctioned in the event of non-obedience, then there *is* an obligation even though it is clearly an invalid one. The existence of this obligation cannot be disputed by the fact that the gunman had no normative power to create it. In this interpretation, he at least claims that there is such an obligation. This is sufficient for an (invalid) obligation to emerge.

Alternatively, the statement, 'Your money or your life!', can be interpreted as presenting a choice without a normative requirement. According to this interpretation, it is, even from the perspective of the gunman, totally up to the victim to decide whether he or she will hand over the money, but, in the event that he or she does not do so, severe consequences will follow. No requirement to act in a certain way is claimed or involved. Under such an interpretation, there is no obligation, not even a claimed one. Instead, the victim is free to decide and is compelled to undertake the desired action 'only' by exterior circumstances. Because the gunman lacks the capacity to create valid obligations, it is usually irrelevant whether one interprets his statement as an attempt to create an obligation or as a mere threat of violence. There will not be a valid obligation anyway. Therefore, the fulfilment of the gunman's command depends not on the interpretation of his utterance, but mainly on the credibility of his threat.

Nevertheless, the confusion in the question of whether the victim is obliged or also obligated shows the importance of distinguishing between an obligation merely being invalid or being non-existent at all—a distinction that is overlooked when the existence and validity of norms are equated (e.g., by Kelsen 1960, p. 9). While a normative requirement is indispensable for an obligation to exist, its validity concerns, among others, the contingent question of whether the creator had the normative power to enact it. There can be an invalid, but still existing, obligation, which is illustrated by the fact that even unconstitutional obligations can be the subject matter of intensive debate. In contrast to this, there cannot be an obligation without a normative requirement. A proposition about state of affairs without such a requirement is a description or a wish, neither of which are obligations.

The distinction between invalid obligations and non-obligations might not have received much attention for some time because the debate was focused instead on the source of valid obligations. For this question, it was important to establish whether legal norms can be traced back to social facts or whether they can also be founded on morality (Green and Adams 2019, p. 126; Kaehler 2017, p. 24). As important as this debate is, it obscures the question of whether there are social facts that create invalid obligations. This is because, even if there is no legal source for them, such obligations can still arise.

All of this is illustrated in the gunman case. This is because threats (such as that of the gunman) do, according to the first interpretation, refer (a) to an action (the payment of the money), as well as (b) to a person capable of acting (the victim of the robbery), and entail (c) a normative requirement (that the money be paid). Their refutation would be incomplete if one could merely point out that the gunman is acting illegally and also explain that he is, possibly, making an invalid claim. The same holds for illegal contractual obligations. One can only understand them if one conceives of them as obligations which, on the one hand, claim to be legal, and, on the other, violate the law. This would be incomprehensible if invalid obligations ceased to be obligations at all. It is hence not necessary for an obligation that its normative requirement holds. But it is indispensable that there be such a requirement.

One might object that, according to the analysis above, to have an obligation to φ is equivalent to 'one ought to φ', but that one does not have to φ if the obligation is invalid. An invalid obligation can thus, at least at first glance, *not* consist in the fact that one ought to φ. Hence, either the equivalence between an obligation and 'one ought to φ' does not hold, or invalid obligations are no obligations. To solve this problem, one has to distinguish the propositional content of obligations from their truth conditions. If there is a certain obligation φ, then there must be at least the claim that someone has to φ. This concerns its propositional content. But, from this content, it does not follow that he or she does indeed have to φ. The law might, and usually does, entail extensive conditions that have to be fulfilled in order for a certain obligation to be valid. Vice versa, to have an invalid obligation is not equivalent to 'not being obliged to φ'. Instead, it means that one is 'wrongly supposed to φ'. Therefore, even an invalid obligation contains a normative requirement that one ought to φ.

Legal obligations differ from other obligations in that the requirement is a legal one. Only if the law demands certain actions does one deal with a legal requirement. This means, not only that the requirement is based upon law, but also that the requirement itself has a legal character. Only the law can explicate what it means for something to be required by it. This usually includes being enforceable *via* the courts. The specific legal source of the normative requirement might vary, as it can be a statutory norm, an individual command, or a customary rule. But all of these have the same result: that a particular action is required by law. This requirement is an all-or-nothing-issue, i.e., not gradable, whereas moral or customary requirements come in various degrees. In particular, something might more or less be morally obligatory. Respecting the speed limit is morally less required than the obligation to feed ones' children. Contrary to that, both actions are, to the same extent, legally required.

Interestingly, all other properties of moral and legal obligations besides the normative requirement can be the same. Legal obligations can, in the same way as moral obligations, refer to an action or a person. It is not a specific content or person that makes an obligation a legal one, but solely its legal requirement. What distinguishes the threat of a gunman from the command of a police officer is hence not necessarily the requested action, as it can—in both situations—be the same act of handing over money. Nor is it the reference to the person because, in both cases, the obligated person might be the same. Rather, the difference is that the gunman either does not even claim to create a legal requirement or cannot achieve this.

3 Non-necessary Properties

Examination of the invalidity of obligations showed that many of their properties, such as having a considerable weight, are contingent because this could be different. Therefore, such properties can be excluded from a general analysis. Instead, it is important to look at properties from which it is, at least at first glance, not clear whether they are necessary or not.

3.1 Reference to an Obligee

One of the properties that could be necessary for an obligation is reference to an obligee, i.e., a person or institution to whom its fulfilment is owed. Most legal obligations are indeed owed to someone, who is regularly the person who has an interest in their fulfilment. If A has an obligation to pay money to B, then B is the person for the sake of whom the money will be paid. If there is no one for the sake of whom an obligation is to be fulfilled, it will be unclear why it exists. Therefore, obligations without an obligee seem, at first glance, strange.

However, that obligations are owed to a particular person most of the time does not show that there are no obligations at all that are not owed to someone. On the contrary, someone might be supposed to carry out a certain action without there being anyone to whom this action is owed. For instance, there might be obligations not to pollute the environment because this is considered to be unethical. In this case, no one is the obligee of this duty (unless the environment is perceived as an entity to whom an obligation may be owed). Nevertheless, the law might provide for this obligation and empower certain institutions to enforce it. Having the power to enforce an obligation is different from being the person to whom the obligation is owed. There are two separate questions involved that might or might not be answered uniformly. The first question is whether someone can enforce an obligation, the second question is whether there is someone for whose sake an obligation will be carried out. Therefore, even if the state can enforce a certain legal obligation, the obligation might still lack an obligee.

For illustration, consider the case of someone, such as a teacher, who owes a small child a statutory duty of care. In this case, the person to whom the duty is owed is incapable of enforcing it. Therefore, the parents are authorised to do it. But this does not change the fact that it is the child, and not the parents, to whom the duty of care is owed. Similarly, from the fact that the state can enforce obligations not to pollute the environment, it does not follow that the state is, in this case, the obligee.

The question of whether there can be an obligation without an obligee appears not only in law but also in practical philosophy. Kant (1797, MS, AA VI: 442) assumed that an obligation is always owed to a person. Interestingly, one might share this view, as far as morality is concerned, and still deny that legal obligations are always owed to some obligee. For even if there were always a person to whom a moral obligation is owed, the law might not recognise this person as an obligee due to institutional considerations that do not a play a role in morality. For example, a legal system might restrict the number of obligees in order to reduce the number of claims that are brought forward in court. Thereby, it might prioritise the important from the less important obligations and recognise obligations only for a limited set of obligees. There would, then, be legal obligations that are not owed to a particular person although the corresponding moral obligations are.

The result that there can be legal obligations without an obligee can be further illuminated by looking at the reasons for legal obligations. Behind legal obligations there is usually a reason that justifies them and explains their existence. Otherwise, the obligation would be arbitrary and the legislator would have no motivation to enact it. This turns the question of whether obligations are necessarily owed to an obligee into the question of whether the reasons for requiring a certain action always demand that the action be owed to a person or institution. It is unlikely that the answer will always be 'yes'. The plurality of reasons that can justify obligations is so great that it would be surprising if these reasons could never be confined to requiring a certain action and would always demand that this action should be carried out for the sake of a person. For example, construction laws can enforce aesthetic ideals without recognising anyone to whom these obligations are owed. The reason for these obligations can consist in realising aesthetic ideals for their own sake. One might regard such a justification as illiberal (Mill 1859, p. 84) but should not deny that such obligations are at least within the concept of an obligation.

The possibility of having legal obligations without an obligee also helps to understand that there might be obligations without a corresponding right.[6] For if there is no person to whom the obligation is owed, there is no reason to have a rights-holder in whose interest the obligation exists. Thus, obligations without an obligee usually lack a corresponding right. Nevertheless, it is conceptually possible to have a legal obligation that is owed to no one but still corresponds to a right of the state or another person to enforce it. This is especially the case for the obligation not to pollute the environment. It is owed to no one but nevertheless enforceable by the state.

Legal obligations might therefore exist both with and without an obligee. There is no reason to confine the concept of an obligation to only one kind. Only this openness creates the space to recognise the huge variety of obligations. It is the decision of the legislator and not a conceptual matter whether obligations without obligees will be established.

3.2 *Reference to an Obligating Person*

Besides the people who are obligated and the person to whom the obligation is owed, there is usually an institution that created it. Most usually it is parliaments that adopt statutes and private parties that conclude contracts. This might give the impression that obligations exist only due to an obligating person. Is the property of being created by a person thus a necessary one?

Positivist theories of conventionality (e.g., Marmor 2011, p. 75) might, at first glance, support such a thesis, as they deny that there are valid natural obligations. However, the question at this point does not concern the validity of obligations but their existence. The question is merely whether an entity would cease to be an

[6] The question is hotly disputed. See, e.g., in agreement, Bierling (1894, p. 171), and against, Raz (1984, p. 199).

obligation if it were not created by some person. There is no reason to assume so. Neither the reference to an action or to a person, nor the normative requirement would be excluded if it turned out that the obligation was not created (but is, for instance, necessarily given). If an obligation never became part of the law but was always only discussed, it could still have the propositional content of requiring someone to perform a certain action. So far, there seems nothing wrong with the idea of natural obligations even from a positivist point of view. They are conceptually possible (and therefore the subject matter of debate), even though their validity is in dispute. If there always had to be an obligating person, natural obligations could not even be conceived or refuted. This should not come as a surprise because the underlying questions are different. The creation of an obligation concerns the question of how an obligation arose and not the question of what it consists of. The existence of an obligating person concerns only the former so that there is conceptual space to answer the second question freely. This means that the property of being created by a person is not necessary for an obligation.

In some cases, the existence of an obligation without an obligating person has, at least, a *prima facie* plausibility. Let us consider the question of whether there is a general obligation to obey the law. If there is such an obligation, then it exists, not by virtue of an obligation-creating act, but by virtue of reasons such as fairness, respect, equality, etc., (Dagger and Lefkowitz 2021). It is highly implausible that any person or institution be capable of creating such a general obligation because they would already have to rely on law in order to impose such an obligation. But then they would have to presuppose that there is an obligation to obey it. Without such a presupposed obligation, it would remain unclear how anyone could create any additional obligation that would be obeyed.

All of this is not to say that there is a valid legal obligation to obey the law. A careful analysis might show that there is none. The point worth noticing is that conceptually such an obligation could exist even if no person or institution created it. The existence of an obligating person is hence no necessary property of an obligation.

3.3 *Sanctionability*

The final property of legal obligations worthy of consideration is its sanctionability. Kant (1797, MS, AA VI: 231) famously argued that law is connected to force. This suggests that there cannot be a legal obligation without the possibility of a sanction in a broad sense, i.e., a detrimental reaction towards a breach of an obligation. One reason for this thesis is best expressed by the idea that an obligation without a sanction could not be law (Kelsen 1960, p. 52) but merely morality in disguise because it would be totally up to the obligated person as to whether he or she fulfils the obligation or not. If law is to make any difference, so the argument goes (Himma 2020, p. 128), it must provide a sanction.

Interestingly, this argument does not suggest that there cannot be obligations without a sanction. Rather, it is having legal character that supposedly requires a sanction. Sanctions cannot be a necessary part of an obligation, as its central idea that someone ought to carry out a certain action is independent of the legal consequences of its breach. It is perfectly possible that an action is prescribed without any negative consequence for the case of non-execution. Then all the mentioned properties of an obligation are given. If, however, there could be no obligation without a sanction, the possibility of prescribing action would be severely limited. For then, no obligations could exist in situations such as the end of life, where it is physically impossible to implement a sanction later. But, even there, one needs obligations such as not to kill or to insult others.

This argument applies not only to obligations in general but also to legal obligations in particular. The mere fact that it is impossible, in certain situations, to force or to sanction someone should not suffice to exempt him or her from an obligation. On the contrary, the idea that something ought to be done might be most central in situations in which one can rely on nothing other than the fact that there *is* a certain obligation. Granted, there could be prudential reasons not to establish legal obligations which are not sanctioned because they would—contrasted with moral obligations—arguably, not make a practical difference. But this is just a pragmatic consideration that depends, amongst other things, on whether persons might be motivated by the simple fact that they bear a certain legal obligation. It is, at least, not excluded *a priori* that some people are motivated by the fact that something is the law. Therefore, even sanctionless obligations could possibly make a practical difference. A legislator might, for example try, for purely symbolic reasons, to prescribe obligations despite the lack of the opportunity to sanction a breach of them. Therefore, the sanctionability of obligations is not a necessary property of legal obligations.

Even if it were necessary for every legal obligation to be sanctioned, this would not make it an essential property, i.e., a property by virtue of which an entity is an obligation. This is because the normative requirement does not hinge on a sanction. In general, necessary properties do not have to be essential ones (Fine 1994, p. 4). A concept might be based upon only a few properties by virtue of which an entity exists, although, in addition, there are compelling reasons why some further properties would always be present once the other properties are given. If so, there is a property that is, despite its necessity, not essential because it does not belong to the defining properties.

In this way one might argue that every legal obligation is created by a human act, and that, necessarily, the persons whose act created the obligation were born. Nevertheless, it is not essential for an obligation to be created by persons who were born. For this property, though necessary, is not part of the meaning of an obligation. It has nothing to do with the requirement to undertake a certain action. If an entity is an obligation, then it is not one because its creators were born. Equally, being sanctioned is not the reason why an entity is an obligation, but, possibly, its consequence. The sanctionability of an obligation is, therefore, not part of its concept, even if it is necessary. One can perfectly conceive of unsanctioned obligations, whereas one cannot conceive of an obligation that does not refer to an action or a person. This shows that sanctionability—in contrast to reference to an action and person—is not part of the definition of an obligation.

4 Summary

If the previous analysis is correct, it takes little for a norm to contain an obligation. An obligation exists simply if there is a reference to an action, to a person, and a normative requirement that the person performs the action. These three elements capture the central idea that someone is obligated. With the help of these elements, one can distinguish obligations from mere descriptions of what happens in fact and can also distinguish them from the situation that someone is obliged. Physical force or the threat of it might accompany an obligation and thus create the situation in which someone is obliged. But they are not a necessary element of an obligation as the law might confine itself to the mere appeal that something has to be done without foreseeing a sanction in order to enforce it.

Such a minimal conception of an obligation has the advantage that it captures the great variety of obligations that exist in the current as well as the past legal systems and makes them comparable. It helps to ask why, in some cases, obligations are owed to someone, and not in other cases, and why, in some cases, obligations rest on the decision of an obligating person, whereas in other cases they might exist without such a decision, etc.

Most importantly, this characterisation illuminates that obligations are neither material nor immaterial things, but an ontologically ideal state of affairs. To have an obligation is nothing other than to be obligated. Consequently, any analogy of legal obligations to physical objects, as occurs in the debates about the acquisition or destruction of an obligation, must either be avoided or be treated as a mere metaphor.

References

Berto F, Plebani M (2015) Ontology and metaontology. Bloomsbury, London

Bierling ER (1894) Juristische Prinzipienlehre, vol 1. Mohr Siebeck, Freiburg

Carnap R (1956) Meaning and necessity, 2nd edn. University of Chicago Press, Chicago

Dagger R, Lefkowitz D (2021) Political obligation. In: Zalta EN (ed) The Stanford encyclopedia of philosophy. https://plato.stanford.edu/entries/political-obligation

Fine K (1994) Essence and modality. Philos Perspect 8:1–16

Finnis J (1980) Natural law and natural rights. Oxford University Press, Oxford

Frege G (1918) Der Gedanke: eine logische Untersuchung. In: Beiträge zur Philosophie des deutschen Idealismus 1, pp 58–77

Green L, Adams T (2019) Legal positivism. In: Zalta EN (ed) The Stanford encyclopedia of philosophy. https://plato.stanford.edu/entries/legal-positivism/#Bib

Hart HLA (1953) Definition and theory in jurisprudence. In: Essays in jurisprudence and philosophy, vol 1983. The Clarendon Press, Oxford, pp 21–48

Hart HLA (1958) Legal and moral obligation. In: Melden AI (ed) Essays in moral philosophy. University of Washington Press, Seattle, pp 83–107
Hart HLA (1961) The concept of law. Oxford University Press, Oxford
Himma KE (2019) Morality and the nature of law. Oxford University Press, Oxford
Himma KE (2020) Coercion and the nature of law. Oxford University Press, Oxford
Kaehler L (2017) Kelsen and the problems of the social fact thesis. In: Langford P, Bryan I, McGarry J (eds) Kelsenian legal science and the nature of law. Springer, Cham, pp 23–42
Kant I (1797 [1968]) Die Metaphysik der Sitten. Akademieausgabe (AA), vol 6. De Gruyter, Berlin
Kelsen H (1960) Reine Rechtslehre, 2nd edn. Verlag Österreich, Vienna
Mackor AR (2016) Legal doctrine is a non-normative discipline: an argument from abstract object theory. In: Taekema S et al (eds) Facts and norms in law: interdisciplinary reflections on legal method. Edward Elgar, Cheltenham, pp 127–149
Marmor A (2011) Philosophy of law. Princeton University Press, Princeton
Marmor A, Sarch A (2019) The nature of law. In: Zalta EN (ed) The Stanford encyclopedia of philosophy. https://plato.stanford.edu/archives/fall2019/entries/lawphil-nature/
Mill JS (1859 [1991]) In: John G (ed) On liberty. Oxford University Press, Oxford
Raz J (1984) On the nature of rights. Mind XCIII:194–214
Raz J (1986) The morality of freedom. Oxford University Press, Oxford
Rosen G, Falguera JL, Martínez-Vidal C, Rosen G (2021) Abstract objects. In: Zalta EN (ed) The Stanford encyclopedia of philosophy. https://plato.stanford.edu/entries/abstract-objects/
Williams B (1985) Ethics and the limits of philosophy. Harvard University Press, Cambridge

What Is a Legal Obligation?

Stefano Bertea

> *'We are such stuff/As dreams are made on, and our little life/is rounded with a sleep.'*
>
> *(Shakespeare, The Tempest)*

1 Introduction

In this essay, I will be concerned with legal obligation as an aspect of reality, or a specific ontological kind, and will seek to determine what this ontological kind is, or what class this thing we call legal obligation belongs to.[1] The argument I will deploy is premised on the conceptualisation of legal obligation I offered in an earlier study, where my interest was not so much in the *reality* of legal obligation as in its *concept* or *idea*. The difference in focus between these two kinds of inquiries into legal obligation can be stated in the following way. A *conceptualisation* of legal

[1] As this framing of the problem suggests, it is not with any specific instance of legal obligation that I will be concerned, but with legal obligation as such, the thing *generally* referred to when we speak of legal obligation. Or, stated otherwise, I will be offering a description of legal obligation as an ontological *type* rather than trying to arrive at such a description by looking at this or that specific *token* of legal obligation.

I am grateful to Deryck Beyleveld, Lorenz Kaehler, Giuseppe Lorini, and Filippo Valente for their comments on earlier drafts of this work. Responsibility for the views expressed herein and for any error rests solely with me. This work has been made possible by a 3-month fellowship offered by the Durham Institute of Advanced Study, Durham University. I take this opportunity to warmly thank the directors of the institute—Alexander Easton, Nayanika Mookherjee, and Patrick Zuk—as well as the principal of Stephenson College, Rob Lynes, where I resided during the fellowship, for their kind hospitality, outstanding encouragement, and continuous support throughout the period spent researching this article.

S. Bertea (✉)
University of Messina, Department of Law, Messina, Italy

D. Beyleveld, S. Bertea (eds.), *Theories of Legal Obligation*, Law and Philosophy Library 146, https://doi.org/10.1007/978-3-031-54067-7_3

obligation accounts for how legal obligation should specifically and distinctly be *understood* or *conceived*, which is what I refer to as the *concept*, or idea, of legal obligation. The objective of a conceptualisation of legal obligation is to arrive at a theoretically sound or plausible, if not necessary, account of the specific kind of obligation that law engenders. Legal obligation is approached as a notion in its own right, something that needs to be explained and possibly consolidated. By contrast, a study of the *reality* of legal obligation requires one to engage with what a legal obligation, in turn understood as *a piece of the furniture of the universe*, actually *is*. So understood, the focus of a study of legal obligation turns from the question of how legal obligation is best conceptualised—an *epistemological* question—to the question of what kind of entity legal obligation *is* as something out there in the world, which is a question having to do with the *ontology* of legal obligation. So, because I am interested here in the reality of legal obligation (and not in its conceptualisation), the argument that follows offers to explain how legal obligation *exists* (its ontology) as opposed to elucidating how legal obligation should be *conceived*.

Clearly, an enquiry into the ontology of legal obligation will hinge on some fundamental debates not only in legal philosophy but also in contemporary metaethics since, in investigating the existence of legal obligation as a distinct entity, or a portion of reality, we need to consider a set of closely related and conceptually interlinked *meta-normative* questions. Figuring among them is not only the question, 'Does legal obligation exist?', but also a family of related questions, such as, 'What kind of entity is legal obligation?', 'Does legal obligation belong to the physical dimension or psychological dimension, or does it just exist in the mind as a thought?', 'Is legal obligation a merely linguistic statement or does it have an extralinguistic existence?', 'If legal obligation does exist as an extralinguistic entity, that is, as a fact, is legal obligation a natural fact, a social fact, a deontic fact, a psychological fact, or something else?' As the reader will appreciate, addressing these questions raises concerns that lie at the very core of any meta-normative, or metaethical, enquiry, since it requires us to deal with the nature, or quality, of a given normative entity—legal obligation—and its relation to other portions of the factual and normative reality that we experience.

As I see it, this array of questions specifically requires us to search for the privileged or theoretically soundest *referent* of the concept of legal obligation. Otherwise stated, if we want to investigate legal obligation as an ontological type, we should primarily be concerned with the *extension* of legal obligation. In yet other words, if we want to study the reality of legal obligation, we need to establish what kind of entity a legal obligation is in the specific sense of determining what the term 'legal obligation' *refers to*. In addition to enabling us to gain insights into the reality of legal obligation, an inquiry of this kind serves a theoretically useful purpose because the question of the referent of the concept of legal obligation is still unsettled in the literature, being identified with a variety of entities, including (a) sentences, or statements; (b) propositions, or meanings; (c) utterances, or speech acts; (d) states of affairs, or facts; (e) statuses; (f) mental constructs; (g) social practices; and (h) thoughts, or thought-objects.[2] There is, then, a vast plurality of mutually irreducible and even heterogeneous candidates for the role of referent (or

[2] These referents are mentioned in relation to legal norms (inclusive of obligatory legal norms) in Conte (1995), Passerini-Glazel (2017), and Passerini-Glazel (2020, pp. 27–44).

reality) of legal obligation. The purpose of this work, however, is not to survey the plurality of possible referents that legal obligation has been claimed to have. The argument that follows is instead meant to establish, on the theoretical approach here outlined, what single entity can be identified as *the* referent or single reality of legal obligation. In the context of this work, the question, 'What is legal obligation?', is to be understood as meaning, 'What is the most plausible referent of the concept of legal obligation, the kind of thing that legal obligation is?'

In my view, which I defended in an earlier work (see Bertea 2019, esp. pp. 199–262), the *reality* of legal obligation—its ontology—draws on, and partly depends on, the *conceptualisation* of legal obligation—its epistemology. My conceptualisation can be summarised as follows. Legal obligation is to be understood as a reason sourced in the law categorically requiring certain courses of conduct to be carried out on a basis that cannot be exclusively prudential. On this account, which I argued to be Kantian (in a modified meaning of this qualification), legal obligation is conceptualised as a normative kind of necessitation—a standard categorically demanding, as opposed to simply recommending, that those who live under the law act in the prescribed way. Relatedly, complying with legal obligations should presumptively be considered the *right* thing to do, as opposed to what it is *expedient* or prudentially advisable e to do. Thus, legal obligation operates as a genuine rational requirement favouring, or justifying, certain courses of conduct in a binding way. The key to this conceptualisation of legal obligation is the claim that *legal obligation* is to be conceived as a not merely prudential *justificatory reason for action*. From a theoretical perspective informed by the conceptualisation of legal obligation just summarised, establishing the reality of legal obligation therefore requires us to determine what it means for something to be a not merely prudential justificatory reason for action. This, in turn, means that we have to engage with the meta-normative debate on the nature of justificatory reasons for action.

In doing so, I will present an argument based on the following claims. As just indicated, the starting point for the discussion is the view of legal obligation as a *justificatory reason for action* of a given type (one that is not purely prudential). The question, 'What is a legal obligation?', will thus be approached as a search for what a (not merely prudential) justificatory reason for action is—a search for its referent. This search will be pursued from the perspective of a given tradition in meta-normative thought, namely, meta-normative non-naturalist cognitivism (or 'non-naturalism', for short), which fits particularly well with my modified Kantian approach to the conceptualisation of legal obligation.[3] For the purposes of this study, then, I will take non-naturalism as my main meta-normative frame of reference. On the non-naturalist approach, a justificatory reason for action is a *sui generis fact*. I will thus be trying to properly understand this notion of a *sui generis* fact as a way to pin down the reality of legal obligation. This notion, I will argue, is best understood as a *non-natural entity* with *unique traits*. I will argue that legal obligation—as a justificatory reason for action, and so as a *sui generis* fact in a non-naturalist

[3] The coherence between non-naturalism and Kantian philosophy is emphasised by Shafer-Landau (2007) and Skorupski (2010, pp. 1–31), among others.

fashion—is an *abstract, ideational,* and *public object possessing distinctive qualities*.

More analytically, five claims will be made about legal obligation.

(1) Legal obligation is an *abstract* entity that, as such, is specifically distinguished from ordinary, concrete entities.
(2) It is *ideational,* meaning that it exists in thought and is therefore immaterial as opposed to being natural in the manner of a physical or even a psychological phenomenon.
(3) But as an ideational entity it is not a purely personal, subjective, or individually held idea. It is not a private state of mind but something that exists only insofar as it is acknowledged to exist by a plurality of persons. It is a constitutively collective and *public* entity.
(4) As an idea or thought, legal obligation is an *object*, albeit an immaterial one that cannot be reduced to any predicate, attribute, or property of an object.
(5) It is a *sui generis* entity, namely, an abstract reality unlike any archetypical abstract and immaterial object. This is because, unlike paradigmatically abstract objects such as mathematical entities (numbers, pure sets, functions), propositions, and universals,[4] legal obligation is (a) a *created abstractum*, rather than a necessary one, with (b) an existence that is time-bound. For, unlike standard abstracta, legal obligations apply across a span of time, thus are temporally finite, at least from when they begin to take effect.

These claims are the building blocks of the conception that will be defended here in regard to the ontology of legal obligation. But before I set out my argument in full, I need to take care of some preliminaries.

2 Preliminaries

Three points need to be made in order for the argument I will be making for the reality of legal obligation not to be misunderstood. To begin with, the argument is shaped by the assumption that, in the context of the study of legal obligation, it makes sense to investigate not only the *concept* of legal obligation—how we should *think* about legal obligation as something that exists out there in the world—but also its reality, or what that something *is*. That is to say, I take it to be the case that legal obligation (or the term ‘legal obligation’) possesses both intension and extension. The *intension* of legal obligation concerns the meaning, form, and force of obligation such as it issues from the law. An enquiry into the intension of legal obligation thus seeks to determine the essential features of legal obligation as a distinctive *idea*. By contrast, the *extension* of legal obligation is its *referent*, namely, what the

[4] For an overview of the recent debates on abstract objects and an indication of the paradigmatic instances of those objects see, for instance, Cowling (2017, pp. 69–105) and Plebani (2020).

concept of legal obligation refers to in the world, or what can be pointed to as the entity that legal obligation in the world consists of.[5] A study of the extension of legal obligation is accordingly grounded in the assumption that legal obligation is not just a concept but also an entity. In other terms, the term 'legal obligation' should not be taken as something we say in a manner of speaking—legal obligation as a placeholder in a linguistic practice—nor as just a manner of thinking—legal obligation as a concept to which no actual reality corresponds, but rather as standing for 'something', that is, for an entity, for a piece of reality. In this study, then, I start out from the premise that legal obligation requires an ontological stance or has metaphysical status: it is a specific kind of *thing* and thus refers to a discrete object. And, if legal obligation can be so approached, as something that *is*, then it makes sense to ask what kind of entity it is: linguistic, or mental, or factual, and so on. Or, stated otherwise, if legal obligation exists not only as a concept but also as an entity, as I believe it does, then we should want to know what that entity is, or what the thing is which the concept refers to. This will be the basic premise and assumption behind the argument that follows.[6]

Secondly, even if the idea of this inquiry into legal obligation is to pin down its *reality*, I will not be approaching this reality in the vein of *scientific* realism. Instead, I will follow the Kantian tradition of philosophy, which denies that we have direct access to the reality of what we experience, denying that we can grasp the reality of things independently of the categories of thought and the conceptual schemes framing our experience of the world around us. On this epistemological approach, what I am calling the *reality* of legal obligation depends partly on our *cognition* of legal obligation. This reality, then, is to an extent *constructed*: it is partly determined by our minds as we conceptualise legal obligation. This amounts to saying that there is a close and unbreakable connection between our *conceptualisation* of legal obligation and its *reality*. So, in offering an account of the reality of legal obligation—an account of what legal obligation *is*—I do not pretend that we have an unmediated access to such a reality, or that we can access it independently of the way in which we conceptualise it. The view, more forcefully stated, is that we cannot *immediately* grasp what legal obligation is, without going through epistemic processes that end up ultimately shaping the kind of thing legal obligation is. To put it in a slogan, the *metaphysics* of legal obligation is contingent on its *epistemology*: our conceptualisation of legal obligation, along with the

[5] For a similar understanding of the intension-extension distinction as it applies to the normative, see Di Lucia and Passerini-Glazel (2017, p. 12).

[6] This assumption is criticised by Narvaez-Mora (2015), among others. Narvaez-Mora (2015, p. 45), claims that 'it makes no sense to assert the ontological character of norms', including norms that set out obligations. He accordingly advocates a 'legal theory without entities' (ibid., pp. 56–59). I argue, by contrast, that while legal norms and obligations are undoubtedly constructed, and thus could not exist without their human makers, they would not be able to function as norms and obligations without a reality to which they correspond or on which they rest, which is to say that they cannot function entirely as fictions, as might be the case with properly fictional entities such as money. Because I cannot take the time here to make a proper case for this ontological stance, I will just ask the reader to go along with this ontological stance for the sake of argument.

categories through which we cognise it, guides and filters our experience with its reality.

It is fair to ask, at this point, whether this way of getting at the ontology of legal obligation is so reliant on its conceptualisation as to undercut the distinction between the two, in that the ontology of legal obligation ultimately comes down to, and indeed coincides with, its conceptualisation. At which point one might ask, 'Why bother with the ontology of legal obligation to begin with?' The reason for doing so is twofold. For one thing, I am making the basic assumption that legal obligation does in fact exist as a real entity in its own right—that it does have an ontology. As mentioned, I cannot mount anything like full defence of this assumption here, so it will have to be taken as given for the sake of argument. And, for another thing, even on my Kantian approach to the concept and reality of legal obligation—an approach on which the metaphysics of legal obligation is dependent on its epistemology—it is one thing to ask about the *reality* of legal obligation—what kind of entity legal obligation *is*, or how legal obligation can be claimed to *exist*—and another to inquire into its *concept*, asking how it is possible to *conceive* of legal obligation. And, even if the former question, on the Kantian approach, cannot be answered independently of the latter, this is not to say that there is no such thing as a reality of legal obligation. It is only to recognise that this reality is not a self-standing or concept-independent entity. Moreover, it is merely to concede that we do not have a direct insight into reality or an unfiltered, unprocessed view of it. In this investigation into the reality and existence of legal obligation, then, I will be dealing not directly with that reality and existence but with the conditions subject to which legal obligation can be *conceived* as a real entity or as existing. These are conditions for the possibility of *thinking* about legal obligation, or forming a *concept* of it as something that can be said to *exist*. This clearly limits the scope and ambition of this investigation, since its purpose is not to peer directly into legal obligation as a real entity but to set out the most plausible conceptual scheme within which to frame and understand its reality. Much less am I pretending to get at a purported 'essence' of legal obligation: I am only interested in its reality, while recognising that this reality cannot be described independently of how we *think* about legal obligation. So, while the account of legal obligation offered in this essay does not pretend to give us a direct view of its reality—but rather seeks to describe this reality such as it can or must necessarily be conceived—this does not amount to denying the same reality. It merely recognises that we are not equipped to fully bridge the gap between thought and reality.

This takes us to the third and final preliminary point. This is that even if the investigation into the reality of legal obligation I am embarking on is qualified in the sense just explained, which investigates this reality indirectly through the lens of how it must be conceptualised, the resulting account remains tethered to the same reality, not by describing how legal obligation is understood within a specific community, but by describing how it *must* be understood regardless of the community we belong to. What the account seeks to do, in other words, is to arrive at how legal obligation must be understood in light of the premises we must *all* accept if we are to engage in any rational discourse about obligation. For the argument will point out that certain premises are necessary, or fundamental, in that we cannot ignore them without depriving ourselves of even thinking about legal obligation. The study, then, is shaped by an interest in the essential conditions of conceivability of legal obligation: the argument concerns what can be assumed to be the scheme of thought through which we *have to* understand legal obligation. What the argument posits, in other words, is that, insofar as we think coherently and clearly, we cannot but acknowledge that legal obligation is what the argument offered below claims it is. This is to say, the claims about legal obligation that will be defended are claims about legal obligation not as a cultural construct—a specific view that *some* people may have of this concept—but as something we cannot but recognise as legal obligation, or something we must *all* recognise as such because this is how legal obligation must necessarily appear to and be experienced by us. It is in this sense that this work proposes to investigate what legal obligation *is*, for it seeks to uncover the ontology (or reality) of legal obligation by describing the conditions for the conceivability of legal obligation. These are understood as *necessary* conditions, ones we cannot avoid if we as human beings are to have any understanding of legal obligation and any sensible engagement with it. And, if we can identify these conditions, by describing the basic concepts and categories without which we would not even be able to converse sensibly about obligation, and *legal* obligation in particular, we will not just be describing ourselves as human beings (versus describing particular communities of human beings) but will also be describing the thing we are engaging with as human beings, namely, in this case, legal obligation itself. The account here offered can in this sense be understood as concerned with what legal obligation *is*—offering as full a view of legal obligation as is humanly possible—even if it does so through the lens of our basic framework for *thinking* about legal obligation as an entity that is not independent of that activity.

The main thrust of this preliminary discussion, then, is that this study is concerned not with legal obligation as an *idea* but with legal obligation as an *entity*. And even though this entity is dependent on the conceptual and epistemic constructs through which we engage with it, these constructs are understood as ones absent which we could *not* engage with it (as is the case with the whole of the reality that surrounds us). So, if this investigation attempts a general conceptual scheme, its intended outcome is more than a framework of thought designed to help us better understand legal obligation, for this scheme or framework is understood as *necessary* for us to be able to engage with legal obligation. As a result, in providing such a scheme or framework, we are at the same time providing a picture of the thing the scheme or framework is *for*, namely, legal obligation itself—legal obligation not just as an idea but also as a distinct kind of entity in the world.

3 What Legal Obligation Is

In this section, I offer an account of the reality of legal obligation. As mentioned, the argument is embedded in my modified Kantian conceptualisation of legal obligation as a not merely prudential *justificatory* reason for action. Insofar as legal obligation is understood as a justificatory practical reason, the question, 'What is a legal obligation?', can be reformulated as, 'What is a *justificatory* reason for action?', or, more specifically, 'What is the theoretically soundest referent of the notion of a justificatory reason for action insofar as this referent constitutes legal obligation?'

The candidates for this role, as they emerge from the meta-normative research conducted to date, are of two main kinds: (a) subjective mental states, or psychological conditions, which gives us a *psychologism* about reasons, and (b) facts, which gives us a *factualism* about reasons.[7] A fact, in turn, has been understood to be (1) a linguistic entity, (2) an external performance, or (3) a thought-object. As a linguistic entity, the reality of a justificatory reason is (1) a statement, or proposition, taking the form 'the fact that …'. Such a statement is then further characterised as either a syntactic structure (the sign or string of words following 'the fact that' formulation), a semantic unit (a meaning), or a pragmatic term as an individual utterance or speech act. As external conduct, the reality of a justificatory reason is (2) taken to consist in an objectively determinable action, be it an individual act or a social practice. Finally, as a thought-object, the reality of a justificatory reason is (3) a public, or collective, entity capable of being true or false. An entity so understood is additionally characterised as either a part of the natural world or something immaterial or non-natural.

We can now ask which of these candidate referents of a justificatory reason most plausibly singles out what a legal obligation is. The psychologistic approach to justificatory reasons can be discounted on the ground that, on the Kantian approach here advanced, legal obligation can hardly be reduced to a psychological state.[8] For we can have a legal obligation to do something without necessarily feeling obligated to do that thing or believing ourselves to be so obligated. True, there may well be certain psychological states typically associated with the existence of a legal obligation and with our doing or not doing what is legally obligatory. For instance, complying with a legal obligation is typically *believed* to be a burden and is more often than not *felt* to be entailing sacrifice and renunciation. Moreover, not doing what is legally obligatory is commonly associated with a feeling of guilt: an act carried out in breach of a legal obligation is typically experienced as blameworthy, and the otherwise law-abiding

[7]A critical discussion of psychologism and factualism can be found in Dancy (2000, pp. 1–25), Alvarez (2010, 2017), Wiland (2012) and many others. For a defence of factualism, which in relation to justificatory reasons is now the dominant view, see Darwall (1983), Raz (1990), Smith (1994) and Scanlon (1998). Davidson (1963), Williams (1981, 1995), Schroeder (2008), and Goldman (2009) are instead committed to different versions of psychologism.

[8]The contrary view is associated with different forms of meta-normative noncognitivism, which defines reasons in terms of different psychological states, such as emotions, inclinations, pro-attitudes, or desires. See, for instance, Ayer (1936, 1984), Blackburn (1984, 1993, 1998), and Gibbard (1990, 2003, 2012).

individual who carries it out is likely to feel the moral weight of that choice of action. But no matter how regularly legal obligation may be accompanied by a *belief* that we have an obligation to do something or a *feeling* that we are so obligated or a sense of *guilt* for not fulfilling that obligation, it is one thing to have these cognitive and psychological states, and another to have an obligation, legal or otherwise; nor can a legal obligation be reduced to a conditional statement to the effect that if we *feel* obligated to do something, then we *are* obligated to do that thing. There is no internal state, in other words, that can be pointed to as necessary for an obligation to exist. In fact, part of the meaning of an obligation is precisely that it holds *regardless* of what we may individually think about it or how we may feel about it. Indeed, it would defeat the very point of an obligation if it turned out that it was contingent on the agent's beliefs, feelings, and other internal states, be they cognitive or volitional. Otherwise stated, as an entity in the world, legal obligation is not internal to the agent and so cannot be equated with any subjective state or condition. Just as a practical choice is justified not by the way in which we feel about it but by the factual grounds on which it rests, so legal obligation as a justificatory reason comes into being not through any accompanying belief, feeling, or subjective experience of the agent but through the factual basis on which it is validated.

This takes us to the factualist view. It begins with the thesis that a legal obligation qua fact is a linguistic entity (in turn understood in a syntactic, a semantic, or a pragmatic sense). This thesis certainly has some intuitive appeal because language is typically and paradigmatically the means we use to express legal obligations. But this does not mean that legal obligations are thereby reducible to the language through which they are expressed and brought into being. From the fact that legal obligation is introduced and conveyed linguistically it does not follow that the linguistic entities through which this is done (whether they are signs, meanings, or speech acts) are themselves legal obligations. We might be tempted to make that inference if we consider that the law itself is typically expressed in language, and we often speak of that language *as* law, for example, when we say, 'The law says, or the Constitution says this or that'. But even here we have to concede that this manner of speaking is figurative so that we would get only an incomplete picture of the law if we equated the law with its language, not least because that language always needs to be interpreted and cannot do the work of the law simply by virtue of its being written into law. Also, we simply cannot equate legal obligation with the linguistic entities through which it is formulated because legal obligations can come into being without any corresponding linguistic formulation.[9]

Legal obligation is also not reducible to an external performance. No doubt, legal obligation is constitutively linked to the practical domain (the sphere of action) in both its individual form (the act done by an individual subject) and its collective form (the social and conventional practices habitually followed by groups of individuals). But it cannot be reduced to what people *do*, for it consists in a standard or

[9] A case in point is pictorial, or drawn, obligatory norms. On nonlinguistic norms (inclusive of obligatory norms), see Lorini and Moroni (2020, 2021, 2022) and Loddo et al. (2021).

directive in light of which what they are doing (the way they are acting) can be made sense of and assessed as compliant or noncompliant. We cannot even make sense of the way people are behaving, or tell whether or not their behaviour is obligatory, just by looking at their behaviour alone, without a benchmark in light of which to make such a judgment. And that benchmark cannot itself be a course of conduct. It needs to be a *standard* for conduct. So, while legal obligation is connected to courses of conduct, it cannot be equated with them. The relation between legal obligation and behaviour, in other words, is not one of identity (otherwise we would not even be able to distinguish the meaning of 'legal obligation' from that of 'behaviour'). It is, instead, the relation that holds between that which *regulates* (a directive, standard, or norm) and that which is *regulated* (behaviour). The latter (be it individual or collective) is the *object* and *subject matter* of legal obligation. Hence, it cannot itself be understood as legal obligation: it cannot, on its own, be used as a basis on which to make out the scope and meaning of legal obligation. In short, legal obligation cannot be analysed without remainder into any behaviour or pattern of behaviours but is instead best understood as that which *governs* such behaviour.

We are thus left with only one plausible view of the reality of legal obligation, namely, the view of it as a thought-object. But how is this thought-object to be understood? Two points are worth making here. For one thing, it cannot be a psychological state, for as we just saw, that would be tantamount to making legal obligation conditional on one's *feeling* obligated, which contradicts the very thing that distinguishes obligation as such (thus, legal obligation) within the normative, which is its being independent of how you or I happen feel about it. And, for another thing, and relatedly, legal obligation cannot be an *individual* affair either—something that you or I can decide on for ourselves. It is instead *public*. Just as it cannot be a subjective *feeling*, so it cannot be a subjective, and hence *individual*, thought or thought process, and for the same reason, which is that legal obligation can only make sense in the context of a *community*, one consisting of the plurality of individuals who are subject to the law. An obligation that someone established on their own and for themselves alone would not be an obligation proper, much less a legal obligation, but something we may feel compelled to do only in a psychological or aspirational sense and not in a properly necessitating sense (under which we are bound to do something even if we may not see it that way).

We thus have a view of legal obligation as a justificatory reason for action that accordingly can be reduced neither to a psychological state nor to a private choice but is instead a public thought-object. But what is a thought-object? How are we to conceive of this peculiar fact in with which we are identifying the referent of a legal obligation, the thing that can be pointed to in pinning down how it exists in the world? The three avenues that can be pursued in answering this question are non-cognitivism, naturalism, and non-naturalism. There is no definitive argument for any of these three broad theories, and so I will not be taking the time to get into that debate. But the foregoing discussion does already give us some guideposts. In particular it suggests that two of these approaches are ill-fitting: these are the non-cognitivist approach, since it leans toward a view of obligation as dependent on psychological states, and the naturalist approach, which would commit us to a scientistic understanding of thought-objects as natural facts,[10] thereby undercutting their normative force or at least making it difficult to explain how legal obligation might possibly carry any such force. I will therefore run with the non-naturalist approach, taking a leaf out of contemporary meta-normative non-naturalism.[11] Accordingly, here I will seek to gain insight into the reality of legal obligation by specifying what a non-natural fact is.

On the non-naturalistic approach, what we are calling non-natural facts—understood as primitive and irreducibly normative facts—are an ontological kind distinct from empirical, or ordinary, facts in both an epistemic and an ontological sense. In an *epistemic* sense, what distinguishes non-natural facts is that they can be accessed via epistemic processes that are both a priori and synthetic, whereas our knowledge of natural facts is empirical and a posteriori.[12] In an *ontological* sense, the distinction depends on the way the ontology of non-natural facts is accounted for, and there are two such accounts that we find in non-naturalism. On one account, non-natural facts are worldly, robust, substantive objects with their own ontological status.[13] Insofar as normative facts are so understood, they provide a solid ontological basis for legal obligation, for they are claimed to be facts proper—real entities irreducible to the language used to describe them (that is, to any linguistic formulation of them), which makes them objects with their own distinct ontological existence. What is peculiar about non-natural facts so understood is that they are non-empirical, primitive, and irreducibly normative. On the other account, non-natural facts are, by contrast, (true) propositions. This is a nominal—or noncommittal and merely formal—understanding of facts, which so conceived have no (real) ontological counterpart outside the linguistic, or propositional, realm.[14] They are, in other words, facts in name only, since nothing substantive or actual corresponds to them. This nominal and deflationary view of justificatory reasons as non-natural facts can be described as quietist, and the same can therefore be said of the reality of legal obligation as a kind of justificatory reason. As a non-natural fact, in other words, legal obligation is no more than a proposition, and one at that, while understood as 'true', lacks any corresponding entity in the world. But this quietist account of the ontology (or reality) of legal obligation was previously rejected, arguing that it is misleading to characterise legal obligation as no more than a linguistic entity. For this reason, in what follows I will be going with the *robust* non-naturalistic account of normative facts as having a substantive reality in the world. In short, legal

[10] Meta-normative naturalism comes in two main varieties: one is reductionistic, examples of which are Harman (1977), Brandt (1979), and Railton (1986, 1989), and the other is non-reductionistic, an approach defended in Sturgeon (1988, 1992), Boyd (1988), Sayre-McCord (1988), and Brink (1989), among others.

[11] The most influential statements of this theoretical approach can be found in Audi (2004), Crisp (2006), Dancy (2004), Shafer-Landau (2003), Enoch (2007, 2011), and Parfit (2011).

[12] This point is made by Skorupski (2010, pp. 401–419).

[13] For a defence of this position see, for instance, Enoch (2007); Enoch (2011), pp. 85–99.

[14] See Raz (1999, pp. 15–35), Skorupski (2002), and Parfit (2011, pp. 475–487).

obligation will be understood as a non-natural fact in a worldly, substantive, and thus firmly ontological sense of the term.

On the non-naturalist approach here endorsed, then, a justificatory reason—thus legal obligation as such a kind of reason—is a non-natural fact, understood not empirically as belonging to the natural or psychological world of causation investigated by the natural sciences, nor even linguistically as no more than a proposition that is true even without any empirical reality against which to ascertain its truth, but rather as a sui generis fact. Legal obligation is a primitive and irreducibly normative entity but a fact, nonetheless, having a real existence in a robustly ontological sense. So, the question we now have to turn to is, 'What is legal obligation as such a *sui generis* fact – one that is non-natural, i.e., primitive and irreducibly normative, yet worldly?'

Since non-natural facts are understood as primitive and irreducibly normative, they cannot constitutively be further analysed. They are entities that can neither be reduced to nor analysed into other entities. Still, it is possible (and I think instructive) to clarify what features are necessarily associated with justificatory reasons as non-natural facts and thus with legal obligation as such a fact, and specifically as a justificatory reason for action. I will do so by focusing on the two aspects that non-naturalists take to be fundamental to non-natural facts (and so to justificatory reasons and thus to legal obligation as justificatory reasons for action). For one thing, they are *facts* (have facticity) and, for another, they are facts in a peculiar, *sui generis* sense (have sui genericity). Let us, therefore, further specify these two aspects of non-natural facts as the kind of thing that justificatory reasons are, and as the kind of thing that legal obligation as a justificatory reason is. This will set the stage for the account of the reality of legal obligation that will be defended here, giving us a preview of what lies at its core.

It was just noted that non-natural facts are, in the first place, *facts*: they are non-natural and non-empirical but still facts in the robustly ontological sense that they have an actual existence in the world and, as such, they can be described as having three properties: they are *abstract*, *ideational*, and *public*. What it means for them to be abstract is that they are not concrete. Relatedly, what it means for them to be ideational is that they are ideas or thoughts: they are therefore immaterial (neither physical nor psychological) and thus not part of the causally ordered world. What it means for them to be public is that these are not the individual thoughts or ideas of this or that person but are collective: they are recognised by an entire community of people. But as non-natural facts, they are nonetheless *facts*. This means that, as mentioned, they are not predicates, attributes, or properties but are rather the thing to which a property, attribute, or predicate is ascribed. They are, in other words, objects (albeit in a narrow, discriminating, and less than all-encompassing sense of this term, as will be specified shortly).

This takes us to the *sui generis* quality of non-natural facts as the kind of reality to which belongs a justificatory reason (and so legal obligation as such a reason). There are two properties in particular that make them *sui generis*: first, they are *created*, rather than found (and are thus artefacts), and second, they are temporal but not spatial. The first of these properties makes them *sui generis* even within the realm of abstract objects, since these are paradigmatically construed as mathematical entities, propositions, universals, and the like. In fact, unlike these entities—broadly understood as being *found*, or discovered—the non-natural entities forming the reality of legal obligation are, as just mentioned, *created*. Hence a distinction is drawn in the literature between (a) standard abstract objects—the abstractions that, paradigmatically, are not anyone's construction and so are not dependent for their existence on anyone understanding them to exist—and (b) the niche class of abstract objects that are known as *created abstracta*. The latter do depend for their existence on someone thinking them into being and are, in this sense, a thing apart from the abstractions of science, mathematics, and the like. But what also makes these created *abstracta* specifically distinct from standardly abstract objects is that, as just mentioned, they are *temporal*. In fact, while created *abstracta* and standard abstractions alike are non-spatial (neither occupy space), the latter are non-temporal, too, in a way that the former cannot be. In other words, created *abstracta* (a) must necessarily at least have a creation date—a moment of inception—and (b) may also have an expiration date, a moment when they are understood to no longer exist—in contrast to standard abstract objects, for which there is no point in time in which they begin or cease to exist. As created *abstracta*, then, the non-natural facts making up the reality of justificatory reasons (and so of legal obligation as such a reason) are *sui generis* in this second sense, too, by virtue of their being temporal.

In summary so far, I have argued that the reality of a justificatory reason—and so of legal obligation as such a reason—is to be located in non-natural facts of a specific kind, in that they are (1) abstract, (2) ideational, (3) public, (4) objectual, and (5) *sui generis*. So far, I have just looked at these ontological properties in outline, and now and for the remainder of this discussion I will inspect each of them from up close so as to firm up the argument that is being made about legal obligation and what it consists of.

3.1 Legal Obligation: Abstract

In the literature on what exists in the world, all entities (or objects, in a broadly encompassing sense of this term) are distinguished into abstract and concrete.[15] This abstract-concrete distinction thus gives us a fundamental ontological dividing line, in that the two classes (the abstract and the concrete) are understood to be at once exhaustive of what exists and exclusive of each other.[16] The distinction is exhaustive in that the two classes account for *all* that exists (nothing can be said to exist outside these two classes of objects); and it is exclusive in the sense that what exists must

[15] Here the term 'object' is used in an all-encompassing sense to refer to any existing entity, along with its properties, predicates, and relations.

[16] On this distinction, see Cowling (2017, pp. 69–105).

either be abstract or concrete (no object can be both abstract and concrete). To be sure, there are different methods for drawing the distinction between abstract and concrete, and no firm consensus exists on what counts as one and what as the other.[17] But we do have a broad picture of what is archetypically an abstract entity, with a cluster of standard features they tend to be associated with (or, conversely, a cluster of opposite standard features they tend to lack).[18]

To begin with, with some notable exceptions, abstract entities can be characterised as *necessary* existents, as opposed to contingent ones, since they can be neither created nor destroyed and are therefore not dependent on any concrete event, action, or circumstance. Moreover, abstract entities are *causally inefficacious*, or inactive: in stark contrast to concrete entities, they exist outside the causal order of the world, having no causal power or relations or any active causal role in the world. Related to this, abstract entities are *immaterial*: they are not physical objects like chairs and tables. From this it follows that, even though they have the ontological status of 'things', they cannot be sensed or perceived (they are in this sense non-sensible). Nor does their *existence* depend on someone feeling, perceiving, or experiencing them: even in a world devoid of sentient beings, they would continue to exist; they are not contingent on anyone's psychology (they are in this sense non-psychological)—this being an implication of their necessity. Epistemically, their imperceptibility means that they cannot be discovered by means of empirical investigation. The existence of abstract objects can instead be discovered through epistemic processes such as postulation, synthetic a priori reasoning, and inference to the best explanation. In that respect, even if abstract entities are causally inert, they are argued to exist on the basis that they are useful, or even indispensable, for the functioning of our best scientific models, metaphysical theories, or other human practices, such as practical deliberation.[19] To continue, abstract entities are claimed to have *no spatial location*, or even to exist outside spacetime. The lack of the *spatial* element is widely accepted in the literature as an essential feature of abstract entities, but not so the lack of the *temporal* dimension: it is generally agreed that an

[17] On this point, see Cowling (2017, pp. 1–22), Plebani (2020), and Falguera et al. (2022). Some frame the distinction by way of example, looking at paradigmatic and intuitively indisputable cases of abstract and concrete objects in order to arrive at what is abstract and what is concrete: mathematical entities, for example, will undeniably be recognised as paradigmatically abstract entities, while tables will be recognised as solidly concrete. Thus, on this approach, anything like a mathematical entity counts as abstract, while anything like a table counts as concrete (so long as the differences and similarities are relevant). Others instead choose to arrive at abstraction 'by considering the common features of several objects or ideas and ignoring the irrelevant features' (Falguera et al. 2022, p. 8). And others still see the distinction between abstract and concrete as primitive and so unanalysable—something we can take at face value on the ground that it is ubiquitous in ordinary language. Nor are these the only approaches to the distinction: for a sense of the full range of methods and approaches, see Cowling (2017, pp. 69–105), Plebani (2020), and Falguera et al. (2022).

[18] This characterisation of abstract objects is largely indebted to Cowling (2017, pp. 69–105).

[19] For clear statements of this, see Brink (1989, pp. 182–197), Copp (1990), Railton (1998), Schafer-Landau (2003, pp. 98–115), Field (2005), Fine (2005), Enoch (2007), Skorupski (2010, pp. 401–419), and Cowling (2017, pp. 47–57).

entity can be abstract and non-spatial but still be temporal.[20] Either way, abstract entities are clearly distinct from concrete entities, which can only exist in space *and* time: nothing can be called concrete that exists outside of either space or time. Abstract entities are also characterised as *public* and *mind-independent*: they are public as *intersubjective* entities recognised by more than one person; they are mind-independent in that, just as they exist without anyone perceiving or feeling them, they also exist without anyone *thinking* them, that is, regardless of anyone's mental states or mental acts at any given time.[21] Finally, on at least some accounts, abstract entities are understood to only enjoy a *weak* kind of existence: they exist in a sense that is less robust than that associated with concrete entities. Stated otherwise, there is no substantive fact—no fact of the matter—corresponding to an abstract entity.[22] In sum, abstract entities are typically understood as necessary, causally inert, immaterial, non-sensible, imperceptible, public, mind-independent, non-spatial entities, which may also be non-temporal, and which on some accounts exist only in a weak sense.

Now, if we compare this cluster of traits with the features that can plausibly be associated with the reality of legal obligation, we should be able to conclude that, from an ontological point of view, legal obligation—as a justificatory reason whose reality is that of a non-natural fact—is properly categorised as an abstract entity. The close continuity between abstract entities and legal obligation can be made to emerge in a number of respects. First, not unlike archetypically abstract entities, legal obligation incorporates a kind of *necessity*: normative necessity. For what one is obligated to do is something that ought to be done as a matter of necessity. True, legal obligation is a *construction*, and therefore something that does not necessarily exist, at least not in the same sense in which archetypical cases of abstract objects do. But the existence of created abstract entities (and so of entities that do not necessarily exist) is widely acknowledged, so much so that a specific category of abstract entities—the previously discussed created *abstracta*—has been introduced in research on abstract entities. At the same time, legal obligation is inseparable from necessity of the normative kind, since this is the kind of necessity without which a standard cannot even qualify as obligatory. Hence the thesis that normative necessity is a characteristic feature of what is obligatory, as distinct from other non-normative conditions as well as from normative statuses (such as permissions and privileges).

The normativity of legal obligation also means that legal obligation does not feature in the causal order of the world: just like typical abstract entities, legal obligations lack causality.

Furthermore, legal obligation is best characterised as *non-sensible*, for even though it establishes a relation between agents, and these agents typically have a

[20] That abstract entities need not be atemporal emerges in Lowe (1995, pp. 513–518), Plebani (2020, pp. 1–3), and Falguera et al. (2022, sec. 3.5.2).

[21] This is noted in Falguera et al. (2022), section 3.5, among others.

[22] This view is defended in Linsky and Zalta (1995), Azzouni (1998), Yablo (1998), Maddy (2011), Linnebo (2018), and Leng (2020).

physical existence and a psychology, neither of these two traits describes the relation itself (the one by which they are bound to act in certain ways in relation to one another). Legal obligation, in short, is neither a physical nor a psychological constraint, for it may be associated with, but is ultimately irreducible to, compulsion. That legal obligation cannot be reduced to compulsion in the psychological sense is widely agreed on in contemporary legal philosophy. The different conceptions of legal obligation defended by legal theorists are reducible to a basic dichotomy of models of legal obligation: the empirical model and the normative one. However, the empirical model, which seeks to explain legal obligation entirely in terms of the way people in fact behave or are likely to behave when they are said to be under an obligation, is all but defunct today.[23] To briefly elaborate on the empirical model, we have a legal obligation insofar as the law requires us to behave in some way and (a) we actually behave accordingly (matter-of-fact compliance) or (b) we are more or less likely to behave accordingly, since undesirable consequences will follow or are likely to follow any noncompliant behaviour (compliance under threat of force). The problem with this model is that it fails to grasp the 'ought' of legal obligation. For, on this model, any connection between what we have a legal obligation to do and what we ought to do is merely contingent and occasional, or at best probabilistic. This is why the normative model of legal obligation nowadays commands wide acceptance. On this view, legal obligation cannot be defined by the course of action we *in fact* take or are more or less *likely* to take in light of the consequences of failing to do what the law requires. Rather, legal obligation is understood as a requirement singling out the course of action we *ought to* take (or ought not to take), regardless of whether we actually act accordingly or are likely to do so. In contrast to the empirical model, the normative model rests on the claim that obligation is conceptually linked to what we *ought* to do. On this view, in short, an obligation to do something implies a prescription saying that this is what can legitimately be demanded of us or exacted from us. This view finds broad support in common sense: intuitively, it makes sense to claim that legal obligation means that some behaviour ought to be carried out. And so it is that legal theorists with diverse backgrounds and philosophical agendas conceive of legal obligation as an 'ought', in turn inflected as

[23] In legal philosophy, we find at least two different basic variants of the empirical model of legal obligation: the predictive account and the imperatival account. An account of legal obligation can be qualified as predictive insofar as it describes legal obligation in terms of the likelihood of our being sanctioned for disobeying the behaviours described in a legal system (with the connection between obligation and punishment in being purely probabilistic). This view is theoretically associated with the pragmatic and instrumentalist strand of legal realism (see, for instance, Holmes 1896), and with the Law and Economics movement (see Cooter 1984 and Kornhauser 1999). The second variant of the empirical model—the imperatival account—provides a different definition of legal obligation, which too is purely fact-based. An account can be qualified as imperatival if it ties legal obligations to what the law commands us to do. The idea of a legal command is in turn tied to the idea of a sanction, whether real or potential, since those who introduce this command are usually in a position to enforce it. This means that for a legal obligation to exist, there must be some kind of pressure, whether physical or psychological, that someone (the enforcer) exerts on someone else (the person or persons bound by that obligation). The imperatival account is paradigmatically advanced in Austin (1998, pp. 11–15).

a practical and normative necessity.[24] Directly flowing from the normative model so construed is that, insofar as (1) an analytical connection does get recognised between 'ought' and obligation, and (2) some conceptual gap can be said to exist between 'is' and 'ought', legal obligation cannot be satisfactorily characterised solely on the basis of sensible or material elements (whether physical or psychical).

The normative quality of legal obligation comes with a further implication, which is that legal obligation cannot be discovered by means of empirical investigation. In this sense, like the paradigmatically abstract entities previously discussed, legal obligation is *imperceptible*. That is, in order to determine whether a legal obligation exists, we need to rely on nonempirical epistemic methods that are not based on perception. Related to this, legal obligation stands in a relation of conceptual continuity with abstract entities in that both are *mind-independent* in one specific sense.[25] Legal obligation, in other words, is not reducible to anyone's mental contents or acts: it exists even if no one feels, pictures, or thinks about it. And, not unlike paradigmatically abstract entities, legal obligation is a *relational* entity and so a public one, rather than a private matter or an individually held status. For obligation is a normative status under which some individuals are accountable to others for doing certain actions. On this basis, in order for an obligation to exist, it must not only be acknowledged, but acknowledged by a *plurality* of people: it cannot exist as something controlled and recognised by a single individual or institution. In other words, when an obligation is in place, someone must be entitled to expect something—an action or restitution—from someone else, who in turn has to grant that claim. This is why the claims associated with legal obligation are best characterised as constitutively shared, or at least shareable. Finally, whilst legal obligation can be said to exist in a substantive, or robust, sense, the thesis has been influentially defended that obligation, as a justificatory reason, exists in a purely nominal sense, and thus in a sense that is clearly distinguishable from the sense of existence associated with concrete objects.[26]

[24] Worth mentioning among the proponents of this normative view of obligation are, at least, Kelsen (1934, 1945, 1967), Hart (1958, 1994), Beyleveld and Brownsword (1986), Dworkin (1986, 2006, 2011), Raz (1990), Hurd (1999), Coleman (2001), Marmor (2001), Shapiro (2001, 2002, 2014), and Finnis (2011).

[25] More specifically, legal obligation is not dependent on anyone deciding for themselves whether or not they are bound by an obligation. In that respect, legal obligation is both created and collective. It is *created*, for it would not exist but for the people who bring it into being but can only be created if recognised by others (those to whom it is understood to apply. And once it is so recognised, no single individual can decide that it does not apply to them or does not exist for any of those to whom it applies. This makes it possible to say that obligation is *created*—and therefore *not* completely mind-independent—while not depending for its existence on the mind of any single individual. In a slogan, legal obligation is *individually* mind-*independent* but *publicly* mind-*dependent*. Or (otherwise started) it is dependent on *collective* recognition for its *existence*, but independent of *individual* recognition for its *scope* and *content*. I would like to express my gratitude to Filippo Valente to bring these points to my attention.

[26] As mentioned, this deflationary view is defended in Raz (1999, pp. 15–35), Skorupski (2002), and Parfit (2011, pp. 475–487).

This continuity between legal obligation and abstract entities is not undermined in any decisive way by the *temporal* nature of legal obligation. True, abstract entities are typically said to exist outside space, and even outside time, whereas legal obligation exists *in* time. For legal obligations are introduced at a specific time, can be modified at some later stage, and may be extinguished thereafter. However, on the one hand, the temporal existence of legal obligation is not coupled with any spatial existence: while legal obligations apply to courses of conduct and conduct necessarily takes up space (that of the people who engage in it), legal obligation itself does *not* take up space. In short, while the *scope* of legal obligation is spatial, its *existence* is not. As to its spatiality, then, legal obligation does not differ from other abstract entities. On the other hand, as mentioned, the thesis is far from consolidated that abstract entities necessarily lack temporal existence. Whilst it is widely accepted that abstract entities exist outside space, more controversial is the claim that they *all* exist outside *time*. Hence, this discontinuity between legal obligation and abstract entities is merely possible and arguably inessential.

In sum, legal obligation shares with abstract entities the vast majority of properties by which the latter are defined, namely, necessity (of a normative kind), causal inertness, non-sensibility, immateriality, imperceptibility, publicity, mind-independence, and, on some views, weak, or nominal existence. The only significant difference between legal obligation and abstract entities lies in the artificial and temporal existence of the former. These traits find no parallel in paradigmatically abstract entities, which are uncreated and have an existence that is not spatiotemporal. However, these differences are not so salient as to commit us to the conclusion that legal obligation is not abstract. For we can recognise that legal obligation is created and exists in time without denying that it is abstract in a peculiar, *sui generis* sense.[27] An entity can be created and stretch across time and still be abstract. That applies to legal obligation, which from an ontological point of view is an abstract entity due to being a justificatory reason for action and thus a non-natural fact.

3.2 Legal Obligation: Ideational

We have just seen that, as a justificatory reason for action, and so as a non-natural fact, legal obligation is best characterised as an abstract entity. This takes us to a further property of legal obligation: its being ideational, as opposed to being causal in the manner that material and sensible entities are. There is a twofold sense in which legal obligation can be said to not inhabit the causally ordered world. For one thing, as mentioned, legal obligation is a *normative* relation, as opposed to a physical constraint, so it does not belong to the physical world of coercion. For another, legal obligation does not inhabit the sphere of consciousness—that of mental states as psychic processes, states, and conditions. The specific sphere in which legal

[27] The *sui generis* quality of legal obligation is further examined below in Sect. 3.5.

obligation can be found, then, is separate from both the physical and the psychological domain. Drawing on Gottlob Frege's seminal account, Karl Popper refers to this domain—neither purely physical nor purely psychological as World 3.[28] World 3 is the realm of ideations and thought structures, as distinct from both physical entities and psychological states.

To briefly elaborate, we all are familiar with the external world of physical, sensible, and sense-perceivable things. This is World 1 in Popper's nomenclature. This domain is distinguished from, and cannot be reduced to, the domain of subjective experience, which includes our psychological processes, states, and conditions. This is what Popper calls World 2. Like World 1, World 2 is a domain of causation that is nonetheless not material in the same sense in which World 1 is, since World 2 is purely psychical rather than physical. Worlds 1 and 2 are made accessible to us by the natural sciences. Finally, Popper introduces the realm inhabited by shared creations of the mind, and these may also include institutions. What inhabits this realm are neither the external objective entities of World 1 nor the private, subjective, individual entities of World 2. This further realm therefore cannot be reduced to the causal order of the physical and the psychical (Worlds 1 and 2), and Popper calls it World 3.

This is where I think legal obligation finds its rightful place, in this third realm that shares none of the different ways of causation operating in Worlds 1 and World 2. As a normative form of necessitation, legal obligation is noncausal and thus can be seen to belong in the distinctive realm of shared ideas, collective thought-constructs, public ideations, and institutional frameworks making up World 3. It is in this sense that I understand legal obligation as an ideational entity. What I mean is that legal obligation is ontologically akin to ideas and thought constructions. The ideational quality of legal obligation can thus be specified as follows: (a) legal obligation exists *in* and *as* thought, but (b) it does so in a way that is distinctively mind-*independent* (it is therefore not part of World 2).[29] For legal obligation exists independently of anyone's judgement: it does not come into existence by virtue of someone cognising it or judging it to be an existing reality. Quite to the contrary, legal obligation exists *despite* our recognising it and independently of any other mental state we may have. Legal obligation, in sum, is a thought-structure independent of any thinking being. Or, stated otherwise, legal obligation is at once a thought and an entity. As a thought it is ideated. As an entity it is independent of our thinking. It is, in short, a mind-independent ideation.

[28] See Popper (1968). Similar claims have also been made in Bolzano (1837), Brentano (1874), and Frege (1918). A similar understanding of legal standards (inclusive of the obligatory standards of law) is defended in Amselek (1991). See also the discussion in Weinberger (1986a, b).

[29] Note that even as a *mind-independent* entity in this *ontological* sense, legal obligation is understood here as *concept-dependent* in the *epistemic* Kantian sense previously outlined, where the idea, as noted, is that reality exists independently of us even if our access to it is filtered through the conceptual lens we use to process and cognise the same reality.

3.3 Legal Obligation: Public

An additional distinctive quality of legal obligation is its publicity—its public existence. Legal obligation is not an immaterial entity that is privately conceived and understood to exist by only a single individual but is rather public. This property flows from its very grammar as a relation. By definition, an obligation is something that someone is bound to do because *others* in the community think they have to do it, and because an obligation is owed not to oneself but to *others*. That goes double for a *legal* obligation, but even more importantly, this makes obligation (and legal obligation with it) an inherently *intersubjective* thought-construct, and so a shared entity, or at least one that is held up as such (as an idea that *can* be shared).

The publicity of legal obligation can be further specified and clarified by reference to the ongoing meta-normative debate on the publicity of justificatory reasons.[30] One main issue in that debate is whether or not justificatory reasons for action are necessarily public normative standards. What is meant by a 'public' normative standard, as I would distil this concept from that debate, is not just a standard that takes the interests of others into account as a basis on which they should have a reason for acting as the standard prescribes or allows. This is no doubt a component of publicity, but it does not in itself make a standard public. For while it may take into account a range of interests that is not limited to those of the agent who is introducing or asserting the standard for an entire community of other agents, it notably does *not* take into account the views that these other agents *themselves* may have about what it means to take their interests into account. It follows that in order for a normative standard to be public in the relevant sense, it must not only address the interests of all the agents to whom the standard is meant to apply, but must do so by giving these agents a reason that justifies to them why they ought to follow the standard: this justification may only be presumptive, to be sure, but it must be addressed to an entire public (all those to whom the standard applies), which accordingly includes anyone who may reject the reasons put forward as justification for the standard. In short, a normative standard is public if, in stating a reason for acting accordingly, it takes into account not only the interests of all those to whom it applies but also their viewpoint, or what the standard looks like from their perspective, given their concerns, and in light of what *they* understand to be in the public interest. The standard can be inclusive by responding to the interests of others, but it does so from a standpoint that is exclusive to its proponent—or on the basis of a justificatory reason that only its proponent can endorse, or a justificatory reason that disregards the reasons that others may have for committing the standard—it remains essentially private. A normative standard is therefore, by contrast, *private* if it fails

[30]Among the major contributions to this debate are Nagel (1970, pp. 90–98), Nagel (1986, pp. 164–188), Darwall (1983, pp. 117–167), Parfit (1984, pp. 142–143), Pettit (1987), McNaughton and Rawling (1991, 1995), Korsgaard (1996a, pp. 275–310); Korsgaard (1996b, pp. 132–145); Korsgaard (2009, pp. 191–206), O'Day (1998), Norman (2000), LeBar (2001), Gert (2002), Willigenburg (2002), and Wallace (2009).

under either of these two tests of publicity: if it fails to take the interests of others into account (it is literally self-interested) *or* if it does take their interests into account but on the basis of reasons that do not take their *viewpoint* into account.

As I see it, there are two important dimensions to the sense of publicity at issue in the debate on the publicity of justificatory reasons. First, as much as there may be an inherent grammar or 'syntax' of publicity as a relational concept, it is not just this formal aspect that defines the publicity of justificatory reasons (their being addressed to *others*) but their substantive aspect, meaning their content and force, and so the authoritative power they can exert in making claims on others. A reason for action, in other words, does not become public simply by being 'made public', or made known to those who are to act on it as a reason for action: if it is to apply to agents other than the profferer—and thus extend its scope as a properly public reason—it needs to also be able to exert some kind of authoritative force, this by making the right kind of appeal to its addresses. And this takes us to the second point about publicity, namely, that justificatory reasons for action are public entities in a sense that is more demanding than mere intelligibility. In order for a justificatory reason for action to qualify as public, in other words, it needs to do more than simply come across to others intelligibly or be expressed in a way that others can understand, making sense to a group of individuals who are not just the person proffering the reason. A justificatory reason is public, in the sense in which publicity is debated in this context, if it is shared in a deeper and denser sense, having to do with the second prong of the two-pronged test of publicity previously introduced. Publicity, more to the point, is primarily about whether a justificatory reason can or ought to be recognised by others as a reason for action. This is a test of mutual recognition under which a reason for action qualifies as public if it can be regarded as worthy of consideration, invoking values that have broad appeal, such that it would be unreasonable for others to reject the same reason unless they can do so on the basis of other reasons that others ought to themselves recognise as worthy of consideration. Essential to this test is the idea that reasons for action need to be intersubjective: they cannot just appeal to one agent (the one proffering the reason) but must be able to appeal to *others* as well (to people other than the profferer). In this intersubjectivity—which is key to publicity—lies the element that makes a reason for action properly justificatory. A reason for action can justify the normative standard for which it is proffered as a ground of action only so long as it is intersubjective, that is, only so long as it draws on values of broad appeal that have gained recognition among a community of agents, such that these reasons can properly make a *normative claim* on these agents, one they cannot reject without coming across as unreasonable, in the strong sense of having exited the practical realm of reason and reason-giving. And in this intersubjectivity to which reasons owe their justificatory force lies the element that specifically distinguishes reasons for action in the normative sense proper from other kinds of reasons—reasons that do not *justify* a standard to others so much as they simply *explain* what the standard entails, or else reasons that *compel* others to act accordingly (neither of which are reasons proper, in that they cannot make a normative claim on anyone other than the profferer, and so are not intersubjective).[31]

To understand legal obligation as a public normative standard, then, is to appreciate that this standard cannot be framed exclusively from the standpoint of a single individual's concerns—for in that case it would fail as a justificatory reason for action—but must be framed on a shared basis, one that draws on a common stock of ideas, values, and principles. Or, what amounts to the same thing, a legal obligation cannot qualify as a public standard if the reasons and concerns that make up its rationale are ones that other individuals may legitimately reject. Insofar as one has a legal obligation, the action that is demanded by that standard is supported by considerations that others cannot refuse to treat as a sound basis for action without misunderstanding the situation at hand. One's legal obligation is thus an essentially public consideration in a specific sense: it ought to be recognised as a presumptively sound or valid demand not only by the obligee (the person to whom the obligation is owed) but also by everyone else, including those who may have different, or even conflicting, interests. Conversely, idiosyncratic preferences, private motives, personal interests, and the like are not a solid basis of legal obligation. For no consideration can qualify as a justificatory reason for action, and so as a legal obligation, unless it is public—unless it can and ought to be intersubjectively acknowledged as a plausible supporting ground of action. That is, the publicity of justificatory reasons for action implies that legal obligation exists as a standard that inherently commands recognition by anyone with a basic appreciation for what it means to offer and accept reasons in the practical realm. Hence, whenever there is a legal obligation to act in some way, those to whom the obligation applies cannot simply decide that it does not. This is because, conceptually, an obligation (including a legal obligation) cannot qualify as one unless it is grounded in reasons for acting accordingly and unless these reasons are sound: they have gained public recognition, such that, even if they may not be decisive in getting others to act on the obligation they support, they cannot be rejected out of hand. It is the publicity of legal obligation that endows it with this normative force (a force in virtue of which we have to explain ourselves to others before we can count ourselves out as not subject to the obligation at hand). And it is this trait that conceptually distinguishes legal obligation from a non-reason-like statement as to why other ought to behave as required. Legal obligation, in this sense, differs in kind from a private standard that everyone apart from the endorser can simply ignore in reflecting on the basic practical question of how to act. This characterisation configures legal obligation as a public statement in the non-trivial sense that anything we qualify as legal obligation exists in a shared space, namely, a space we all inhabit, we all ought to take care of, and we all are responsible for.

---

[31] This idea can be rephrased in Korsgaard's (1996a, p. 301) words as follows: a practical reason essentially makes normative claims on different agents by exerting its 'authority over other people and yourself at other times', which means that 'to say that you have a reason is to say something relational' (emphasis in the original).

In conclusion, legal obligation exists as an intersubjective normative entity: it is essentially public. The publicity of legal obligation means that the force of legal obligation transfers across agents and their courses of conduct, such that legal obligation cannot be equated with an idiosyncratic or privately held consideration: it is an entity that other agents cannot refuse to acknowledge, and if they do refuse, they are signalling to everyone else that they are unwilling or unable to engage with them in the public space of reason-giving—the space occupied by legal obligation.

3.4 Legal Obligation: Ontologically an Object

I have so far referred to legal obligation generically as an entity. But what precisely does that word mean in this context? This is the question to which I will now turn. I will claim that legal obligation as an entity is properly an *object*, but in a narrow and discriminating sense of this term, where objects are distinguished from the predicates, attributes, and properties that can be ascribed to them. Legal obligation, in short, is a *thing*, as distinct from what can be *predicated* of things.

This understanding of legal obligation is premised on the view that our world contains a variety of entities and objects that do not exhaust our ontology. Worldly entities can in turn be catalogued as either objects or nonobjects.[32] The latter typically include predicates, attributes, and properties. Both objects and nonobjects possess a distinct and respectable ontological status: ontologically, both objects and nonobjects are entities in the world. They exist. However, their way of existing is different. Objects are entities that can *have* predicates, attributes, and properties and are thus irreducible to predicates, attributes, and properties. For what is *predicated* of something cannot, by definition, *be* that thing (what a property takes as its subject matter cannot itself be that subject matter). And the same goes for attributes and properties: what is attributed to a term cannot *be* that term, and what *bears* a property cannot *be* that property.[33] Which is why the reality of objects exceeds, and cannot be reduced to, the reality of their predicates, attributes, and properties. Correspondingly, nonobjects (predicates, attributes, properties, and the like) are borne, held, or instantiated (by objects). They are features, traits, characteristics, qualities, or modes of being. As such, they constitutively are not objects themselves, since otherwise they would be identical to objects, as opposed to being borne, held, or instantiated by them. To rephrase this point, far from *being* predicates, attributes, and properties (these being typical non-objects), objects *instantiate* and *exemplify* predicates, attributes, and properties.

[32] On this point, see Armstrong (1989) and, for a more recent discussion, Rettler and Bailey (2017).

[33] The relevant distinction here, then, is between 'bearing' entities (objects) and 'borne' entities (nonobjects). Nonobjects are entities that other entities (objects) can exemplify and instantiate. Nonobjects therefore need to be kept ontologically distinct from what exemplifies and instantiates them (namely, objects).

In the theoretical framework explored here, legal obligation is an *object* (albeit a specific kind of object). Hence, legal obligation is a *thing*, and so can be described as having predicates, attributes, or properties that, by definition and necessarily, cannot *be* the thing they are predicated of, attributed to, or found to possess. Legal obligation, therefore, belongs to the ontological class 'object', as distinct from the class 'nonobject'. Legal obligation is, in this sense, not a property, attribute, or predicate, but something that bears, possesses, instantiates, or exemplifies properties, attributes, and predicates.

3.5 Legal Obligation: Sui Generis

I have so far argued that legal obligation is an abstract object of a certain kind: one that is ideational and public. In this section, I will home in on the peculiarities of legal obligation as an *abstract* object. For, on closer inspection, it emerges that legal obligation is not a standard abstract object, a paradigmatic instance of one, but a peculiar instance occupying a special position among other abstract objects.

Firstly, let us quickly review the grounds for the claim that legal obligation is an abstract object. Unlike concrete objects, and very much like abstract entities, legal obligation is not a physical, material thing. True, legal obligations govern courses of conduct, which exist as parts of the physical and material world: human conduct and behaviour have a physical and material existence. So, too, the parties involved in a legal obligation (the obligee and the obligor) are often embodied creatures (even if this is not necessarily the case, since they can be institutional entities). But even if the *scope* of legal obligation and its operation are well within the physical realm, legal obligation itself is a non-sensible relation (an immaterial bond). In this sense, legal obligation stands in stark discontinuity with standard instances of nonabstract, or concrete, objects. For the latter are typically material, sensible, causally efficacious, and spatial entities, while legal obligation possesses none of those traits. Which is why it is best classified as an abstract object.

As further support for this conclusion, consider that legal obligation is associated with a normative power, and even if this power can be observed in time and space—by looking at the behaviour of those who are subject to a legal obligation—the obligation itself lacks any spatial dimension. Likewise, even if legal obligations apply to contexts occupying a determinate space (regions, territories, jurisdictions), this spatial element relates not to legal obligation itself but to its compass, or field of operation. So, while legal obligation might operationally be said to unfold in space, the same cannot accurately be said of their existence. Legal obligation (as distinct from its operation) is an abstract object that is inherently non-spatial. Finally, just like paradigmatic cases of abstract objects, legal obligation is a mind-independent entity. Legal obligation and standard abstract objects alike exist even if they are not the contents of any subjective state or condition of the mind: while there may certainly be attitudes, feelings, and perceptions by which legal obligation is typically accompanied, they are not what legal obligation consists of or what makes it real.

But while legal obligation, for the reasons just given, is best understood as an abstract object, it is, as noted, an abstract object of a peculiar kind. For unlike paradigmatically abstract objects, legal obligations are both *created* and *temporal*. This makes legal obligation similar to abstract objects such as artworks, scientific models, and games. These are all human creations, and they all have an existence associated with time coordinates. So, like other types of abstract human artefacts, legal obligation belongs to a special subset of *abstracta*: those that are created and thus temporal.[34]

As far as temporality is concerned, we should be able to see that even as an abstract entity, legal obligation exists in time, since it arises at a given point in time, persists for a definite period (during which it may also undergo modifications and amendments), and normally disappears, or is extinguished, at some stage. This is unusual for abstract objects, since core cases of abstract objects, such as mathematical entities and propositions, are thought to be timeless and universal. In fact, the temporal dimension is key to Adolf Reinach's claim that legal obligation needs to be classified as an abstract object in a very narrow sense, for it makes legal obligation distinct not only from concrete objects but also from ideal ones, to which it is not possible to assign specific time coordinates.[35]

As far as createdness goes, we have seen that legal obligation is an artificial object, for it would not exist but for the (human) act through which it comes into being. And this, too, is not a typical trait of abstract objects, only some of which can be characterised as created. This can be appreciated by looking at Platonism as the broad family of views allowing for the existence of abstract objects (thus populating our ontology with concrete as well as abstract objects).[36] Only on certain versions of Platonism, grouped under the banner of expansive Platonism, is it argued that created abstract objects exist, thus extending 'the domain of abstract entities far beyond the realm of paradigmatic abstracta',[37] while in the downsized world of austere Platonism, created *abstracta* have no citizenship.[38] So, while Platonists of all stripes are united by a shared commitment to the existence abstract objects, only some of them include created objects among these *abstracta*. As a created object, then, legal

[34] And even within this special subcategory of abstract objects, legal obligation has a distinct place. For, while it presents some analogies with other created and temporal abstract objects, it is at the same time discontinuous with most of them in a number of important respects. Hence, we should look at legal obligation as distinctive even within the subset of created and temporal abstract objects.

[35] See Reinach (2012, pp. 8–17). For a thorough discussion of Reinach's view of legal obligation, see Lorini and Loddo (2023). In relation to legal norms in general, a similar point is made in MacCormick and Weinberger (1986, pp. 13–16) and Weinberger (1986b, pp. 37–41).

[36] Here Platonism is contrasted with nominalism, which holds that there are no abstract entities, whether created or otherwise.

[37] Cowling (2017, p. 5).

[38] For an introduction to Platonism, in its various renderings, see Cowling (2017, pp. 23–68).

obligation occupies a niche position in the realm of abstract objects, considering that even among those who are committed to a rich ontology inclusive not only of concrete objects but also of abstract ones, there is suspicion about the idea that the latter depend on human activity for their existence, that is, that they are created, and hence temporally situated—which further underscores the *sui generis* quality of legal obligation as an abstract object.

4 Conclusions

In this essay, it was argued that legal obligation is an abstract, ideational, public, and *sui generis* object. As an entity, in other words, legal obligation is an *object*, as distinct from a property; it is *abstract*, rather than concrete; it is *ideational*, rather than physical or psychological; and it is *public*, as opposed to being private or individually held. And in the category of abstract objects, legal obligation as a created and temporal *abstractum* is *sui generis*, so much so that only an expansive and tolerant form of Platonism recognises these created *abstracta* as having a robust, rather than merely nominal, existence—one that, by contrast, is rejected in both nominalism and austere Platonism. These ontological theses about legal obligation are best understood in the context of a theoretical effort aimed at contributing to a new development (of an old tradition) in meta-normative studies, namely, new non-naturalism. I should therefore briefly outline this context in closing this discussion.

In a critical argument taking aim at meta-normative non-naturalism, Jonas Olson observes two recent and closely related trends in meta-normative research.[39] One of these is the revival of non-naturalism, which Olson describes as the thesis that there exist *normative* properties and facts, and that these are conceptually and ontologically distinct from *natural* properties and facts.[40] The other trend consists in a renewed interest in *reasons*.[41] This trend recognises a foundational role for justificatory reasons in understanding normativity. In turn, the idea of a justificatory reason is claimed to be conceptually primitive, in that it cannot be analysed into any more elemental normative notions. It is through this idea of a reason that the connection between the two trends is formed. For, as Olson points out, it is reasons that account for the distinction drawn in contemporary non-naturalism (or new non-naturalism,

---

[39] See Olson (2009).

[40] As mentioned, this revival is mainly owed to Audi (2004), Crisp (2006), Dancy (2004), Shafer-Landau (2003), Enoch (2011), and Parfit (2011).

[41] The gist of this approach is summarised in Joseph Raz (1999, p. 28) where it is claimed that 'the normativity of all that is normative consists in the way it is, or provides, or is otherwise related to reasons'. The same idea is stated as follows in Scanlon (1998, p. 17): a reason is a fundamental notion, since 'any attempt to explain what it is to be a reason for something seems to me to lead back to the same idea: a consideration that counts in favour of it'. 'Counts in favour how?' one might ask. 'By providing a reason for it' seems to be the only answer'. Arguments for this thesis can also be found in Dancy (2004, pp. 15–37), Dancy (2009), Parfit (2011, pp. 31–38), Raz (2009), Raz (2011, pp. 13–101), and Scanlon (2014, pp. 1–15).

as Olson calls it) between the normative and the natural, since the former (but not the latter) is structured around the notion of a justificatory reason. And through this combination of theses—namely, (a) that the normative exists ontologically and conceptually apart from the factual, and (b) that the distinction is owed to the role of justificatory reasons (which are foundational in the normative but absent from the factual)—contemporary non-naturalism in all its varieties seeks to make a strong case for itself.[42] For this approach makes it possible to dispense with the obscure and questionable idea of intrinsic goodness in shaping the normative, as old-school non-naturalism failed to do,[43] and to replace this idea with that of a justificatory reason understood as a primitive fact.

Contrary to Olson, who advances strong reservations on reason-based non-naturalism,[44] I endorse the premise that the combination of the revival of non-naturalism and preoccupation with reasons as fundamental, primitive, and non-analysable can be argued to support the assertion that new non-naturalism is a respectable meta-normative position. In my view, the combination of the trends described by Olson can actually be used to support the claim that new non-naturalism—the reason-based variant of non-naturalism—is a better candidate for establishing the nature of normative facts and properties than old non-naturalism—the intrinsic-goodness-driven version. The argument offered in this work should be interpreted as a contribution to, and specific application of, this new development of non-naturalism, which is here used to determine the reality of a given normative object—legal obligation. Indeed, I think that an account of the nature of legal obligation along the lines put forward by new non-naturalism—this is what I sought to start doing in this work—should be found quite tempting, especially by those embracing a Kantian approach to legal studies in general and legal obligation in particular. As argued in this essay, it means to view legal obligation as a primitive, fundamental, and unanalysable non-natural fact providing the bedrock of the normative dimension of law. This thesis, I believe, is very much in line with the Kantian tradition of practical philosophy.

References

Alvarez M (2010) Kinds of reasons. Oxford University Press, Oxford

Alvarez M (2017) Reasons for action: justification, motivation, explanation. In: Zalta EN (ed) The Stanford encyclopedia of philosophy, Winter 2017 edition. https://plato.stanford.edu/archives/win2017/entries/reasons-just-vs-expl/

---

[42] As mentioned, this is something that Olson denies.

[43] Traditional non-naturalism is mainly associated with Moore's (1903, 1912, 1922) body of work.

[44] In making the case that new non-naturalism is not an advance on old-school non-naturalism, Olson (2009) argues that the two conceptions are equally vulnerable to key objections, such as the extension fallacy, the supervenience argument, the queerness objection, and the redundancy argument.

Amselek P (1991) Law in the mind. In: Amselek P, MacCormick N (eds) Controversies about law's ontology. Edinburgh University Press, Edinburgh, pp 13–29
Armstrong D (1989) Universals: an opinionated introduction. Westview, Boulder
Audi R (2004) The good in the right: a theory of intuition and intrinsic value. Princeton University Press, Princeton
Austin J (1998) The province of jurisprudence determined (1863). Ashgate, Dartmouth
Ayer A (1936) Law, truth, and logic. Gollancz, London
Ayer A (1984) Freedom and morality. Oxford University Press, Oxford
Azzouni J (1998) On 'On what there is'. Pacif Philos Q 79:1–18
Bertea S (2019) A theory of legal obligation. Cambridge University Press, Cambridge
Beyleveld D, Brownsword R (1986) Law as a moral judgment. Sweet & Maxwell, London
Blackburn S (1984) Spreading the word. Oxford University Press, Oxford
Blackburn S (1993) Essays in quasi-realism. Oxford University Press, Oxford
Blackburn S (1998) Ruling passions. Oxford University Press, Oxford
Bolzano B (1837) Wisserschaftlehre. Seidel, Sulzbach
Boyd R (1988) How to be a moral realist. In: Sayre-McCord G (ed) Essays on moral realism. Cornell University Press, Ithaca, pp 307–356
Brandt R (1979) A theory of the good and the right. Oxford University Press, New York
Brentano F (1874) Psychologie vom Empirischen Standpunkt. Dunker & Humblot, Leipzig
Brink D (1989) Moral realism and the foundations of ethics. Cambridge University Press, Cambridge
Coleman J (2001) The practice of principle. Oxford University Press, Oxford
Conte AG (1995) Studio per una teoria della validità. In: Conte AG (ed) Filosofia del linguaggio normativo, vol I Studii 1965–1981. Giappichelli, Torino, pp 55–74
Cooter R (1984) Prices and sanctions. Columbia Law Rev 84:1523–1559
Copp D (1990) Explanation and justification in ethics. Ethics 100:237–258
Cowling S (2017) Abstract entities. Routledge, Oxford
Crisp R (2006) Reasons and the good. Oxford University Press, Oxford
Dancy J (2000) Practical reason. Oxford University Press, Oxford
Dancy J (2004) Ethics without principles. Oxford University Press, Oxford
Dancy J (2009) Reasons and rationality. In: Robertson S (ed) Spheres of reasons. Oxford University Press, Oxford, pp 93–112
Darwall S (1983) Impartial reason. Cornell University Press, Ithaca
Davidson D (1963) Actions, reasons and causes. J Philos 60:685–700
Di Lucia P, Passerini-Glazel L (2017) Two semiotic shifts in the philosophy of norms: meaning shift and referent shift. Phenomenol Mind 13:10–18
Dworkin R (1986) Law's empire. Fontana, London
Dworkin R (2006) Justice in robes. Harvard University Press, Cambridge
Dworkin R (2011) Justice for hedgehogs. Harvard University Press, Cambridge
Enoch D (2007) An outline of an argument for robust meta-normative realism. Oxf Stud Metaethics 2:21–50
Enoch D (2011) Taking morality seriously: a defense of robust realism. Oxford University Press, Oxford
Falguera JL, Martínez-Vidal C, Rosen G (2022) Abstract objects. In: Zalta EN (ed) The Stanford encyclopedia of philosophy, Summer 2022 edition. https://plato.stanford.edu/archives/sum2022/entries/abstract-objects/
Field H (2005) Recent debates about the a priori. In: Gendler T, Hawthorne J (eds) Oxford studies in epistemology. Oxford University Press, Oxford, pp 69–88
Fine K (2005) Our knowledge of mathematical objects. In: Gendler T, Hawthorne J (eds) Oxford studies in epistemology. Oxford University Press, Oxford, pp 89–109
Finnis J (2011) Natural law and natural rights, 2nd edition with postscript (1st edn: 1980). Oxford University Press, Oxford

Frege G (1918) Der Gedanke: Eine Logische Untersuchung. Beiträge zur Philosophie des Deutschen Idealismus 1:58–77
Gert J (2002) Korsgaard's private-reasons argument. Philos Phenomenol Res 64:303–324
Gibbard A (1990) Wise choices, apt feelings. Oxford University Press, Oxford
Gibbard A (2003) Thinking how to live. Cambridge University Press, Cambridge
Gibbard A (2012) Meaning and normativity. Oxford University Press, Oxford
Goldman A (2009) Reasons from within: desires and values. Oxford University Press, Oxford
Harman G (1977) The nature of morality. Oxford University Press, Oxford
Hart HLA (1958) Legal and moral obligation. In: Melden A (ed) Essays in moral philosophy. University of Washington Press, Seattle, pp 82–107
Hart HLA (1994) The concept of law (with a postscript, or. ed. 1961). Clarendon, Oxford
Holmes OW (1896) The path of the law. Harv Law Rev 10:457–478
Hurd H (1999) Moral combat. Cambridge University Press, Cambridge
Kelsen H (1934) The pure theory of law. LQR 50:474–498
Kelsen H (1945) General theory of law and state. Harvard University Press, Cambridge
Kelsen H (1967) Pure theory of law. University of California Press, Berkeley
Kornhauser L (1999) The normativity of law. Am Law Econ Rev 1:3–25
Korsgaard C (1996a) Creating the kingdom of ends. Cambridge University Press, Cambridge
Korsgaard C (1996b) The sources of normativity. Cambridge University Press, Cambridge
Korsgaard C (2009) Self-constitution. Oxford University Press, Oxford
LeBar M (2001) Korsgaard Wittgenstein and the Mafioso. South J Philos 39:261–271
Leng M (2020) Is there a fact of the matter about the existence of abstract objects? In: Falguera J, Martinez-Vidal C (eds) Abstract objects: for and against. Springer, Berlin, pp 111–130
Linnebo Ø (2018) Thin objects: an abstractionist account. Oxford University Press, Oxford
Linsky B, Zalta E (1995) Naturalized platonism versus platonized naturalism. J Philos 92:525–555
Loddo O, Lorini G, Moroni S (2021) Deontic artifacts. Investigating the normativity of objects. Philos Explor 24:185–203
Lorini G, Loddo O (2023) Legal objects: essence and existence. In: Hopkins Burt C, De Santis D (eds) The new yearbook for phenomenology and phenomenological philosophy, vol 21. Routledge, London, pp 39–54
Lorini G, Moroni S (2020) How to make norms with drawings: an investigation of normativity beyond the realm of words. Semiotica:55–76
Lorini G, Moroni S (2021) Multiple functions of drawings. J Urban Design 26:374–394
Lorini G, Moroni S (2022) Non-propositional regulation. Philos Investig. https://onlinelibrary.wiley.com/doi/full/10.1111/phin.12343
Lowe E (1995) The metaphysics of abstract objects. J Philos 92:509–524
MacCormick N, Weinberger O (1986) Introduction. In: MacCormick N, Weinberger O (eds) An institutional theory of law. Kluwer, Dordrecht, pp 1–30
Maddy P (2011) Defending the axioms: on the philosophical foundations of set theory. Oxford University Press, Oxford
Marmor A (2001) Positive law and objective values. Oxford University Press, Oxford
McNaughton D, Rawling P (1991) Agent-relativity and the doing-happening distinction. Philos Stud 63:167–185
McNaughton D, Rawling P (1995) Value and agent-relative reasons. Utilitas 7:1–47
Moore GE (1903) Principia ethica. Cambridge University Press, Cambridge
Moore GE (1912) Ethics. Oxford University Press, Oxford
Moore GE (1922) The conception of intrinsic value. In: Moore GE (ed) Philosophical studies. Routledge, London, pp 253–275
Nagel T (1970) The possibility of altruism. Princeton University Press, Princeton
Nagel T (1986) The view from nowhere. Oxford University Press, New York
Narvaez-Mora M (2015) Expressing norms. Revus 25:43–70
Norman R (2000) Public reason and the 'private language' argument. Philos Investig 23:292–314
O'Day K (1998) Normativity and interpersonal reasons. Ethical Theory Moral Pract 1:61–83

Olson J (2009) Reason and the new naturalism. In: Robertson S (ed) Spheres of reason. Oxford University Press, Oxford, pp 164–182
Parfit D (1984) Reasons and persons. Clarendon Press, Oxford
Parfit D (2011) On what matters (3 volumes). Oxford University Press, Oxford
Passerini-Glazel L (2017) Normative experience: deontic noema and deontic noesis. Phenomenol Mind 13:96–107
Passerini-Glazel L (2020) Le realtà della norma, le norme come realtà. LED, Milan
Pettit P (1987) Universality without utilitarianism. Mind 72:74–82
Plebani M (2020) Recent debates over the existence of abstract objects: an overview. In: Falguera J, Martinez-Vidal C (eds) Abstract objects: for and against. Springer, Berlin, pp 1–14
Popper K (1968) Epistemology without a knowing subject. In: Logic, methodology, and philosophy of science III, North Holland, Amsterdam, pp 333–373
Railton P (1986) Moral realism. Philos Rev 95:163–207
Railton P (1989) Naturalism and prescriptivity. Soc Philos Policy 7:151–174
Railton P (1998) Moral explanation and moral objectivity. Philos Phenomenol Res 58:175–182
Raz J (1990) Practical reasoning and norms. Oxford University Press, Oxford
Raz J (1999) Engaging reason. Oxford University Press, Oxford
Raz J (2009) Reasons: explanatory and normative. In: Sandis C (ed) New essays on the explanation of action. Palgrave, Houndmills, pp 184–202
Raz J (2011) From normativity to responsibility. Oxford University Press, Oxford
Reinach A (2012) The a priori foundations of the civil law. De Gruyter, Berlin
Rettler B, Bailey A (2017) Object. In: Zalta EN (ed) The Stanford encyclopedia of philosophy, Winter 2017 Edition. https://plato.stanford.edu/archives/win2017/entries/object/
Sayre-McCord G (1988) Moral theory and explanatory impotence. In: Sayre-McCord G (ed) Essays on moral realism. Cornell University Press, Ithaca, pp 256–281
Scanlon T (1998) What we owe to each other. Harvard University Press, Cambridge
Scanlon T (2014) Being realistic about reasons. Oxford University Press, Oxford
Schroeder M (2008) Having reasons. Philos Stud 139:57–71
Shafer-Landau R (2003) Moral realism. Oxford University Press, Oxford
Shafer-Landau R (2007) Ethics as philosophy: a defense of ethical nonnaturalism. In: Shafer-Landau R, Cuneo T (eds) Foundations of ethics. Blackwell, Oxford, pp 210–221
Shapiro S (2001) Legality. Harvard University Press, Cambridge
Shapiro S (2002) Law, plans, and practical reason. Leg Theory 8:387–441
Shapiro S (2014) Massively shared agency. In: Vargas M, Yaffe G (eds) Rational and social agency: essays on the philosophy of Michael Bratman. Oxford University Press, New York, pp 257–293
Skorupski J (2002) The ontology of reasons. Topoi 21:113–124
Skorupski J (2010) The domain of reasons. Oxford University Press, Oxford
Smith M (1994) The moral problem. Blackwell, Oxford
Sturgeon N (1988) Moral explanations. In: Sayre-McCord G (ed) Essays on moral realism. Cornell University Press, Ithaca
Sturgeon N (1992) Nonmoral explanations. Philos Perspect 6:97–117
Wallace J (2009) The publicity of reasons. Philos Perspect 23:471–497
Weinberger O (1986a) Facts and fact-descriptions: a logical and methodological reflection on a basic problem for the social sciences. In: MacCormick N, Weinberger O (eds) An institutional theory of law. Kluwer, Dordrecht, pp 77–92
Weinberger O (1986b) The norms as thought and as reality. In: MacCormick N, Weinberger O (eds) An institutional theory of law. Kluwer, Dordrecht, pp 31–48
Wiland E (2012) Reasons. Bloomsbury, Oxford
Williams B (1981) Internal and external reasons. In: Williams B (ed) Moral luck. Cambridge University Press, Cambridge, pp 101–113
Williams B (1995) Internal reasons and the obscurity of blame. In: Williams B (ed) Making sense of humanity. Cambridge University Press, Cambridge, pp 35–45

Willigenburg T (2002) Shareability and actual sharing: Korsgaard's position on the publicity of reasons. Philos Invest 25:172–189
Yablo S (1998) Does ontology rest on a mistake? Proc Aristotelian Soc 72:229–261

Part II
Theoretical Perspectives on Legal Obligation

Why Any Legal Positivist Idea of Legal Obligation Is Untenable: A Kantian-Gewirthian Synthesis

Deryck Beyleveld

1 Introduction

Legal positivists hold that legal obligations are not necessarily moral obligations. Obligation-asserting rules of legal systems are, indeed, not necessarily morally valid and I have never asserted that they are. What I hold is that compliance with an obligation-asserting rule of a legal system is *an obligation* only if there is a moral obligation to obey the rule, and a *legal* obligation (i.e., something rendered an obligation by being required by an obligation-asserting rule of the legal system) only if the legal system is morally authorised to promulgate it. If legal positivists agree with this, there is no dispute between us. There is only genuine disagreement between us if they hold, which I think they do, that a legal obligation is *simply* what an obligation-asserting rule of a legal system requires to be done. My aim is to explain why I hold my position. However, this requires engagement with fundamental issues of epistemology, metaphysics and philosophical anthropology not normally addressed in jurisprudential debates about legal obligation. In essence, my argument is as follows. By denying a necessary conceptual connection between law and morality (a system of rules governed by a material categorical imperative, one with a substantive content), legal positivism portrays legal obligations as hypothetical imperatives, which obligations cannot be if a material categorical imperative exists. Human agents, being finite and embodied, necessarily adopt

John Adenetire, Stefano Bertea, Roger Brownsword, Patrick Capps, Marcus Düwell, William Lucy, Shaun Pattinson, Stuart Toddington, and Kenneth Westphal, commented helpfully on drafts of this essay. My thanks to all of them.

D. Beyleveld (✉)
Durham University, Durham Law School, Durham, UK
e-mail: deryck.beyleveld@durham.ac.uk

D. Beyleveld, S. Bertea (eds.), *Theories of Legal Obligation*, Law and Philosophy Library 146, https://doi.org/10.1007/978-3-031-54067-7_4

hypothetical imperatives. But understanding the concept of a hypothetical imperative requires understanding the concept of a categorical imperative, while understanding *having* the concept of a categorical imperative requires assent to Alan Gewirth's Principle of Generic Consistency. This analysis, a Kantian metaphysical exposition of the concept of a categorical imperative, proves that a material categorical imperative exists *unless* only hypothetical imperatives *can* exist, or human agents *cannot* have free will. But the concepts of a hypothetical imperative and a categorical imperative are co-dependent, and Kant's transcendental exposition of the concept of a categorical imperative demonstrates that the impossibility of free will is unknowable.

1.1 My Dispute with Legal Positivism

As a reference point, I take a legal system to be a social practice or institution in a specific geographical territory or domain of behaviour with rules for permissible, required and prohibited action that are identified by the set of rules applied (by and large effectively) *as a matter of empirical fact* (for whatever reason, and by whatever means) (the system's 'secondary rule of recognition', as H L A Hart 1961 terms it, its 'SRR') by those whose actions in accord with the system's SRR are necessary for the continued existence of the system (its 'officials').

There is no good reason for legal positivists to take issue with this or with my view that for a *legal* obligation to exist it must be validated by the SRR of a legal system. Where we differ is over whether validation of an obligation-asserting rule by the SRR of a legal system is sufficient to create an obligation.

According to 'normative positivists' (e.g., Hart 1962 and Hans Kelsen 1967), legal obligations (unlike coercive threats) provide normative (justificatory) reasons for obedience that are like moral obligations in that 'Agnes has *an* obligation (whether legal or moral) to do X' *means* 'Agnes strictly (categorically) ought to do X (i.e., ought to do X regardless of what she wants to do)'. But 'Agnes has *a legal* obligation to do X' *simply means* 'Agnes strictly ought to do X according to the SRR of her legal system'.

Despite this, Kelsen insists that the existence of a legal *obligation* presupposes 'the basic norm' of a legal system, according to which the system's SRR—its 'historically first constitution'—strictly ought to be applied and obeyed, so that 'Agnes has a legal obligation to do X' *means* 'Agnes strictly ought to do X according to the basic norm of her legal system' (1967, p. 46).

Because Kelsen is a moral relativist (1967, pp. 63–69), this *might* suggest that he is not a legal positivist after all, but a relativistic legal idealist, someone who thinks that the validity of a law rests on a moral judgment, but that there are no moral judgments that everyone rationally must accept. But I think not. One form of moral relativism accepts that there are rules (e.g., 'Treat like cases alike') that must be agreed to by everyone (because they are analytic) but considers that there is no analytic criterion of relevant similarities, so that they lack any matter or substance that everyone rationally must accept, leaving their content open to individual or group opinion. Another form holds that belief in categorically binding rules is rationally optional, even if it requires them to be assigned a unique content. In either case, it can be an objective fact (something to which everyone must agree) that Agnes has an obligation to do X *only if* this means that, *according to* someone or some group, Agnes strictly ought to do X. This is why Kelsen holds that the meaning of legal *validity* is a 'subjective' 'ought', while a legal obligation is an 'objective' 'ought', one that strictly ought to be applied and obeyed *according to* the basic norm of a legal system (which provides the reason for the validity of the system's assertions of obligation) (1967, pp. 7–8). However, because a basic norm does not exist independently of the SRR it 'validates', it is not an end in itself. Consequently, validation by it does not make an SRR a rule that strictly ought to be applied and obeyed. It merely signifies that the system's officials must act according to the system's SRR in order to perform their roles as its officials. Since the SRR of a legal system exists only by being accepted by its officials, it is their acceptance that indirectly generates Agnes's legal obligations. As Kelsen says, the basic norm is

> the ultimate (but in its character conditional and therefore hypothetical) reason for the validity of the legal order. (1967, p. 46)

So, while Hart thinks that presupposition of a basic norm is unnecessary and that Kelsen's view commits him to legal idealism (1962, pp. 105–107), it merely signifies what Hart himself holds: that the officials of a legal system, *behaving as its bona fide officials,* necessarily adopt the system's SRR and the rules it validates as 'standards for their conduct' (ibid., p. 113), though they may do so for any reason whatsoever (ibid., p. 198–199).

According to 'non-normative positivists' (Hart's 'imperativists', Kelsen's 'realists', e.g., John Austin 1955), 'Agnes has a legal obligation to do X' *means* 'Agnes ought to do X in order to avoid the threat of punishment or nullity if she acts contrary to the rules of her legal system'. Legal 'obligations' are *merely* orders of the officials of a legal system backed by generally effective threats of punishment or nullity.

This presupposes that it is unconditionally irrational to regard *any* rules as categorically binding, ones that Agnes ought to obey whether she wants to or not. Given the *normative* idea of an obligation as that of a categorically required action, non-normative positivism does not merely presuppose moral relativism. It presupposes adeonticism (the view that there cannot be any categorically binding rules because the concept of a categorically binding rule is incoherent).

However, both normative and non-normative positivists subscribe to the 'sources thesis', the view that legal obligations are generated simply by being required by rules of a legal system, which means that they are generated directly in non-normative positivism by the coercive purposes of its officials, and indirectly in normative positivism by the officials choosing to regard an SRR as the normative justification for their conduct. Hence, both forms of legal positivism portray legal obligations as hypothetical imperatives, 'oughts' that are generated, in the final analysis, by understanding what must be done to achieve someone's merely accepted purposes.

Regardless of their personal views about the epistemic status of *moral* claims, when relating moral obligations to legal obligations, legal positivists treat 'Agnes has a moral obligation to do X' *as* 'Agnes strictly ought to do X according to criteria that are not necessarily adopted by a legal system'. This is because they clearly cannot hold that moral obligations are ones that are *necessarily* adopted by a legal system without making them necessary criteria for legal validity.[1]

Clearly, 'obligations' *according to* a legal system will not *necessarily* be 'obligations' *according to* some other criterion or system of rules. Thus, the sources thesis coupled with legal positivism's characterisation of moral obligations grounds its 'separation' (or 'separability') thesis, according to which Agnes can have a legal obligation to do X that is contrary to morality.

Against legal positivism, I hold that 'Agnes has a legal obligation to do X' *means* 'The SRR of Agnes's legal system strictly requires her to do X *in consequence of which* she rationally must agree that she strictly ought to do X'.

So defined, Agnes can have a legal obligation (as against merely being claimed to have one) only if a categorical imperative (an imperative that *everyone* rationally must accept) validates the SRR of Agnes's legal system. Because an obligation *is* a strict 'ought', *no* obligation can be a hypothetical imperative (direct or indirect). No strict 'ought' can be generated by a merely accepted or effective rule. Validation by another rule cannot convert what is asserted to be an obligation into an obligation, *unless* the validating rule itself strictly ought to be applied and obeyed. Obedience to the validating rule must either be an end in itself, or the validating rule must be permitted or required to prescribe what strictly ought to be the case by a rule that requires obedience to itself as an end in itself. Genuine obligations are categorically binding rules, because what they prescribe is either an end in itself or is justified by a material (substantive) rule to which obedience is an end in itself, and ultimately by a *single material* categorical imperative (one with which *all* practical precepts must be consistent *unconditionally,* that provides criteria capable of distinguishing obligatory, permissible, and impermissible conduct from each other in a rationally unquestionable way).

Iredell Jenkins (1959–1960, pp. 1–2) claims that no genuine dispute exists between legal positivists and natural lawyers (whom he, like Kelsen, designates 'legal idealists') because their definitions of *legal* obligation serve different purposes. Legal positivists *as such* are interested in what *are* legal obligations, whereas natural lawyers *as such* are merely interested in what *ought to be* legal obligations.

The interest Jenkins attributes to legal positivists is instantiated by empirical questions like, 'What does Agnes need to know about the rules of her legal system to avoid the risk of being taken to court, fined or imprisoned?' *If* this sort of question were dispositive, legal obligations would be determined by the SRR of Agnes's legal system. Because legal positivists routinely think that they can refute the natural lawyer's claim that there is a necessary conceptual connection between legal and

[1] From this, it follows that positivists cannot *coherently* believe that there is a material categorical imperative, even if they consider that their belief cannot be shown to be rationally necessary.

moral obligation by pointing to legal systems that lay down rules as obligations that they consider (and I would agree) are morally invalid (such as various Nazi laws), they clearly think that this kind of question is dispositive. But this is not my kind of question *as a natural lawyer.* It is also not, 'What ought to be legal obligations?' It is, 'Under what conditions does Agnes actually have an obligation to obey an obligation-asserting rule of her legal system *because* it is an obligation-asserting rule of her legal system?' If legal positivists agree with my answer to *this* question, there is no dispute between us. However, whereas I do not contest their answer to *their* factual question, they do contest my answer to *my factual* question by implying that being required by an obligation-asserting rule of Agnes's legal system is not only necessary *but also* sufficient for Agnes to have a legal obligation to obey the rule, whereas I claim that it is *only* necessary.

I hold my view because I think of morality as a system of rules governed by a categorical imperative *and* believe that a single material categorical imperative exists. From this perspective, legal positivism does not offer a concept of a legal obligation *as an obligation,* merely a characterisation of the rules that officials of a legal system must observe *in order to perform their roles within the system.* What legal positivists say *are* legal obligations are merely what legal systems *claim* are obligations.

Consequently, I am not interested in what ought *to be* legal obligations because this presupposes that there can be legal obligations that are not what they ought to be (i.e., not obligations *as such*). Instead, my interest is in what legal systems ought *to claim* are obligations. But, given the existence of a single material categorical imperative, determining this requires knowing what actions *are* obligatory, and 'Agnes has a legal obligation to do X' is true only if this statement is validated by the SRR of her legal system, the SRR is *morally* authorised, *and* there is a moral obligation to do X.

Thus, in claiming that obligations are facts, my view is not that what legal systems claim are obligations are *necessarily* moral obligations. It is that they are not obligations unless they are moral obligations. It also does not rule out moral obligations to obey rules of a legal system that are, *in themselves,* immoral. What I take to be *the* categorical imperative requires legal systems to be instituted and to make some of their own rules. Thomas Hobbes (1962) is right that, human nature being what it is, human agents will inevitably have disagreements that lead to conflicts that threaten a peaceful social existence by restricting their freedoms and even by endangering their lives. To avoid such conflicts, they must sometimes defer to the wishes of others, which (as an ongoing social arrangement) requires legal systems to be instituted. However, the categorical imperative specifies the conditions under which Agnes may or ought to agree to such governance, which conditions are those under which the authority of the categorical imperative is legitimately delegated to a legal system. These are that the legal system's SRR itself, and any rules and actions it validates, not be in clear violation of the categorical imperative. Of course, even rule makers who try to apply the categorical imperative in good faith can misapply it. However, failure to observe it does not *necessarily* mean that what are thereby claimed to be legal obligations may or should be disobeyed. A material categorical imperative can require obedience to rules of a legal system that, *in themselves,* are immoral in order to prevent more immoral consequences that can arise from disobedience. But such obligations are grounded in overriding moral obligations that exist independently of the legal system. They are non-legal moral obligations rather than legal obligations.[2]

The guiding idea here is that, according to *the* material categorical imperative, important (indeed, basic) *moral* values require legal systems to be instituted. These values generate a *prima facie* moral obligation to obey the rules of a legal system *unless* the moral defects of the rules outweigh, or at least cancel, the values that generate the *prima facie* obligation. Because of the nature of the moral values requiring the institution of legal systems, these defects must be very serious for this to be the case.

The Hobbesian need to prevent life-threatening conflicts also grounds the 'non-positivism' of Robert Alexy (2009), who holds that obligation-asserting rules of legal systems are legally valid *unless* they are very seriously morally invalid *because* 'certainty' (the umbrella term Alexy uses to convey the value of having a legal system) must be weighed *against* morality. But only if Alexy's 'certainty' is itself a moral value assigned by the material categorical imperative can it withstand conflict with *any* moral value (Beyleveld and Brownsword 2019).

The need to protect life and other values of the greatest importance for a peaceful social existence, is also behind Hart's claim that there is a 'minimum content of natural law' (1961, pp. 189–195). But Hart treats these values as shared independently by positive law and morality, not as values positive law categorically ought to serve *because* they are moral values.[3]

In short, I hold that legal systems are not merely permitted (Hart) or required (Alexy) to *recognise* moral values; they are unconditionally required to be *ruled by*

[2]Obligations of any kind are facts, just not morally neutral facts. The *factual* nature of obligation-asserting rules of a legal system *as rules of a legal system,* their '*L*egal' nature, i.e., 'their 'legal *vs* non-legal' nature, is empirical; but their *factual* nature *as obligations* (their normative validity, their '*l*egal' nature, i.e., their 'legal *vs* illegal' nature) is morally regulated (Beyleveld and Brownsword 1986). Using this case convention, what I call a 'legal system' in this paper is a '*L*egal system', while a '*l*egal system' is a '*L*egal system with a morally authorised SRR'. There can be morally invalid '*L*aws' but not morally invalid '*l*aws'. In other words, a '*L*aw' (a rule of what of what I have called a 'legal system') is not a '*l*aw' if it is morally invalid.

[3]When distinguishing moral obligations from legal ones, Hart (1962, pp. 169–171) claims that breaches of moral obligations are always *mala in se,* whereas some breaches of legal obligations are merely *mala prohibita,* involving acts that are not wrong in themselves, like driving on one side of the road rather than the other. But this does not show, as Hart seems to think it does, that breaches of rules requiring driving on one side of the road rather than the other are not breaches of moral obligations. While morality (what I consider to be the categorical imperative) does not specify the correct side of the road on which to drive, it does specify that there must be an enforceable rule requiring all drivers going in one direction to drive on the same side of the road because this is necessary to protect life and other moral values, and it will only recognise an obligation to obey such a rule if doing so serves moral values.

moral values.[4] In other words, the *practical* difference between my natural law theory and legal positivism is that the former makes moral evaluation of legal systems *rationally* obligatory whereas the latter portrays this, at most, as *rationally* optional (Beyleveld and Brownsword 1985).

In essence, legal positivists conceptualise legal obligations from the viewpoint of officials of a legal system, or academics teaching students about the practice of lawyers, on the model of a game like tennis. Anyone wanting to play tennis must play according to the rules of tennis. Analogously, to be an official of a legal system, one must 'play' according to the rules of the legal system. This model is fine *if all* legal positivists *as such* are trying to do is provide an account of how legal systems operate that assists someone *to predict* how it is likely to respond to certain events and actions. The problem is that one is only bound to abide by the rules of tennis if one wants to play tennis. But the 'game' of officials of a legal system, *their* purpose, is to manage the imposition of its rules on *everyone* in the territory of their legal system. It is 'the enterprise of subjecting human conduct to the governance of rules' that purports to have general authority over all to whom it can be effectively applied (Fuller 1969, p. 96). Consequently, relative to this *characterising* purpose of a legal system (which is built into the concept of a legal system that I share with legal positivists), legal positivists need to explain why those who do not want to abide by the rules of a legal system *strictly* ought to do so. It is only by doing this that their conception of a legal obligation can be an articulation of the concept of a legal system. As John Finnis (1984, pp. 15–19) puts this, they need to explain why *everyone must* conceive of legal obligations from the partial standpoint of the practically reasonable person *qua* official rather than from that of the impartially practically reasonable person *qua* person (i.e., from the purely instrumentally rational viewpoint of persons as officials rather than from the universal viewpoint of the morally rational person as such). They can only justifiably evade this demand if there is no ascertainable substantive practical standpoint that all human agents rationally *must* share.

Thus, the dispositive *factual* question is, 'Does a categorical imperative with "a unique matter" exist?' I answer affirmatively, and legal positivists, whatever they personally believe, *must* answer negatively (or, at least, say that the answer *cannot be known*). Without demonstration of the absolute rational necessity of their belief about the existence of a categorical imperative, any arguments presented by one side against the others merely presume what they purport to prove. If no proofs are possible, no genuine dispute about *the concept* of legal obligation can exist between

[4] 'Exclusive positivism' (as against 'inclusive positivism') holds that legal systems *may not* recognise moral values. One possible ground for this is non-normative positivism. Another, compatible with normative positivism *ala* Kelsen, is to hold that legal systems claim exclusive (categorical) materially relative authority within their own territories, so cannot recognise moral standards *as such* (i.e., as having universal authority *independent* of recognition by a legal system). I do not, however, see why *(from a legal positivist perspective)* this precludes holding (which is all I take inclusivists to do) that a legal system may have an SRR that incorporates principles, like those of the United Nations Declaration of Human Rights 1948 (UDHR) (which the UDHR says have independent universal authority), on the understanding that they only have *legal* authority on account of this incorporation, because this does not violate the sources thesis.

normative and non-normative positivists or between legal positivists and myself. All views about it must then be considered purely optional, driven by incommensurable presuppositions between which there can be no rational arbitration, just verbal quibbling.

1.2 The Nature of My Argument

The aim of my argument is to prove that there is a single material categorical imperative, the Principle of Generic Consistency (PGC),

> Act in accord with the generic rights of your recipients as well as of yourself. (Gewirth 1978, p. 135)[5]

According to Gewirth, it is 'dialectically necessary' for all human agents to accept the PGC. By this, he means that it is unintelligible for any human agent (e.g., Agnes) to think it permissible to adopt *any* view on reasons for action inconsistent with the view that the PGC is *the* categorical imperative because, by incurring such inconsistency, Agnes implies that she lacks the capacities necessary to have any view about reasons for action in the very act of having a view about reasons for action, thereby implying that she is not an agent.

As I will explain, the connection between Gewirth's dialectically necessary method and the existence of the categorical imperative is such that it entails that to justify *any* legal positivism requires *proof* that the concept of a categorical imperative is incoherent. But legal positivism cannot provide this because it requires the coherence of the concept of a hypothetical imperative, which, I claim, requires the coherence of the concept of a categorical imperative.

Gewirth's dialectically necessary method operates within Agnes's understanding of herself as a human agent (i.e., from within human agential self-understanding, 'HASU'). As a human agent, Agnes chooses purposes to pursue. But human agents are not omnipotent, so Agnes cannot achieve her purposes just by having them. She needs to employ means to achieve them. She is also subjected to forces, factors, and circumstances that can hinder or prevent her from being able to achieve, or even from being able to try to pursue, any purposes at all. She has emotions and desires that can be overwhelming and conflict, and senses that are limited in the inputs they can receive. Her physical existence can be threatened and ended. In addition, she has limited knowledge and understanding, no matter how brilliant and learned she is. Such factors generate the GCAs, which are shared *as categories* by all finite

[5] Generic rights (GRs) are rights to 'GCAs' (the generic conditions of the agency of finite embodied agents, like human agents), which are things needed to be able to act at all or to have any general chances of acting successfully, regardless of one's purposes (like, e.g., life) (Gewirth 1978, pp. 52–63). It is not necessary for present purposes to detail what the GCAs are. The example of life will be sufficiently illustrative. Recipients are agents other than oneself who stand to be affected by one's actions.

embodied agents, though what will interfere with them or support them can vary between species of such agents and between individual such agents of the same species. For example, (physical) life is a GCA for all finite embodied agents, but something, e.g., peanuts, might be a deadly poison for Agnes but not for another human agent. Thus, applying the PGC, though not the argument for it, requires empirical information about Agnes's *specific* circumstances, make-up and needs. My discussion is confined to human agents, although its logic applies to all possible finite embodied agents.

A lynchpin of both Gewirth's and Kant's arguments for a categorical imperative is the following analytic proposition: 'Agnes cannot be the unique agent she is without being a human agent and cannot be a human agent without being *an* agent (an agent *at all*), whilst, at the same time, *she* cannot be *an* agent without being the unique human agent that *she* is'.

I contend that the absolute rational necessity of Agnes's commitment to the PGC as *the* categorical imperative is revealed simply by her understanding the nature and implications of this biconditional relation, which entails and explains a co-dependency between the concepts of a categorical imperative and a hypothetical imperative.

I will refer to Kant repeatedly because I consider that he and Gewirth employ the same *methodology* when arguing for the existence of a categorical imperative.[6]

However, there are *material* differences between Kant and Gewirth. First, the PGC is not the 'Formula of Humanity' (FoH) as *Kant interprets it.* The FoH states:

> So act that you use humanity, whether in your person or in the person of any other, always at the same time as an end, never merely as a means (Kant 1998a, GMM AK 4:429)[7]

Kant says that the FoH provides the 'Formula of Universal Law' (FUL)

---

[6] My understanding of Kant's argument has changed in important ways over the years and is still being refined. Unlike the most widely accepted current view, I hold that Kant presents the same argument in *Groundwork of the Metaphysics of Morals (GMM)* (Kant 1998a) and *Critique of Practical Reason (CPrR)*, (Kant 1997), in both of which (not merely in *CPrR)* free will is the *ratio essendi* of the categorical imperative (the property that human agents must have for it to be possible for the categorical imperative to apply to them) cognised as an apodictic (i.e., a rationally absolutely unquestionable) synthetic a priori proposition in being produced by HASU solely by itself (Beyleveld and Düwell 2020). I cite Kant to acknowledge debts, and because I consider that he and Gewirth are best understood in a dialogue with each other in which Gewirth's argument is not an argument from prudential self-interest (which almost all its critics mistakenly take it to be) but a genuine Kantian argument, which is an argument from and within HASU (see also Beyleveld 2015, 2017).

[7] I follow the standard practice in Kant scholarship of referring to the Prussian Academy citation (AK volume number: page number), rather than page numbering in translated texts, except for *Critique of Pure Reason (CPuR)* (Kant 1932), where I use the standardly used 'A: B' system, in which 'A' refers to the page numbering in the first edition and 'B' to the page numbering in the second edition. Because of the extensive references I make to Kant and the significance of the work in which he says things, it is important to indicate this by direct or abbreviated reference to the title of the work as well as the date of the work in the reference list. I will also use the abbreviation instead of 'ibid' where appropriate.

> Act only in accordance with that maxim through which you can at the same time will that it become a universal law (GMM AK 4:420)

with 'a matter' *(GMM* AK 4:436).[8] In essence, my argument aims to establish that the PGC is the correct interpretation of Kant's FoH on Kant's own basic premises.

Secondly, while I agree with Kant that free will is a capacity Agnes must possess for a categorical imperative to be capable of applying to her, I have concerns about some of the things he says about its nature. I also have some disagreements with him about what the categorical imperative requires in its application; but these need not concern us here.

2 The Argument

2.1 There Can Be Only One Categorical Imperative

A categorical imperative is a wholly unconditional imperative, one that applies (and can only apply) to human agents simply because they are finite embodied agents. Thus, *all* rules for human actions must be consistent with a categorical imperative. *Nothing* can evade, modify, or nullify *any* of its commands.

Therefore, as Kant (1998a, *GMM* AK 4:421) says, *if* there is a categorical imperative, there can be only one. The reason is obvious. Incompatible imperatives that each govern all practical precepts would cancel each other out, whereas compatible wholly unconditional imperatives can only exist if they are combinable into one imperative, each being a formula that reveals different aspects of one imperative.

This, however, does not preclude the existence of multiple categorically binding imperatives because 'Agnes categorically ought to do X' can signify that doing X is what *the* categorical imperative categorically requires Agnes to do given her own particular characteristics and circumstances. The difference between a categorical imperative and a mere categorically binding imperative is that a categorical imperative governs *all* practical precepts, so prescribes what ought to be done regardless of what *anyone* wants to do in all circumstances, whereas there are circumstances in which Agnes can be categorically bound to do something (i.e., regardless of what

[8] I take 'humanity in a person' to refer to the capacities necessary for Agnes to be an intelligible addressor and addressee of practical precepts, in having which Agnes possesses 'dignity', and that these necessary capacities are the a priori powers of HASU. As I will explain later, treating humanity in persons as an end in itself, not merely as a means (i.e., respecting the dignity of persons as a value beyond price), requires the GRs to be granted to human agents under the will conception of a right, according to which Agnes may release other human agents from the duties they owe her correlative to her GRs *as part of the specification of each GR.* Thus, the correct specification of, e.g., the GR to life is that it imposes a duty on other agents to respect Agnes's life in accordance with her will. However, what Kant (1998a, *GMM* AK 4:429) says about treating one's existence as an end in itself does not accord with this, because he holds that the FoH imposes a *prima facie* duty against self-destruction, whereas the PGC *prima facie* grants Agnes a right to end her life or have it ended.

she wants to do) that someone else (say, Brian) is not categorically bound to do.[9] On the basis that morality is a set of rules governed by a categorical imperative, *the* categorical imperative is *the* moral law, and mere categorically binding imperatives are moral laws, which are justified (directly or indirectly) by *the* moral law.

2.2 *Conditions to Prove the Existence of a Categorical Imperative*

Agnes can only genuinely affirm, deny, or doubt the existence of a categorical imperative if she understands its concept. But simply by understanding the concept of a categorical imperative Agnes must (categorically ought to) assent to 'Think and act only in accord with the strict requirements of a categorical imperative!'

Because the idea of a categorical imperative is one with which *all* practical precepts must be consistent unconditionally, the only thing that a categorical imperative can and must comply with is the idea of itself, the idea of a universal law as such (the law of a pure, i.e., unconditional, reason—reason that is its own explanation, an end in itself), which entails that simply understanding the concept of a categorical imperative requires assent to its existence as the FUL (Kant 1998a, *GMM* AK 4:420). In other words, by understanding the concept of a categorical imperative, Agnes must judge in accord with the criterion for possible categorically binding imperatives, which is specified by the FUL.

Some will object that understanding the concept of a categorical imperative requires assent to the FUL only *if* a categorical imperative exists independently of this understanding, *and* that Kant thinks so too. I disagree. As I will explain later, the purpose of Kant's argument in the third section of Kant (1998a) *(GMM* III), which he promises *(GMM* AK 4:420, 445) is where he will prove that the categorical imperative really exists, is not to show that Agnes is rationally necessitated to believe that there is a categorical imperative. It is to show that, by requiring her to assent to the FUL simply by being able to understand the concept of a categorical imperative, her rational capacity is not in conflict with itself by presupposing that Agnes has a capacity for free will yet is subject to the principle that every observable event has a mechanistic cause. In any event, any objection to the claim that understanding the concept of a categorical imperative requires assent to its existence as the FUL (and not merely assent to its taking the form of the FUL *if it exists*), presupposes that nothing can exist unless its existence depends on (hence requires explanation by) something *outside of* understanding, so that a categorical imperative cannot exist just by being elicited by understanding its concept, by being a 'fact of pure reason' as Kant (1997, *CPrR* AK 5:31) puts it. But this presupposition illegitimately rules out the existence of a categorical imperative from the start because

[9] An alternative way of saying this is that there can be multiple categorical imperatives only if there is one *supreme* categorical imperative.

a *categorical* imperative is possible only if it can exist as a fact produced by a capacity for understanding necessarily shared by all finite embodied agents (like human agents) without the mediation of anything else.

Nevertheless, *if* this 'imperative of understanding' is *merely* analytically contained *in the freestanding concept of* a categorical imperative, then it is an idea without any necessary *practical* significance for Agnes. To be genuinely action-guiding, and not an empty formalism, two conditions must be satisfied. First, the FUL must be a fact of understanding *by* being a strict requirement of HASU. In other words, the categorical imperative of *pure* understanding must be contained in the concept *of* Agnes understanding what is contained *in her understanding* the concept of a categorical imperative (i.e., a statement of what is contained in the concept of Agnes *having* the concept of a categorical imperative).[10] Secondly, understanding the FUL as a fact of HASU must require Agnes to accept that it has a unique substantive content. However, because the categorical imperative as the FUL commands that Agnes judge in accord with the criterion for possible categorically binding imperatives, and a *categorical* imperative is possible only if Agnes *can* be unconditionally (autonomously) motivated, a third condition must be satisfied. It must be coherent for HASU, the self-understanding of a being whose will is affected by heteronomy, to postulate the existence of such an imperative.

2.3 The First Condition

A hypothetical imperative for Agnes is one that she must accept by virtue of understanding that having or doing Y is necessary for her to achieve a heteronomous purpose X (one she has chosen to pursue but is not unconditionally required to pursue). The particular purposes Agnes chooses to pursue, coupled with the abilities and biological characteristics (both physical and psychological) that she possesses (which, together with the physical and social environment she occupies, affect the

[10] In an influential article, David Enoch (2006) says that Gewirth and Kantians like Christine Korsgaard ('Self-constitution: agency, identity and integrity', unpublished manuscript given in the Locke Lectures at Oxford University, May and June 2002) try to get the existence of a categorical imperative out of the concept of action or of being an agent. He argues that this commits them to Humean internalism (the view that only heteronomous incentives can provide reasons for action, so only hypothetical imperatives can exist), and then rightly ridicules the idea that a categorical imperative can be justified on this basis. I make no comment on Korsgaard, but neither Gewirth nor Kant tries to get the existence of a categorical imperative out of the concept of being an agent or of action. They derive assent to it from understanding *having* HASU (out of understanding what is involved in understanding oneself as possessing agency). As an internalist, Gewirth requires good reasons for Agnes to act to serve purposes *coherently acceptable* to her *as an agent,* not (like Humean internalists) to serve purposes she is prepared to accept as a matter of empirical fact. Enoch appreciates that his targets are moral objectivists who reject moral intuitionism. He accuses them of trying, incoherently, to marry moral objectivism with Humean internalism because he mistakenly thinks that a priori intuitions and heteronomous incentives are the only possible reasons for action (see Beyleveld 2017).

means she has to pursue and achieve purposes), make Agnes the particular human agent that she is. Thus, a hypothetical imperative for Agnes is one that she must accept in order to understand the *relationship* between the *particular* things that make her the *particular* human agent that she is. *In this way,* a hypothetical imperative is a fact of HASU conditioned by an individual's circumstances and particular purposes.

On the other hand, a categorical imperative for Agnes is a strict requirement of her understanding the *relationship* between understanding what it is for her to be the particular human agent that she is and understanding what it is for her to be an agent at all. *As such,* a categorical imperative is a fact of HASU *per se,* one conditioned only by the conditions of its possibility.

This is what Kant means when he says that if a categorical imperative exists it must 'already be connected (completely a priori) with the concept of the will of a rational being as such' (1998a, *GMM* AK 4:426) but 'not contained in it' *(GMM* AK 4:420 fn). He reasons thus. If there is a categorical imperative, what makes it *categorical* is its autonomy, its existence not depending on *any* heteronomous factors (factors that are not given to Agnes's understanding solely by itself). A will that can *only* act for a reason that is free in this way is purely rational, necessarily moved to act purely by having the idea of a law that necessarily governs every possible will, the moral law *as such.* For such a will, acting in accord with the idea of such a law would be a law of its nature. Since Agnes does not possess such a will, such a law can (if at all) govern her behaviour only as a categorical *imperative* because the fact that her will is affected by heteronomy is what makes it possible for her not to be motivated to act by the thought of the moral law *as such.* But this means that a categorical imperative must be connected entirely a priori with the concept of the will of a rational being as such (i.e., be ascertainable simply by understanding the concept of the will of a purely rational agent) that (because it is an imperative) cannot be contained in this concept. Given that the idea of Agnes (as the particular agent that she is) is the idea of Agnes subject to heteronomy, and the idea of Agnes (as an agent at all) is the idea of Agnes abstracted (because she is a human agent) *not from heteronomy* per se, but from *the heteronomy that characterises her as the particular agent that she is,* what Kant *means* when he says that the categorical imperative is a synthetic a priori proposition is (though not in as many words) that it is the law of HASU, the a priori law of the agential self-understanding of a heteronomously affected agent. In other words, it is the law that is ascertained by Agnes understanding what it is for *her* as a particular human agent to be an agent at all, which is what Gewirth means when he calls the PGC a dialectically necessary proposition. Thus (for human agents), *if* a categorical imperative exists, action in accord with the strict requirements of HASU must be an end in itself, which entails that the categorical imperative of understanding can be, and is, a fact of understanding only by being a fact of HASU. *As such,* it is properly designated the 'Imperative of HASU' (IHASU): 'Think and act only in accord with the strict requirements of HASU!'

It cannot be overstressed that the idea of *Agnes* as an agent at all is not the idea of Agnes abstracted from heteronomy *per se.*

According to Bernard Williams (1985, p. 63), Kant's argument fails because Agnes cannot be a rational agent and no more (*an* agent unaffected by heteronomy). But Kant need not (and does not, at least not clearly) suppose that she can be.[11] While Agnes cannot be anything *other than* herself (the particular human agent that she is), she cannot be herself if she is not *at the same* time *an* agent (Beyleveld 2013). This, which describes the biconditional relationship between Agnes as the particular human agent that she is and Agnes as an agent at all, does not entail that she cannot think or act in accord with a categorical imperative. As I will explain later, it is sufficient for my purposes (as Kant claims it is for his) that it be coherent to think that, when Agnes does something, she *can* be doing this simply because it is, and she perceives it to be, rational (i.e., that it be intelligible for her to think that rational explanation can be its own explanation). This claim of sufficiency is grounded in non-empirical claims about human psychology (which might be termed 'transcendental phenomenological'). I consider that these constitute the very foundation of Kant's transcendental philosophy, which is nothing other than the elucidation within HASU (the only place from which any human understanding can proceed) of the fundamental principles that limit and govern HASU.

(1) There is no thinking without self-consciousness, and no self-consciousness without an 'I', a thinking subject (the nature of which *as a transcendent substance, i.e., as existing independent of this thought,* is unknowable). Whatever Agnes makes of Descartes's '*Cogito ergo sum*', she cannot deny '*Cogito ergo cogito*', that *she* can only know or think anything if *she* has the power to think, which requires *her somehow* (but in an unknowable manner) to be endowed with the capacity to understand and to be able to know that she is.
(2) Having the concept 'I' and the concept 'not-I' (the concept 'other than I') necessarily go together.
(3) Human self-consciousness is necessarily human agential self-consciousness. This is because the idea of it can only be thought to arise due to the operation of inchoate faculties of the human mind (capacities for sense-perception, feeling, and desire) coupled with a priori powers of HASU (which include powers of understanding, judgment—including imagination—and reason, which may be designated collectively 'Understanding' or 'Reason') producing felt resistance to *behaviour-implementing* desires by giving rise to feelings and sense-experiences that are not automatically produced by having the originating desires.

[11] In my opinion, Agnes cannot be both a particular agent *and* a *purely* rational agent, unless she has previously been affected by heteronomy *(perhaps*, *after* her physical death). Indeed, Agnes cannot coherently imagine *now* that *she is* a rational agent and no more. But she can imaginatively understand (using the reflective power of judgment that enables her to form general concepts—as against the determinative power of judgment that enables her to apply general concepts to specific things) what it is for *something* to be a rational agent and no more, for this is presupposed by being able to comprehend that Agnes cannot be a purely rational agent.

Given this, human agents *are* required to think that thought and action in accord with the strict requirements of HASU is an end in itself. The idea of a categorical imperative is the idea of an imperative compliance with which is an end in itself, and the only way in which this compliance can be an end in itself is by Agnes being strictly required to think that the categorical imperative exists simply by understanding what is involved in the idea of her having its concept. In short, because understanding the idea of a categorical imperative *does* postulate (i.e., render rationally undeniable by itself) that there is a categorical imperative, and *all* human understanding requires use of the *a priori* powers of HASU, Agnes is required to think that action in accord with the strict requirements of HASU is an end in itself, its own explanation.

2.4 The Second Condition

The IHASU as the FUL is not a material categorical imperative and can be provided with a *necessary* substantive content only if this is revealed simply by understanding the concept of HASU. Gewirth's dialectically necessary argument for the PGC demonstrates that the IHASU has a substantive content and reveals what it is. The logic of its reasoning is as follows.

2.4.1 Agnes Must Act in Accord with Her Need for the GCAs

As a human agent, Agnes necessarily acts to achieve purposes she has chosen. Understanding this requires her to assent to P: 'If doing or having Y is necessary for me to do X, then I must do or have Y or give up trying to do X'.

P displays itself both as a statement about what Agnes can do and as a statement about what she ought to do.

As a statement about what Agnes *can* do, P is Pa: 'If doing or having Y is necessary for me to do X, then if I do not do Y or secure my having Y, I will not be able to do X'.

That Agnes must accept Pa depends only on Agnes understanding what it means for something to be necessary for her to have or do for her to be able to achieve a purpose she has chosen to pursue, which is part of Agnes understanding what it is for her to be the particular human agent she is. Since Agnes cannot be the particular human agent that she is without being an agent, she must accept Pa simply by virtue of understanding what it is for her to be an agent at all. That Agnes will not be able to do X without Y is a fact about human agency that is *cognised* by HASU. But it is not a fact *of* HASU because it is not *created solely* by HASU.

P, as a statement about what Agnes *ought* to do, is the 'Principle of Hypothetical Imperatives' (PHI): 'If doing or having Y is necessary for me to do X, then (provided only that I can) I strictly ought to do Y (or secure my having Y) or give up trying to do X'.

The PHI is a fact of HASU. Because Agnes must assent to it simply by virtue of understanding the way in which P is contained in the concept of her being an agent at all, it is contained in and created by HASU.

The PHI structures any necessary matter the IHASU might have. This matter is provided by the fact that it is contained in understanding the concept of any finite embodied agent that there are GCAs, conditions necessary for Agnes, whoever she might be, to pursue or achieve any purposes by her own actions. Coupled with the dialectical necessity of the PHI, this renders it dialectically necessary for Agnes to accept *Alpha*: 'I (Agnes) strictly ought to secure my having the GCAs, *unless* I am willing to suffer generic damage to my ability to act' (which I will abbreviate as $\{Alpha\}_{Agnes}$).

Alpha is a substantive imperative that Agnes must consider to be categorically binding on her. It is the Gewirthian correlate of Kant's contention that Agnes must consider her existence to be an end in itself.

Kant (1998a, *GMM* AK 4:429, 437–438) thinks differently.[12] What he says suggests that he thinks that, because Agnes needs to be alive to be able to pursue or achieve any purpose at all, the fact that she unconditionally ought to act in accord with the IHASU means that Agnes's duty to defend her life cannot be to defend her life for the sake of continuing to be able to act (i.e., cannot be a duty to treat as an end in itself her capacity to use her life as a means to her ends as against a duty to defend her life whether she wants to be able to act or not).[13]

But a categorical imperative is not a construct of being an agent, but a construct of HASU. As such, it does not prescribe that Agnes must have her life in order to be (to become or to remain) an agent, but what Agnes must do in order to carry out her dialectically necessary commitments *when she is an agent*. It merely governs, through her self-understanding, what she *as an existing agent* may or must do if she is to act in accord with HASU.

The point is that action for its own sake is not an end in itself. Only action in accord with HASU is an end in itself. Therefore, since the PHI is dialectically necessary for Agnes (i.e., $\{\text{PHI}\}_{\text{Agnes}}$), she is only categorically bound to defend her life

[12] However, in *The Metaphysics of Morals* (Kant 1991, *MoM* AK 6:238), Kant says that Agnes may do anything to others that they accept, and 'That is *rightfully mine (meum iuris)* with which I am so connected that another's use of it without my consent would wrong me' (ibid., AK 6:246), both of which seem to imply his adoption of the will conception of a right. Nevertheless, he is adamant that Agnes has duties to herself not to harm or debase herself in a way that contradicts this implication (ibid., AK 6:421–428). The general reason he gives against killing oneself, which fits what he says in *GMM,* is that '[t]o annihilate the subject of morality in one's own person is to root out the existence of morality itself from the world, as far as one can, even though morality is an end in itself' (ibid., AK 6:422–423).

[13] Please note that I do not assert that Agnes's duty to defend her life is a duty that is conditional on her willingness to act. I assert that her unconditional duty, which she must accept whether or not she is willing to act, is 'Agnes ought to defend her life if she is willing to act'. Note too, however, that once (but not until) it is shown that Agnes's dialectically necessary commitments are collectively universal (which I will do shortly), Agnes's autonomy over her existence will be restricted by Brian's parallel dialectically necessary autonomy over his existence.

as a means to her ends, i.e., in accord with *Alpha,* which requires Agnes to act prudentially. But the reason why she must accept *Alpha* is wholly unconditional (that it is dialectically necessary for her to accept that there are GCAs and to act in accord with the PHI). Viewed in terms of its *justification* rather than its content (which is prudential), *Alpha* is categorical. In short, the dialectical necessity of *Alpha* for Agnes renders it categorically imperative (i.e., in order to comply with HASU) for her to treat her life (and her GCAs generally) as generically *instrumental* to achieving her purposes.[14]

It should, therefore, be clear that the argument does not derive a categorical imperative from a hypothetical one. It derives assent to the existence of a categorical imperative as a strict requirement of understanding the concept of a categorical imperative *given as* a strict requirement of understanding the concept of a hypothetical imperative *given as* a strict requirement of HASU (the powers of which are presupposed by any human understanding, which renders the strict requirements of their exercise unquestionable). Thus, the PGC is not found *simply* within the concept of a hypothetical imperative, but within understanding the concept of a hypothetical imperative *as given in* HASU. Normative positivism implies that the originating act of coercive power involved in instituting a legal system is an exception to David Hume's (1888, Book III, Part I, Section I) contention that a strict 'ought' cannot be derived from any *empirical* or *purely* theoretical 'is'. But there is no exception to Hume's claim. Normative positivism's implication *reduces* a strict 'ought' to an empirical 'is'. It does not *deduce* the former from the latter, but simply identifies 'right' with 'might'. In my argument, the 'is' that constitutes the strict 'ought' that grounds all strict 'oughts', is (interpreting Kant 1997, *CPrR* AK 5:31) neither an empirical fact nor an a priori intuition, but the sole fact of coherent HASU in being a rationally necessary presupposition of any possible understanding by a human agent, thus a principle that every human agent rationally must accept.

---

[14] Elsewhere *(GMM* AK 4:422) Kant maintains that the reason why Agnes cannot think it permissible to commit suicide 'when it threatens more troubles that it promises agreeableness' is that the maxim of this action could not become a universal law of (her) nature because this idea entails that the 'feeling' that impels 'toward the furtherance of life' must be the same as that which impels to self-destruction, which is self-contradictory. This claim stems from his view that the FUL must be applied as stating *'[A]ct as if the maxim of your action were to become by your will a* **universal law of nature'** (ibid., AK 4:421), which expresses his view that to deny a perfect duty is to incur a contradiction in conception. A contradiction in conception is, indeed, incurred on the assumption that the categorical imperative requires Agnes to *be* a *purely* rational agent (an agent not heteronomously affected). But such an agent would surely have no conception of being mortal. It could not have any feelings impelling self-destruction. In any case, Agnes is not such a being and cannot aspire to *be* such a being. Her nature as a heteronomously affected being makes her capable of 'self-love' of a kind that can both impel towards the furtherance of her life as well as towards self-destruction. The fact of the matter, however, is that, insofar as the categorical imperative is grounded in agency, this is only in agency as its *ratio essendi.* Cognitively, it is grounded in unconditionally *rational human* agency (i.e., in HASU), which means (contrary to Kant) that Kant's idea of contradictions in conception, as against contradictions in the will, has no role in justifying maxims of the human will, which are necessarily governed by the dialectical necessity of the PHI.

That Agnes *always* acts by choosing means she perceives to be necessary, sufficient, or at least conducive to achieving what she wants to achieve, does not gainsay this. A categorically binding requirement for Agnes to do S requires her to want to do S regardless of what she *just happens* to want to do. It specifies that she ought to want to do S *simply because* HASU strictly requires her to do S. That Agnes categorically ought to do S presupposes that she can do S for two possible reasons: either by wanting to do S simply by understanding that it is a strict requirement of HASU, or by wanting to do S for some other reason. As Kant explains, most fully in *MoM (*Kant 1991), when Agnes does so for the first reason, she acts out of respect for the moral law, i.e., both rightly and virtuously. When she does so for the second reason, she only acts in accord with the moral law, i.e., merely rightly. When Agnes does S, she can never be certain that she is doing so purely out of respect for what is categorically required of her. However, the existence of categorically binding requirements does not require Agnes to know when she is acting purely out of respect for the moral law. It merely presupposes that it is possible for her to know what the moral law requires her to do, and that it is coherent for her to think that she can act purely out of respect for it.[15]

At this point, some might wonder why I have said nothing about Kant's distinction between *Wille* and *Willkür,* which he draws in both *GMM (*Kant 1998a) and *CPrR* (Kant 1997), though he does not develop his views on it fully until *MoM* (Kant 1991) and *Religion (*Kant 1998b). In *GMM,* he tells us that *Wille* is nothing other than practical reason (AK 4:412). But he also uses the term to designate the spontaneity that characterises pure practical reason, which gives the moral law to Agnes, in which it is contrasted with *Willkür,* which he associates with Agnes's capacity to choose purposes and draw up maxims for herself. Kant uses the distinction to explain the possibility of evil actions. Fortunately, for the purposes of this paper, I do not need to present and justify my own view on this, as the relationship between *Wille* and *Willkür* is a matter of considerable contention so that any worthwhile discussion of it would take us too far afield.

[15] Likewise, the fact that very few human agents might, in practice, be able to understand my argument sufficiently to know that it is sound does not mean that it is of no use practically. Parallel things can be said about all normative theories and scientific theories, and the application of the PGC takes all of this into account, part of which involves its justification of the existence of legal systems. If it is sound, what matters for practical purposes is not whether human agents act out of respect for the categorical imperative, but that they can be brought to act in accord with it for reasons that do not violate it *(cf.* the justification of the 'Doctrine of Right' in Kant 1991, *MoM).* Of course, experience shows that achieving such a goal in accordance with any normative theory universally is a pipe dream. This is just a fact about the human condition. It is, to coin a metaphor, an 'original sin' of human existence. It is part of the reason that leads Kant to argue that the *summum bonum,* the 'utopian end' prescribed by the categorical imperative, requires Agnes to have faith that God (a perfectly good and omnipotent being) exists and that she is immortal. I agree with this *only if* 'having faith' is for Agnes to hope, but neither believe nor disbelieve, that God exists and that she is immortal (e.g., Beyleveld 2009, 2012, 2016). I comment further on this later.

2.4.2 Agnes Must Value Action in Accord with Other Agents' Need for the GCAs Equally

Just as *Alpha* instantiates the IHASU for Agnes, HASU requires Brian to accept *Beta*: 'I (Brian) strictly ought to secure my having the GCAs, *unless* I am willing to suffer generic damage to my ability to act': i.e., $\{Alpha\}_{Agnes}$ entails $\{Beta\}_{\mathrm{Brian}}$.

This means that a dialectically necessary commitment to secure the GCAs is distributively universal, what Kant calls a 'subjective principle' (1998a, *GMM* AK 4:429). But, unless *Alpha* and *Beta* are both collectively universal ('objective principles', *each* binding *both* Agnes and Brian), there can be no categorical imperative, merely a supreme categorically binding rule for each human agent. Any basic strict 'oughts' will be essentially and irreducibly egoistic.

However, according to Kant (ibid.), *GMM* III will demonstrate that human agents necessarily share the 'ground' of their 'subjective principles', which entails that *Agnes* must consider that *Brian's* existence is also an end in itself, so adopt the FoH (and *vice versa*).

This shared 'ground' is possession of the capacity for free will, which Kant designates the *ratio essendi* of the categorical imperative (1997, *CPrR* AK 5:4 fn). So, when he (1998a, *GMM* AK 4:447) claims that Agnes necessarily presupposes that she has free will, he is not claiming (as he is usually taken to be doing, which I myself once thought he did) that the necessity of this presupposition is the *ratio cognoscendi* of the moral law. He is claiming that the capacity for free will is the *ratio essendi* of the moral law, the *ratio cognoscendi* for which is that Agnes must consider rational nature to be an end in itself (*GMM* AK 4:428–429), by which I take him to mean that it is dialectically necessary for her to act in accord with the IHASU in the form of the FUL. In other words, the fact that the *ratio cognoscendi* of Agnes's subjective principle is that her assent to it is a strict requirement of HASU means (see, formally, Gewirth's ASA below) that she must regard being *an* agent, constituted by her possession of the a priori powers of HASU in which resides her capacity for free will, as the *ratio essendi* of the moral law. Because she must suppose that all agents have the capacity for free will, it follows that she must act in accord with Brian's subjective principle as well as her own, which commits her to the FoH.[16]

Gewirth (1978, p. 110) also holds that being a human agent is the *ratio essendi* of the PGC, although he does not explicitly identify free will as the property of human agency that makes it so, and the PGC has a different content from Kant's

[16] Further to comments I have already made about this, while Kant (1998a, *GMM* AK 4:429) says that this means that the *physical* existence of human agents must be considered to be an end in itself, I consider that it establishes only that it is obedience to *what is commanded by* the a priori powers of every agent's HASU *in their harmonious use—possession of which powers* constitutes *the possession of humanity in their persons*—that must be considered to be an end in-itself by every agent! And Kant (2000, *CPoJ* AK 5:293–295) says as much when he explains the '*sensus communis*' (see further infra).

FoH. Nevertheless, his argument for the collective universalisation of Agnes's (and Brian's) dialectically necessary commitments *formally* mirrors Kant's.

To set it up, Gewirth (1978, pp. 78–82) first argues that $\{\mathit{Alpha}\}_{\text{Agnes}}$ is equivalent to $\{\text{I (Agnes) have the GR}\}_{\text{Agnes.}}$ This is because, in order to act in accord with *Alpha,* Agnes must have the GCAs, and will not have them if Brian interferes with her possession of them or fails to assist her to secure them when she needs his assistance. Consequently, it is dialectically necessary for *her* to think that Brian ought to act in accord with her need for the GCAs according to her will (i.e., unless *she* is willing to suffer generic damage to her ability to act), which is what it means for it to be dialectically necessary for *her* to think that she has the GR.

The fact that Brian does not *necessarily* need *Agnes* to have the GCAs means that the fact that Agnes necessarily needs to have the GCAs does not, *without more,* demonstrate that *Brian* categorically ought to accept that Agnes has the GR (i.e., that $\{\text{Agnes has the GR}\}_{\text{Brian}}$). But this is irrelevant because the argument for the dialectical necessity of the PGC *for Agnes* is conducted strictly from within Agnes's dialectically necessary viewpoint, not Brian's. As such, Agnes need not take account of anything that Brian thinks or must think, *unless* it is dialectically necessary for *her* to do so. The *only* condition that Agnes's thought that she has the GR must meet in relation to Brian's thinking at this juncture is that if there is anything that it is dialectically necessary for *Agnes* to think is dialectically necessary for Brian to think, then what is dialectically necessary for Brian to think must not *prohibit* Brian from granting that Agnes has the GR. Because dialectically necessary commitments are *distributively* universal, $\{\mathit{Beta}\}_{\text{Brian}}$ entails that it is dialectically necessary for Agnes to recognise that it is dialectically necessary for Brian to hold *Beta* (i.e., $\{\{\mathit{Beta}\}_{\text{Brian}}\}_{\text{Agnes}}$).[17] So, for Agnes to be justified in holding that she has the GR, *Beta* must *permit* Brian to act in accord with *Alpha.* In other words, *given* $\{\mathit{Alpha}\}_{\text{Agnes}}$ and that Agnes must have the GCAs in order to act in accord with *Alpha,* it is enough for Agnes to be justified in holding that she has the GR that it is not *contrary* to *Beta* for Brian to accept that he ought to act in accord with *Agnes's* dialectically necessary needs. Crucially, and decisively, *Beta* does *not prohibit* Brian from acting in accord with the idea that Agnes has the GR. This is because doing so will not *necessarily* interfere with his possession of the GCAs and, even when it does (which it can), *Beta (being structured by the PHI)* permits Brian to allow such interference.

Gewirth's collective universalisation argument, which he calls the 'Argument from the Sufficiency of Agency' (ASA) (1978, p.110), then proceeds essentially as follows.

---

[17] The reason why dialectically necessary requirements are distributively universal is because Agnes represents any agent. So, whatever HASU requires of her (i.e., for her to defend her possession of the GCAs unless she is willing to suffer generic damage to her ability to act), HASU must *in parallel* require of Brian (i.e., for him to defend his possession of the GCAs, unless he is willing to suffer generic damage to his ability to act). But this presupposes that the a priori powers of Agnes's agential self-understanding are the same (in kind) as Brian's. To suppose otherwise is to suppose that Agnes cannot coherently conceive even the *possibility* of there being any agent other than herself. On the supposition that Brian's powers of HASU are different *in kind* from Agnes's, neither can intelligibly think *anything* about what the other might or might not think or do.

(1) *If* {I (Agnes) have the GR}$_{\text{Agnes}}$ *entails* {Being a human agent is the *ratio essendi* for my having the GR}$_{\text{Agnes}}$ *then* {All human agents also have the GR}$_{\text{Agnes}}$.
(2) To deny {Being a human agent is the *ratio essendi* for my having the GR}$_{\text{Agnes}}$, Agnes must claim, 'In order for me to have the GR, it is necessary for me to have some quality D that I do not necessarily possess by being a human agent', i.e., 'Without having D, I cannot have the GR'.
(3) But, by considering that without having D she cannot have the GR, Agnes contradicts {I (Agnes) have the GR}$_{\text{Agnes}}$. But Agnes cannot intelligibly do this because her dialectically necessary commitments are postulated by what she must think in order to think of herself as being a human agent at all.
(4) *Therefore,* {I (Agnes) have the GR}$_{\text{Agnes}}$ *entails* {Being a human agent is the *ratio essendi* for my having the GR}$_{\text{Agnes}}$, *which* (given that Brian is a human agent) *entails* {Brian also has the GR}$_{\text{Agnes.}}$
(5) *Therefore,* because dialectically necessary requirements are distributively universal, {All human agents have the GR}$_{\text{Agnes \& Brian}}$: i.e.,{PGC}$_{\text{All human agents}}$).[18]

Critics of Gewirth (including some avowed Kantians, like Christine Korsgaard 1996, pp. 133–134) routinely depict Gewirth's dialectically necessary requirements as prudential ones, which (like Enoch) depicts Gewirth as trying to ground a categorically binding imperative in a hypothetical one. But, as already explained, this is a complete misrepresentation. While Agnes does have a compelling prudential reason to act in accord with *Alpha,* this is not what makes it dialectically necessary for her to adopt *Alpha.* Agnes has dialectically necessary commitments because she possesses the a priori powers of HASU, and it is the *harmonious* operation of these powers that renders it dialectically necessary (and not *only* prudentially rational) for her to act in accord with her generic needs. And it is the fact that Agnes and Brian, as agents at all, necessarily possess the same powers in kind of HASU that is responsible for the collective universality of *Alpha* and *Beta* on account of their status as dialectically necessary commitments. In a nutshell, HASU (which makes human agency, characterised by free will and the existence of the GCAs in synthesis, the *ratio essendi* of the PGC) is the *ratio cognoscendi* of the PGC.

Both Kant's and Gewirth's arguments for a categorical imperative are encapsulated in Kant's claim that the *sensus communis*, by which he means reason/understanding constituted by the harmonious exercise of the a priori powers of HASU,[19] is governed by three principles.

[18] That this derivation constitutes a deduction of a strict 'ought' from a theoretical 'is' (the fact of being a human agent), does not contradict what I have previously said. This is because it only holds as a strict requirement of HASU, as a fact of HASU (so as a morally loaded fact), not as a fact of *being* a human agent without this imputation.

[19] The *sensus communis* is the *a priori faculty of judging* present in common human understanding (which is the capacity of 'healthy' understanding that 'is the least that can be expected of anyone who lays claim to the name of human being'), which in its reflection takes account (a priori) of everyone's way of representing in thought, in order *as it were* to hold its judgment up to human reason as a whole. (Kant 2000, *CPoJ* AK 5:293)

These are: 'Think for yourself', the 'maxim of understanding': 'Think from the viewpoint of everyone else', the 'maxim of the power of judgment'; and 'Think in accord with yourself', the 'maxim of reason' (Kant 2000, *CPoJ* AK 5:294–295).

The maxim of reason is derived by combining the other two maxims *(CPoJ* AK 5:295), and these maxims govern all human reasoning (Kant 2009, *Logic* AK 9:57). It is clear, however, that the maxim of reason, in its practical application, is formally the FUL (and, substantively elaborated, the FoH/PGC), and that the first two maxims are related by the fact that Agnes and Brian cannot be agents at all unless they possess the a priori powers of HASU, whilst, at the same time, as human agents, being affected by heteronomous factors that render them the particular agents that they are.

Just as the ideas of 'I' and 'not-I' are necessarily connected in either idea, being the thesis and antithesis of a synthetic 'I-not-I', so too are the ideas of an individual human agent and a community of human agents. But the biconditional relation that constitutes this synthesis is not one of identity or equivalence, except in normative weight. One arm cannot be reduced to the other. Agnes does not *simultaneously* (in community) have no normative control over herself *and* (as an individual) have complete autonomy over everything she does (which conjunction is a contradiction in terms). She exists as 'an-individual-in-community' as someone who must respect the possession of the GCAs of all human agents in the same way that she must respect her own possession of the GCAs. Thus (assuming she is able to do so), she may act to deprive (or risk depriving) herself of the GCAs, or allow others to do so, if and only if doing so does not disproportionately deprive others of the GCAs (or risk doing so) against their will. In this sense, with this qualification, the PGC grants relational autonomy to human agents. Indeed (assuming that doing so will not disproportionately threaten Agnes's possession of the GCAs against her will), Agnes must assist others to secure having the GCAs when they cannot do so unassisted and wish this assistance. Thus, the PGC grants both positive and negative rights to the GRs (Beyleveld 1991, Chap. 10), and does not merely require reciprocity (the granting of the GRs equally to human agents), but mutuality (a duty to support possession of the GCAs by human agents co-operatively and collectively when necessary and desired by them) (Gewirth 1996).

Gewirthians (and Kant) are sometimes accused of monological thinking, even of solipsistic thinking (e.g., Werner 2002), because their arguments for a categorical imperative are conducted from within the internal viewpoint of an individual human agent. This accusation is more radical than the claim that the Kantian-Gewirthian collective universalisation argument fails. It is that its method precludes conceiving even the *possibility* of intersubjectivity. But the dialectically necessary method does not portray Agnes's thinking as that of a windowless monad. In HASU, Agnes's

---

Kant contrasts the *sensus communis* with what persons commonly think (meaning 'customarily think'), which he calls the '*sensus vulgaris*' (2006, *Anthropology* AK 7:139). It is a pervasive mistake to think that when he refers to 'common human understanding' as the justificatory resource for his argument, he is referring to the *sensus vulgaris*. He is referring to the *sensus communis* (the powers of thinking that human agents necessarily share).

idea of herself synthetically unites the ideas of the particular and the universal human agent in the 'I-Other' of her human self. Those who doubt the power of the dialectically necessary method to comprehend the dialogical should ask themselves how it is possible to think that *any* human intersubjectivity is possible unless individual human agents have the same powers of understanding in kind that define their capacity to think both their own thoughts and entertain the thoughts of others. Since shared powers of understanding must be supposed, they should then ask themselves how it is possible that having shared powers will not render it possible to have intersubjectivity. I submit that intersubjectivity can only be precluded if the a priori powers of Agnes's HASU are not the powers that must be shared, which entails that these are the powers that must be shared. Therefore, the first-person dialectically necessary method is not only capable of justifying intersubjectivity, but also the *only* method capable of doing so.[20] It is 'mono-dialogical', dialogical within Agnes's HASU as *self*-understanding.

However, the collective universalisation argument does not, without more, establish that Agnes must, *in practice,* grant a real-life Brian the GRs.

First, the argument from Agnes's internal perspective presumes that Brian is an agent, which is fine because, in the argument, Brian represents any existing human agent other than Agnes. But, for Agnes to be strictly required to grant the GRs to a real-life Brian (another human being), she must be strictly required to identify and treat Brian as an agent, and lack of such empathy is aided by the fact that Agnes cannot know directly that a real-life Brian is an agent because she cannot know directly that *any* being *other than herself* possesses the a priori powers of HASU. To have these powers, Brian must have self-consciousness. But Agnes cannot know directly that Brian has self-consciousness without being Brian and, on empirical grounds alone, she can at most know that Brian behaves *as though* he has self-consciousness. Without making purely speculative metaphysical assumptions, Agnes has no *theoretical* basis to infer that Brian is an agent from the fact that he behaves like one.

However (see, e.g., Beyleveld and Pattinson 2000), because the PGC categorically requires Agnes to grant Brian the GRs *if* he is an agent, it requires her to treat him as having the GRs (i.e., as being an agent) if he behaves as though he is an agent. This is because, if he is an agent, she will violate the PGC if she does not identify and treat him like an agent when she can (which is when he behaves like one); whereas, if he is not an agent, she will not violate the PGC if she identifies and treats him like an agent when she can.

Secondly, Agnes must be able to determine, given Brian's specific heteronomous characteristics, what she needs to do to respect his possession of the GCAs, for which she needs empirical evidence (the principles of which are the same as those she must follow to determine whether or not Brian behaves like an agent). These principles, themselves, are grounded in the *sensus communis* because its maxims

[20] Alberto Pirni (2015), in connection with an analysis of elements of Kant's views on the relationship between *Wille* and *Willkür,* also argues that intersubjectivity is embedded in the subjectivity of Kant's supposedly purely monological method.

not only produce the PGC in synthesis, but ground all normative principles of human reasoning, i.e., all fundamental principles of judgment, whether a priori theoretical, empirical, aesthetic, pragmatic, or moral. The overarching point re universalisation, however, is that no uses of the maxims of the *sensus communis* to ground moral rights to real-life agents, directly or indirectly, have any grounding without the a priori universalisation I have sketched. These uses are applications of the PGC as a synthetic a priori principle and cannot be regarded as required for its justification. To think otherwise contradicts that the PGC is apodictic, because these applications (by requiring empirical evidence and collective judgment) are inherently corrigible in ways that do not apply to the reasoning that yields the PGC. Although human agents are capable of errors in judgment about almost everything, they cannot coherently think that they can be in error about absolutely everything. Some propositions simply must be presupposed for it to be meaningful to think that one can be in error about anything at all, and the master such proposition (the proposition in which all such propositions are contained by understanding it) is the IHASU.

Appreciating this is necessary to understand the role of legal systems in generating *moral* rights. Legal systems *can* generate moral rights that are not GRs. But, as already explained in general terms, they can do this only when operating with the authority of the PGC. They have this authority *in full* only when the means and procedures by which they are instituted and the means and procedures by which they issue rights-asserting rules are permitted by the PGC, which means that, taking all circumstances into account, when they do not violate the GR of *any* agent. This must not be misunderstood. The only *absolute* right that human agents have (one from which no human agents can be released by any human agent from their duty to respect it) is the right to expect all finite embodied agents to do their very best to act in accord with the PGC. This right is an *absolute non-generic* right (a component of the PGC itself) correlative to the absolute duty of every finite embodied agent to obey the PGC. This means that the GRs granted by the PGC to any human agent are capable of being overridden by the GRs of other finite embodied agents (and only in this way). This overriding must be in accord with a criterion of needfulness for agency (which operates on the basis that not all GCAs are equally needful for action because interference with them can have varying degrees of *generically* negative effects on Agnes's ability to act or to act successfully) (Gewirth 1978, pp. 350–353). Some cases of weighing are clear; others are open to judgment, of which nothing more can be expected than that they be made in good faith. Furthermore, because the GRs are rights under the will conception, in principle, *discretionary non-generic* rights (rights acquired in indirect applications of the PGC) require the *actual* consent to the procedures that generate them of those required to recognise them, and this is impossible in 'public' as against 'private' law. This means that discretionary non-generic moral rights that are granted by a legal system must be necessary for the protection of GRs (i.e., proportionate, *per* the criterion of needfulness, to the dialectically necessary commitments of any affected agents). In other words, all affected human agents must merely be able to agree to them without acting contrary to their dialectically necessary commitments. To spell all of this out is far beyond the ambit of this essay. The point of raising it at all is to make clear that none of this impacts the validity of the Gewirthian argument for collective universalisation because it presupposes its validity.

This is also important when relating my view of rights to Kant's. According to Kant, there is only one 'natural' ('innate' or 'private') right,

> *[f]reedom* (independence from being constrained by another's choice), insofar as it can coexist with the freedom of every other in accordance with a universal law. (1991, *MoM* AK 6:237)

Kant designates all other rights 'acquired' (or 'civil' or 'public'), meaning that their existence requires a legislator able to enforce the actions that the categorical imperative requires. In so doing, he portrays *having* a right (apart from the right to have the categorical imperative complied with) as requiring *the existence of means to enforce* the duty that corresponds to the right. For Kant (the exception apart), a genuine claim right can only exist in a positive legal system able to enforce the corresponding duty, whereas for Gewirthians a claim right resides simply in being reciprocal to the corresponding duty, a positive legal system merely being necessary to enable the right to be protected generally (i.e., to render it effective). Consequently, for Gewirthians, all claim rights, apart from those generated under the indirect applications of the PGC (which might be said to be 'acquired') are 'innate' (directly protected by the PGC).

Kant's position implies that he thinks that moral *duties* rest on their acceptance because Agnes cannot have any moral rights if Brian has no moral duties, and he certainly does not think this. Furthermore, Brian needs the GCAs to honour any duties he has, including his duty to act in accord with the categorical imperative itself (which is correlative to *his and Agnes's* innate moral right to freedom from coercion). Thus, because Agnes cannot sincerely be granted a claim right to do something if she is not granted claim rights to the necessary means to exercise it, Kant's innate right to freedom entails innate rights to the GCAs (as categories). Put differently, there is only one innate right if this is the right to have all action governed by the PGC because the PGC *necessarily* incorporates rights to all the GCAs as an innate system of rights. In other words, I agree with Kant *only if,* and only to the extent that, by claiming that there is only one innate right, he means that there is only one *absolute* right, the one right that Agnes has that cannot be rendered ineffective or overridden by any other human agent's rights, the right to have the categorical imperative obeyed correlative to the (sole) absolute duty to obey it, and that he holds that enforceability is only necessary to render moral rights effective.[21]

---

[21] Support for the idea that Kant actually holds this comes from his assertion (1991, *MoM* AK 6:266–267) that 'acquisition' of land is only 'provisional' unless a legislator exists to enforce it. Since by acquisition of land he means a right to own land as property, this implies that any possession implied a priori by the one absolute right itself *is* a right but only a provisional one, by which he means that it is not necessarily effective. This, however, implies that the existence of a legislator to enforce it does not create a right but merely renders it effective in practice. This, furthermore, fits his assertion that '[r]ight and authorization to use coercion ... mean one and the same thing' (ibid., 232), which implies that legislators can only create rights if they act in accord with the categorical imperative.

2.5 Coherence of the Concept of a Categorical Imperative

One move remains open to sceptics. This is to claim that it is incoherent to think that a categorical imperative, *in being* an unconditional requirement, *can* apply to *human* action. The implication of the alleged incoherence is that postulation of the categorical imperative by HASU, which presents its existence as certain without the mediation of any other proposition (Kant 2009, *Logic* AK 9:112), reveals an antinomy in HASU. I need to disprove this claim because I agree with Kant that, once the idea of having the concept of a categorical imperative is understood,

> the question of how the imperative of *morality* is possible [i.e., the question of 'how the necessitation of the will, which the categorical imperative expresses … can be thought' (Kant 1998a, *GMM* AK 4:417)] is undoubtedly the only one needing a solution. *(GMM* AK 4:419)

This contention is central to Kant's argument for the categorical imperative because it helps to explain why he says that showing that it is possible to 'furnish' human agents with 'the idea of freedom' is sufficient to establish the rational necessity of the categorical imperative *(GMM,* AK 4:461).

Prima facie, there are two different (though connected) challenges to the coherence of the concept of a categorical imperative.

The first comes from Humean internalism. The second comes from hard determinism because Kant says that a categorical imperative can only apply to Agnes if she has free will (1998a, *GMM* AK 4:447; 1997, *CPrR* AK 5:4 fn) and that free will and mechanistic causation are incompatible *(GMM,* AK 4:456), and hard determinists allege that every event has a mechanistic cause.

The root problem with both challenges is that neither can succeed unless acceptance of its central thesis is a strict requirement of HASU. But the success of either entails that HASU is impossible. Thus, either challenge can only succeed by rendering itself incoherent. Since this might strike some as too elliptical to be clear, I will respond to each challenge separately.

My argument to the end of Section 2.4.2 is what Kant calls a 'metaphysical exposition' of the concept of a categorical imperative, a metaphysical exposition being

> the clear, though not necessarily exhaustive, representation of that which belongs to a concept … when it contains that which exhibits the concept *as given a priori.* (Kant 1933, *CPuR* B38)

This reveals what the concept of a categorical imperative

> contains, that it [a categorical imperative] stands of itself altogether a priori and independently of empirical principles, and then what distinguishes it from all other practical principles. (Kant 1997, *CPrR* AK 5:46)

Kant also says (1932, *CPuR* A807: B833) that the existence of the categorical imperative is postulated merely by thinking it distinctly, and that

> [c]onsciousness of one's representations that suffices for the *distinction* of one object from another is ***clarity***. But that consciousness by means of which the composition of representations also becomes clear is called ***distinctness***. (Kant 2006, *Anthropology* AK 7:137–138)

In my understanding, to think an *a priori* concept distinctly is to provide a metaphysical exposition of it. Thus, to think an a priori concept *clearly* (e.g., to see how a hypothetical imperative relates to a categorical imperative) is to understand what is contained in that concept, whereas to think that concept distinctly is to understand what it contains *as* being given in and by HASU.

My defence against the charge of incoherence, and more directly against the challenge from hard determinism, is provided by what Kant calls a 'transcendental exposition' (elsewhere 'deduction', e.g., in 1997, *CPrR* AK 5:46–48). This is

> the explanation of a concept, as a principle from which the possibility of other *a priori* knowledge can be understood. For this purpose it is required (1) that such knowledge does really follow from the given concept, (2) that this knowledge is possible only on the assumption of a given mode of explaining the concept. (Kant 1932, *CPuR* B40)

Both my Gewirthian dialectically necessary argument and Kant's argument for a categorical imperative combine a metaphysical exposition of a concept with a transcendental exposition of it, the transcendental exposition being defence of the coherence of the result of the metaphysical exposition (postulation of the categorical imperative) necessitated because the intelligibility of the concept of a categorical imperative presupposes that human agents, who are subject to heteronomy, can have the capacity of free will.

In my opinion, Kant completes his metaphysical exposition in *GMM* by the end of *GMM* II, while *GMM* III performs the transcendental exposition (Beyleveld and Düwell 2020, Chap. 6).

The reason for rejecting the challenge from Humean internalism *as such* has already been given. It is that being able to have the concept of a hypothetical imperative presupposes being able to have the concept of a categorical imperative, the metaphysical exposition of which requires assent to the existence of the categorical imperative.

Agnes certainly might not care that she fails to understand what it is for her to be an agent. But, although Humean internalism implies otherwise, this fact is irrelevant to the existence of a categorical imperative. This is simply because for it to be true that Agnes ought to do X, whether this 'ought' is categorical or hypothetical or not, Agnes must be able *not to care* sufficiently about X to be motivated to do X. It makes no sense to say that Agnes ought (in any imperative sense) to do X if she will necessarily do it or will necessarily not do it. The necessity of a categorical imperative is not that of a scientific law, a necessarily *will* happen, but that of a necessarily *ought to* happen. The existence of a categorical imperative does not presuppose that Agnes will be rendered incapable of violating it by recognising it. Its motivational power is not mechanistic, but autonomous. Thus, Humean internalists need *to prove* that what Agnes wants to do can only be driven by heteronomous purposes, that she *can never* be moved to do X just by recognising that doing so is a strict requirement of HASU. They must prove that if Agnes is moved to act (wants to act) in accord with HASU, some heteronomous purpose *must* be responsible. But it is as impossible to prove this as it is impossible to prove that Agnes, when acting in accord with HASU, is not being driven by some heteronomous purpose. This, however, does not put my position and that of Humean internalists on a par because I need not, must not, and do not deny that heteronomous motivations can and do exist, whereas Humean internalists must deny that any of Agnes's actions can be autonomously motivated.[22]

But this exposes the fatal self-contradiction in Humean internalism and, consequently, in the sources thesis of legal positivism. The intelligibility of both theses requires the intelligibility of the concept of a hypothetical imperative. But this requires the intelligibility of the concept of a categorical imperative. So, Humean internalism and the sources thesis need the concept of a categorical imperative to be coherent at the same time as they require it to be incoherent.

What, then, about the challenge from hard determinism? I agree that a categorical imperative can apply to physically embodied beings like Agnus only if they have a capacity for free will, and that something cannot be mechanistically caused and be an act of free will at the same time (a mechanistic cause being a cause that has a mechanistic cause itself *ad infinitum,* while an act of free will is governed by a kind of reason that is an end in itself, which is to say that freely willed actions are autonomous, i.e., their own explanation). So, if everything that can possibly happen has a mechanistic cause, the concept of a categorical imperative is incoherent.

Kant is aware of this challenge. Furthermore, he himself holds that HASU requires Agnes to hold that every *observable* event has a mechanistic cause, which means that, unless free will and the 'principle of universal [mechanistic] causality' can somehow be combined in Agnes's will, the concept of a categorical imperative will be a mere 'chimerical idea without any truth' (1998a, *GMM* AK 4:456 read with AK 4:445).

The problem with both the hard determinist's objection and the challenge that Kant poses for himself is, as Kant argues in *GMM* III, that a rationally necessary principle of universal mechanistic causation cannot be grounded empirically because mechanistic causes are entirely speculative imputations derived from observed regularities in observable events, as Hume (1888, Book I Pt III Section III) himself insists. Therefore, *if any* principle of universal mechanistic causation is rationally necessary, this can only be shown by demonstrating it to be a necessary presupposition of the possibility of *empirical* knowledge. But as such, it only has *any* application to the explanation of *observable* events (and is justified only when we have a sufficient *exclusive* mechanistic causal explanation of such events because it cannot be asserted with certainty whenever it is coherent to provide a different explanation). Consequently, it has no *justified* application to the presupposition of free will because free will, by its concept, is not an observable event or thing. The

[22]The existence of a categorical imperative (and that of any moral rights) does not depend on Agnes (or anyone else) recognising that it is a strict requirement of HASU. It rests only on it *being* a strict requirement of HASU. This is because human agents do not have to act out of respect for the categorical imperative for it to exist. Its existence only requires it to be *unprovable* that they are *not* able to do so. Equally, Agnes does not need to know that it exists for it to exist. It only needs to be knowable that it exists (for which, *given that acceptance of it is a strict requirement of HASU),* it is only necessary that it be unknowable that it cannot exist.

claim that *everything that happens* has a mechanistic cause is mere speculation, ungrounded materialistic reductionism.

It is an indisputable fact that all human reasoning and attribution of meaning involves use of powers of understanding that are necessary for Agnes to be able to ask questions, to doubt and affirm statements, and to draw inferences, which are the a priori powers of HASU. Consequently, as Onora O'Neill (1989, p. 42) says in her interpretation of Kant's argument, to call into question the categorical imperative on *any* basis is, in the same moment, to call into question the cogency of this basis. Thus, if the concept of a categorical imperative does presuppose a concept of free will that is incompatible with hard determinism, no possible evidence or reasoning can demonstrate that free will cannot exist. Because the categorical imperative is the a priori law of HASU, if the concept of a categorical imperative is incoherent then any thesis about anything is incoherent, to conclude which is *unquestionably* nonsense, which renders the statement that it is unquestionably nonsense *unquestionably* true. As Kant puts this, speculative theoretical reason itself presupposes a spontaneity that it cannot explain (1997, *CPrR* AK 5:48), which must, at least, be consistent *cognitively* with the spontaneity presupposed by the existence of the moral law. In short, my Kantian-Gewirthian argument is that the very idea of the possibility of *any* human understanding, presupposes HASU, which postulates *Alpha,* which presupposes free will as part of its *ratio essendi,* which entails the unquestionable existence of the categorical imperative in the form of the FoH interpreted as the PGC!

It is also worth noting that, because acting purely out of respect for the categorical imperative is what is meant by acting out of free will, this connects the challenge from Humean internalism to the challenge from hard determinism. Therefore, the untenability of the one entails the untenability of the other.

3 What Is Free Will as the *Ratio Essendi* of the Categorical Imperative?

My argument rests on the existence of free will in some sense, and my indebtedness to Kant renders it necessary for me to explain my view of free will in relation to his.

Kant says that free will is the only idea of speculative (i.e., a priori *theoretical*) reason the reality of which agents can know, which enables Agnes to know that human immortality and the existence of God are *possible* (both of which are transcendent things, beyond any possible experience) (1997, *CPrR* AK 5:4). He also says that knowledge that Agnes has free will reveals her real as against her merely apparent nature (1998a, *GMM* AK 4:457), and that Agnes as '*homo noumenon*' gives the moral law to Agnes as '*homo phaenomenon*' (1991, *MoM* AK 6:417–418).

Kant, thereby, suggests that free will is a knowable aspect of the otherwise unknowable noumenal *(transcendent* metaphysical) nature of agents. However, he qualifies his claims about transcendent free will, God (and human immortality), by saying that cognition of them is only for practical purposes (1997 *CPrR* AK 5:48–50, 103, 134). Regarding this, he says that knowledge of the categorical imperative forces theoretical reason

> to grant *that there are such objects,* though it [theoretical reason] cannot determine them more closely and so cannot itself extend this cognition of the objects. … In this they become *immanent* and *constitutive* inasmuch as they are grounds of the possibility of *making real the necessary object* of pure practical reason (the highest good), whereas apart from this they are *transcendent* and merely *regulative* principles of speculative reason. (*CPrR* AK 5:135)

In other words, the *theoretical* knowledge of these objects that is given is purely negative, meaning that it cannot be used for theoretical purposes, and positive only in its use for practical purposes *(CPrR* AK 5:136). Regarding this positivity, Kant assigns different statuses to the postulation of God and human immortality, the *summum bonum,* and free will. The nature of free will is known (being specifiable as the *ratio essendi* of the categorical imperative, which—as the supreme law of HASU—is the supreme law of pure reason as a whole), the *summum bonum* must merely be hoped for *(CPrR* AK 5:83), while faith in God (and human immortality) is merely *morally* necessary (*CPrR* AK 5:125).

But how does Kant justify assigning different cognitive statuses to free will, God (and human immortality), and the *summum bonum?* I agree that the categorical imperative sets the *summum bonum* as an end, meaning that Agnes is required to hold that it *categorically ought* to be achieved**.** This requires her to believe that it *can* be achieved, which requires her to hope that it will be achieved. But in what sense of 'can'?

Kant reasons that Agnes is required to believe that God exists and that she is immortal because this must be true for the *summum bonum* to be capable of being achieved. But believing that God (an omnipotent and perfectly good being) exists entails that this is the best of all possible worlds so that the *summum bonum* will be attained *whatever anyone does,* which entails that there is nothing that anyone categorically ought to do (Beyleveld and Brownsword 2001, pp. 134–141; Beyleveld 2009, 2012, 2016)! Consequently, while Agnes must want the *summum bonum* to be achieved, she can be required to believe *neither* that the *summum bonum* cannot be achieved *nor* that it can actually be achieved. Agnes must hope, but do no more than hope, that God exists and that she is immortal.

Alongside this, the existence of *transcendent* free will (free will of a kind that cannot exist unless hard determinism is impossible, which presupposes that it is a property of a non-material substance) is not justified by Kant's defence against hard determinism. Showing that it is impossible *to demonstrate* that free will is not a property of a non-material substance (which Kant does show) does not show that it is possible for her transcendent nature to be a non-material substance. If it did, it would establish that hard determinism is false (and give us transcendent knowledge for *theoretical* purposes). It leaves open to question the possibility and the impossibility of both transcendent free will and hard determinism, leaving both things unknowable. Put differently, strictly speaking Agnes' knowledge of free will does not show that God and human immortality are possible. It shows that they cannot be known to be impossible.

Therefore, Agnes is required by HASU to assign the same cognitive status to *all transcendent* objects that Kant connects to the apodictic nature of the categorical imperative. They are all objects of rationally required hope, things that Agnes categorically ought to want to exist, but categorically ought not to be committed to the existence of in any sense requiring action beyond what the categorical imperative requires practically.

This entails that free will as the *ratio essendi* of the categorical imperative, the spontaneity that HASU presupposes, cannot be thought of as a transcendent substance. The idea of it as *transcendental* free will must be entirely *ontologically* negative, specifiable *in relation to the idea of a substance* only as the product of an unspecifiable transcendent grounding of Agnes's capacity to think at all (postulated by necessary presupposition of her possession of the a priori powers of HASU). In other words, what Kant can and has established is no more (but no less) than that the only sense in which *transcendent* free will, God (and human immortality), and the *summum bonum* are possible is that neither their ontological possibility nor their ontological impossibility can be known.

And this is what Kant implies at the very end of *GMM* when he says that

> we do not indeed comprehend the practical unconditional necessity of the moral imperative [i.e. (when read in context), we cannot *explain how* free will (in being the *ratio. essendi* of the rationally unquestionable categorical imperative) causes action, because this would contradict the categorical nature of the categorical imperative], but we nevertheless comprehend its *incomprehensibility*, and this is all that can be fairly required of a philosophy that strives in its principles at the very boundary of human reason. (1998a, AK 4:463)

So interpreted, Kant is right that the categorical imperative and *transcendental* free have a different status from God, human immortality, and the *summum bonum.* But this does not explain how he can differentiate the status of the *summum bonum* from that of the other two objects. Kant ought to say that all three are *epistemically* objects of rationally required hope, but that there is something about God and human immortality that does not apply to the *summum bonum* that makes it appropriate to regard them as objects of rationally required 'faith'.

Bearing this in mind, Kant (1932, *CPuR* B xxx) says that he has denied knowledge of God in order to make room for faith. This fits with his view that knowing that God exists is incompatible with the existence of the categorical imperative (1997, *CPrR* AK 5:147), basically for the same reason I have said that being rationally required to believe that God exists is incompatible with the existence of the categorical imperative. He also says that it is not permissible to believe that God does not exist, because

> *pure rational belief [*in God's existence] … [in being] a voluntary determination of our judgment, conducive to the moral (commanded) purpose [the *summum bonum]* … can … often waver even in the well-disposed but can never fall into unbelief. *(CPrR* AK 5:146).

This, however, suggests that Kant thinks that it is rationally necessary to hope that God exists, and rationally permissible to be either a theist or an agnostic, but rationally impermissible to be an atheist, and that it is this combination that constitutes the epistemic status of faith in God. But there is a twofold problem with this. First, the way in which the existence of God is linked to that of the *summum bonum* does not permit them to be differentiated in this way. If belief in God is only rationally permissible, then so too is belief in the *summum bonum.* Secondly, I do not think that the categorical imperative even *permits* belief in either, *unless* acting on this belief does not require Agnes to do anything contrary to what she can ascertain that the categorical imperative requires without reference to God. But this means that faith as practical rather than theoretical belief in God (and human immortality) is constituted merely by acting in accord with the categorical imperative coupled with hope for their existence, and all that distinguishes hope for the *summum bonum* from faith in God and human immortality is that the ideas of the latter are derived from the idea of the former as the ideal end postulated by the categorical imperative. In short, faith in God must signify a hopeful agnosticism.

Is this what Kant is trying to say? It fits with his view (1997, *CPrR* AK 5:4, 2000 *CPoJ* AK 5:451) (contrary, e.g., to that of Kelsen 1967, p. 63) that belief in the existence of God is not necessary to justify the categorical imperative. Indeed, he holds that it is only on the basis of having the idea of an unconditional law that the idea of God (as an omnipotent, wholly good being) can arise (1998b, *GMM* AK 4:408), which entails that belief in the existence of God is not the *ratio cognoscendi* of the categorical imperative, though it might be the reason why some agents believe in its existence. From the perspective of HASU (outside of which Agnes cannot think at all), HASU is the *ratio cognoscendi* of the categorical imperative as the law of itself, and transcendental free will (residing in possession of the a priori powers of HASU) is postulated by the categorical imperative as part of its *ratio essendi.* Furthermore, understood in this way, the categorical imperative and *transcendental* free will are facts of pure reason as a whole, while God and human immortality (as well as *transcendent* free will and the *summum bonum*) are only facts of pure practical reason ('morally certain' but not theoretically certain as well), which, I have argued elsewhere is Kant's view (Beyleveld and Düwell 2020, pp. 96–97).

In any event, my own view may be summarised as follows. As a requirement of the dialectical necessity of the categorical imperative, Agnes is required merely to hope that transcendent free will, God, human immortality, and the *summum bonum* are real possibilities. However, *if* the rational necessity of the categorical imperative is not a deceit that transcendent reality imposes on her, all these things must be real. But HASU itself does not permit Agnes to claim either that transcendent reality is deceitful or that it is not. All that HASU enables Agnes to know about transcendent reality is that *a* transcendent reality exists and must be responsible in a manner that HASU cannot comprehend for her possession of the a priori powers of HASU, hence for everything that HASU requires her to believe. But this means that Agnes is rationally required by *transcendent reality,* by its imposing the lens of HASU on her, to hope that hard determinism is false, that God exists, that she is immortal, and that the *summum bonum* will be brought about. On this basis, making God and human immortality objects of 'faith' is to say that hope for their existence is not simply what the categorical imperative requires but a fact about *the relationship* between Agnes's transcendental nature and her transcendent nature (as are her possession of HASU and her requirement to hope for the *summum bonum*), *as presented by HASU*, which is to say that all that Agnes can know about her transcendent nature is that she is a hoping, fearing, questioning being in having the a priori powers of HASU (which constitutes her possession of *transcendental* free will).

However, to give this the full attention it needs, requires a more concerted Gewirthian dialogue with Kant's rational theology than I have provided here or elsewhere. Furthermore, since I disagree with Kant about what treating Agnes's existence as an end in itself amounts to, I consider that no analysis of what he says about *Wille* and *Willkür* (hence about the nature of free will) can be adequate without a clear view of what he thinks about their relationship to his interpretation of the FoH, which has implications for his rational theology. At the same time, my own analysis of free will is incomplete without a more complete account of the relationship between the PGC and free will than I have provided here. Consequently, everything I have said on this matter is still only preliminary to the required full analysis, which is also necessary for a Gewirthian account of the possibility of moral responsibility for actions that contravene the PGC.

4 Conclusion

Explaining what he calls 'the paradox of method in a *Critique of Practical Reason*', Kant says that

> *the concept of good and evil must not be determined before the moral law ... but only (as was done here) after it and by means of it.* That is to say: even if we did not know that the principle of morality is a pure law determining the will a priori, we would at least have to leave it *undecided* in the beginning whether the will has only empirical or also pure determining grounds a priori, in order not to assume principles quite gratuitously *(gratis);* for it is contrary to all basic rules of philosophic procedure to assume as already decided the foremost question to be decided. (1997, *CPrR* AK 5:63)

If (he continues) we 'begin with the concept of the good in order to derive from it laws of the will', because 'the concept of the good has no practical a priori standard',[23] (I now paraphrase) the criterion of what is good could have no standard other than conformity with feelings of pleasure or the means to achieve what is pleasing. Consequently, what is good could only be determined empirically, which would automatically rule out, not only the possibility of any a priori practical law, but also the possibility of even thinking the concept of one coherently. On the other hand, if the concept of an a priori practical law were first

[23] This is one thing on which I am fundamentally in disagreement with John Finnis (1984), who holds that moral values are known by a priori intuition. Finnis also holds that religion is a basic good, whereas I hold that *if* God (unknowably) exists then God does not require agents to believe in God, and the PGC unequivocally opposes Finnis's sanctity of life position, to identify just two other points of contention.

> investigated analytically it would have been found that, instead of the concept of the good as an object making possible the moral law, it is on the contrary the moral law that first determines and makes possible the concept of the good, insofar as it deserves this name absolutely.[24] (Kant 1997, AK *CPrR* 5:63–64).

Since all forms of legal positivism ground legal obligations empirically as reflecting the will of the powerful (their contingent view of the good), what Kant says sums up the basis of my argument against legal positivism.

Since the categorical imperative is the law of HASU, to define obligations, practical laws, as governed by the categorical imperative rather than as a species of hypothetical imperative is not question-begging. For, once the presuppositions of our positions are fully exposed, legal positivism (but not my Kantian-Gewirthian position) is seen to be incoherent *from its own perspective.* And the bottom line is that coherence from its own perspective is the bare minimum that *must* be required of *any* philosophy, while coherence from its own perspective is (at the same time) *all* that can be required of the elucidation of the fundamental principles of philosophy. Many will disagree, because it is fashionable to hold it illegitimate to insist that second order judgments about first order judgments be capable of being applied to themselves without contradiction. But the only possible justification for this dogma is the manifestly false claim that no criteria of rationality and epistemic status can survive being subjected to themselves. In fact, rather than grounding the possibility of coherent discourse, the disqualification of the demand for coherent self-reflexivity in judgment implies the impossibility of any understanding.

There is a folk saying that breakthroughs in knowledge come from thinking the impossible. Nothing can be further from the truth. New knowledge comes from the ability to think beyond what just happens to be thought possible by others. Literally, it comes from understanding the possible and the necessary, and not merely perceiving the actual, for it is only the ability to think possibility and necessity that enables what is actual *to be thought* and not just felt. It is failure to comprehend this, I believe, that spawns epistemological empiricism and, in turn, Humean internalism, the immediate parent of the sources thesis of legal positivism.

It should be apparent that the implications of my argument go far beyond my disagreement with legal positivism. Attention to my agreements and disagreements with Collingwood (1940, pp. 21–33) is a good entry point to what they are.

Central to his attack on epistemological empiricism, Collingwood rightly says that every statement with a truth value (proposition) implies a question to which it is an answer, and every question presupposes a statement.

---

[24] By this, he means 'the idea of something intrinsically good'. Kant (1998a, *GMM* AK 4:393) says that there is nothing 'good without limitation except a good will', while 'the will is nothing other than practical reason' *(GMM* AK 4:412)—which is to say that to possess a will is to possess the capacity for HASU. This, alone, entails that he holds that to think and act in accord with the strict requirements of HASU is the only thing that is an end in itself (good without limitation), which is what I contend he is saying when he says that the ground of the categorical imperative is '*rational nature exists as an end in itself*' *(GMM* AK 4:428–429) (which is then the only possible ground for holding anything to be good objectively).

However, he claims that there are 'absolute presuppositions', statements that give rise to questions but have no presuppositions, so are not propositions. Absolute presuppositions are neither true nor false, and ground systems of thought between which no rational adjudication is possible. So, for a genuine dispute to exist, disputants must share their questions, which requires them to share their absolute presuppositions.

I agree that, for disputation to be possible at all, disputants must share their *fundamental* presuppositions. But I disagree with Collingwood's claim (which I consider grounds all forms of epistemological relativism and conceptual pragmatism)[25] that there can be multiple absolute presuppositions with no truth value because, for this claim to be intelligible, it must be a statement about all alleged absolute presuppositions, in which case it is self-contradictory because it presupposes a commensurability that it denies is possible. Instead, I have argued in agreement with Kant that, while there can be *no* knowledge without presuppositions, there is one substantive practical presupposition that all human thought presupposes that presupposes only itself.

Some further implications of my argument are:

(1) In order for the idea of any intersubjective understanding or communication to be possible, there must be a single categorical imperative that binds all the thinking (not merely the practical thinking)[26] of all human agents, for the idea that there are multiple incommensurable absolute presuppositions renders intersubjective understanding impossible.
(2) This much, I think, is also appreciated (and argued) by discourse theorists like Jurgen Habermas (1970). But Habermas's discourse-grounding presupposition takes the form of a purely procedural set of rules constituting what he calls 'the ideal speech situation' that must be presupposed if the idea that agents are able to debate and agree substantive rules to govern their conduct is to be intelligible. As such, Habermas's position entails that a legal system cannot be fully legitimate unless the rules by which it governs are products of the ideal speech situation. I agree. But my argument goes further than this in two ways:
    (a) It demonstrates that the ideal speech situation is governed by the PGC, which imposes inviolable substantive constraints on what may be imposed by agreements reached procedurally, much as human rights set minimalistic limits on pluralism.[27] In Gewirthian terms, the PGC has indirect

[25] See my PhD dissertation, *The Epistemological Foundations of Sociological Theory*, University of East Anglia, Norwich 1975.

[26] This is because the categorical imperative is to think as well as to act only in accord with the strict requirements of HASU.

[27] Similarly, I do not think that Lon Fuller's (1969) 'inner morality of law', rules that must be accepted by understanding positive law as a set of rules, is purely procedural. Related to this, while I agree with Ronald Dworkin (1978, p. 216) that morality does not exist in 'a brooding omnipresence in the sky', this is only because a 'transcendental' strongbox does not exist 'in the sky'. It is not a mysterious Platonic realm of ideas. It is constituted altogether mundanely by HASU, being located in Kant's *sensus communis*. As such, moral constraints on positive law also do not exist in

applications, involving what Gewirth calls 'the method of consent' (which grounds pluralistic possibilities); but these are limited in the obligations they can impose by the substantive requirements that the PGC imposes directly.

(b) It implies, because there cannot be any intersubjective understanding without intra-subjective understanding, and all intra-subjective understanding is HASU, that a categorical imperative (the PGC) is not merely a necessary presupposition of the possibility of intersubjective communication, but a necessary presupposition of all thinking, which means that it cannot be questioned intelligibly and is the reason why a categorical imperative really exists.[28]

If all of this does not persuade that my view of legal obligation is correct, then I hope that it will at least make clear why I think that legal positivism is untenable.

References

Alexy R (2009) The argument from injustice: a reply to legal positivism. Oxford University Press, Oxford

Austin J (1955) The province of jurisprudence determined. Weidenfeld and Nicolson, London

Beyleveld D (1991) The dialectical necessity of morality: an analysis and defense of Alan Gewirth's argument for the Principle of Generic Consistency. University of Chicago Press, Chicago

Beyleveld D (2009) Morality and the god of reason. Faculty of Humanities, University of Utrecht, Utrecht. ISBN: 978-90-76912-95-0

Beyleveld D (2012) Hope and belief. In: Jenkins RJ, Sullivan E (eds) Philosophy of mind. Nova Science Publishers, New York, pp 1–36

Beyleveld D (2013) Williams' false dilemma: how to give categorically binding impartial reasons to real agents. J Mor Philos 10:204–226

Beyleveld D (2015) Korsgaard v Gewirth on universalisation: why Gewirthians are Kantians and Kantians ought to be Gewirthians. J Mor Philos 12(5):573–597

Beyleveld D (2016) Gewirth vs Kant on Kant's maxim of reason: towards a Gewirthian philosophical anthropology. In: Bauhn P (ed) Gewirthian perspectives on human rights. Routledge, Abingdon, pp 13–29

Beyleveld D (2017) Transcendental arguments for a categorical imperative as arguments from agential self-understanding. In: Brune JP et al (eds) Transcendental arguments in moral theory. De Gruyter, Berlin, pp 141–159

Beyleveld D, Brownsword R (1985) The practical difference between natural-law theory and legal positivism. Oxf J Leg Stud 5:1–32

Dworkin's morality in a 'discriminatory' sense (as against in an 'anthropological' sense) (ibid., pp. 248–253), according to which (in effect) they exist (variably) in the *sensus vulgaris* of each community constrained only by purely procedural or conventional criteria of rationality.

[28] A corollary of this is that there cannot be an essentially private language (one that others cannot learn). This is not because Agnes learns her language from others. It is because, in order to be able to learn a language, or to invent one for herself, Agnes must be able to think, for which she must have and employ the a priori powers of HASU that she shares with all other human agents. To suppose that Agnes can have an essentially private language is to suppose that she cannot think at all.

Beyleveld D, Brownsword R (1986) Law as a moral judgment. Sweet & Maxwell, London. Reprinted (1994), Sheffield Academic Press, Sheffield
Beyleveld D, Brownsword R (2001) Human dignity in bioethics and biolaw. Oxford University Press, Oxford
Beyleveld D, Brownsword R (2019) Is there really anything wrong with an absolute principle? In: Borowski M (ed) Modern German non-positivism: from Radbruch to Alexy. Mohr Siebeck, Tübingen, pp 279–292
Beyleveld D, Düwell M (2020) The sole fact of pure reason: Kant's quasi-ontological argument for the categorical imperative. De Gruyter, Berlin
Beyleveld D, Pattinson SD (2000) Precautionary reasoning as a link to moral action. In: Boylan M (ed) Medical ethics. Prentice Hall, Upper Saddle River, pp 39–53
Collingwood RG (1940) An essay on metaphysics. The Clarendon Press, Oxford
Dworkin R (1978) Taking rights seriously. Duckworth, London
Enoch D (2006) Agency, shmagency: why normativity won't come out of what is constitutive of action. Philos Rev 115:169–198
Finnis J (1984) Natural law and natural rights. Oxford University Press, Oxford
Fuller L (1969) The morality of law. Revised edition. Yale University Press, New Haven
Gewirth A (1978) Reason and morality. University of Chicago Press, Chicago
Gewirth A (1996) The community of rights. University of Chicago Press, Chicago
Habermas J (1970) Towards a theory of communicative competence. Inquiry 13:360–375
Hart HLA (1961) The concept of law. Oxford University Press, Oxford
Hobbes T (1962) In: Plamenatz J (ed) Leviathan. Fontana, London
Hume D (1888) In: Selby-Bigge LA (ed) A treatise of human nature. Clarendon Press, Oxford
Jenkins I (1959–1960) The matchmaker or towards a synthesis of legal of idealism and positivism. J Leg Educ 12:1–12
Kant I (1933) In: Kemp-Smith N (ed) Critique of pure reason. Macmillan, London
Kant I (1991) In: Gregor M (ed) The metaphysics of morals. Cambridge University Press, Cambridge
Kant I (1997) In: Gregor M (ed) Critique of practical reason. Cambridge University Press, Cambridge
Kant I (1998a) In: Gregor M (ed) Groundwork of the metaphysics of morals. Cambridge University Press, Cambridge
Kant I (1998b) Religion within the boundaries of mere reason. In: Wood AW, di Giovanni G (eds) Religion within the boundaries of mere reason and other writings. Cambridge University Press, Cambridge
Kant I (2000) In: Guyer P (ed) Critique of the power of judgment. Cambridge University Press, Cambridge
Kant I (2006) In: Louden RB (ed) Anthropology from a practical point of view. Cambridge University Press, Cambridge
Kant I (2009) Jäsche logic. In: Guyer P, Wood AW (eds) Lectures on logic. Cambridge University Press, Cambridge
Kelsen H (1967) Pure theory of law. University of California Press, Berkeley
Korsgaard C (1996) Sources of normativity. Cambridge University Press, Cambridge
O'Neill O (1989) Constructions of reason: explorations of Kant's practical philosophy. Cambridge University Press, Cambridge
Pirni A (2015) The community within us: about the distinction between *Wille* and *Willkür*. Estudos Kantianos 3:41–50
Werner M (2002) Minimalistiche Handlungstheorie—gescheiterte Letzbegrunding: Ein Blick auf Alan Gewirth. In: Holger Burckhart H, Gronke H (eds) Philosophieren aus dem Diskurs. Betrage zur Diskurspragmatik. Konigshausen & Neuman, Wurzburg, pp 308–328
Williams B (1985) Ethics and the limits of philosophy. Fontana, London

Gustav Radbruch's Theory of Legal Obligation

Martin Borowski

Gustav Radbruch has become internationally famous for the non-positivistic formula that he coined in 1946. A simplified version of this formula—'Extreme injustice is not law'[1]—has served as a lynchpin of the debate between positivism and non-positivism since the middle of the twentieth century. However, while Radbruch's legal philosophy has received considerable attention in the international debate, it has received less attention in the English debate.[2]

1 The Reception of Radbruch's Legal Philosophy in the English Debate

That Radbruch's greater legal philosophy does not figure more prominently in the debate in English can be explained.

[1] See Sect. 1.4 below.

[2] Exceptions include Paulson (1995), Alexy (1999, 2021), Haldemann (2005), Paulson (2006), Spaak (2009), Dyzenhaus (2010), Bix (2011), and Borowski (2019, 2021).

M. Borowski (✉)
University of Heidelberg, Lehrstuhl für Öffentliches Recht, Verfassungstheorie und Rechtsphilosophie, Heidelberg, Germany
e-mail: martin.borowski@jurs.uni-heidelberg.de

D. Beyleveld, S. Bertea (eds.), *Theories of Legal Obligation*, Law and Philosophy Library 146, https://doi.org/10.1007/978-3-031-54067-7_5

1.1 Translations of Radbruch's Works into English

The first explanation is that only a few of Radbruch's works in legal philosophy have been translated into English. Although his main treatise, *Rechtsphilosophie* (Legal Philosophy) (Radbruch 1973), written in 1932, was translated as early as 1950 into English by Kurt Wilk (Radbruch 1950), an American political scientist, Radbruch's German is peculiar. His style of writing is generally clear, but the language he uses is often 'rich', with many expressions having different levels of meaning. Some of these multi-faceted expressions are central to his theory. Because it even requires some familiarisation for a native German to fully comprehend Radbruch's *Rechtsphilosophie* in the original, it must be far more difficult to comprehend it using Kurt Wilk's 1950 translation. However, the situation is better in the case of Radbruch's two famous post-War articles, 'Fünf Minuten Rechtsphilosophie' (1945) and 'Gesetzliches Unrecht und übergesetzliches Recht' (1946), in which he coined the 'Radbruch formula'. Bonnie Litschewski Paulson and Stanley Paulson have published very knowledgeable translations of both articles (Radbruch 2006a, b), and Stanley Paulson (2006) has written an article explaining the background and significance of Radbruch's two post-war papers.

There are also several works by Radbruch that are integral parts of his greater legal philosophy, but which have not been translated into English. These include his first treatise, *Outlines of Legal Philosophy* (*Grundzüge der Rechtsphilosophie*) (1914), key articles (Radbruch 1924, 1934, 1937/38, 1947) and a short Post-War book, *Primer in Legal Philosophy* (Radbruch 1948).

1.2 Neo-Kantianism as Radbruch's Philosophical Foundation

A second explanation is that Radbruch grounds central parts of his legal philosophy on neo-Kantianism, specifically on the Baden School of neo-Kantianism, characterised by the works of Wilhelm Windelband, Heinrich Rickert and Emil Lask.[3] However, he felt no need to justify his choice of this philosophical account as the foundation of his legal philosophy. At that time, it was the German philosophical state-of-the-art. But now it is hardly familiar in German philosophy and has little counterpart in Anglo-Saxon legal philosophy. This said, there are some similarities with Robert Alexy's analytical non-positivism,[4] which has attracted considerable attention in the international debate conducted in English. However, while these

[3]On the neo-Kantian foundations of Radbruch's legal philosophy, see, in particular, Dreier and Paulson (2003, pp. 238–241); Paulson (2006, pp. 29–32); Paulson (2021, pp. 1–3); and Zhao (2020).

[4]A key sentence in Alexy's characterisation of his argument from correctness is: 'Every legal system lays claim to correctness' (Alexy 2002, p. 34). Footnote 64 in this text reads: 'This statement is the point of departure for a rational reconstruction of Radbruch's somewhat opaque statement: "Law is the reality whose meaning is in serving the legal value, the legal idea"'.

similarities deserve to be explored further, such a demanding project goes beyond the scope of this essay, which is confined to providing a more thorough understanding of Radbruch's legal philosophy.

1.3 H.L.A. Hart's Verdict

A third explanation is provided by the fact that Radbruch's legal philosophy was presented in a rather unfortunate light in the international arena in the middle of the twentieth century. In particular, it was ridiculed by H.L.A. Hart (1958) in his famous article 'Positivism and the Separation of Law and Morals'. In this article, Hart presents Radbruch as a converted positivist. Radbruch

> had himself shared the 'positivist' doctrine until the Nazi tyranny, but he was converted by this experience and so his appeal to other men to discard the doctrine of the separation of law and morals has the special poignancy of a recantation. (Ibid., p. 616)

Radbruch supposedly left the right path—positivism—for emotional reasons rather than convincing arguments, a move for which Hart seems to express sympathy.

> It is impossible to read without sympathy Radbruch's passionate demand that the German legal conscience should be open to the demands of morality. (Ibid.)

But he continues:

> There is an extraordinary naïveté in the view that insensitiveness to the demands of morality and subservience to state power in a people like the Germans should have arisen from the belief that law might be law though it failed to conform with the minimum requirements of morality. (Ibid.)[5]

---

[5] Hart has a point here because Radbruch was, indeed, the originator of the 'positivism legend'. 'Positivism, with its principle that 'a law is a law', has in fact rendered the German legal profession defenceless against statutes that are arbitrary and criminal.' (Radbruch 2006b, p. 6)

One year later he wrote: "'The statute and the law,' with this phrase we believed we had said the same thing with two expressions. Every statute was law to us and every law statute, legal science was nothing other than the interpretation of the statute and adjudication exclusively the application of statutes. We called ourselves positivists, and positivism, regarding the statute alone as law, counts as the blame that German legal science has to bear for the state of the law during the years of National Socialism." (Radbruch 1947, p. 5)

Insofar as this 'positivism legend' refers to 'statutory positivism' and the doctrine of judicial bindingness, it proves empirically false. Apart from a few certainly morally outrageous statutes the regime often pursued its aims either by interpreting blanket clauses in the spirit of the new ideology or even with *contra legem* interpretations of statutes (Müller 1991, pp. 219–234; Paulson 2006, pp. 33–35; Dreier 2015a, pp. 10–12).

That Radbruch himself was aware of this fact (which becomes clear in a passage in section 26 on the free law movement in the *Primer in Legal Philosophy*, Radbruch 1948, p. 79) is just as confusing as the fact that, in 1947, he classified his own 1932 theory as positivistic, even though there are good reasons to understand his Pre-War theory as non-positivistic. (See also Borowski 2021, pp. 646–647).

However, it is somewhat surprising that Hart felt confident to dismiss Radbruch's theory in such a manner, considering that he had little knowledge of Radbruch's wider legal philosophy. Hart familiarised himself with Radbruch's legal philosophy only from short excerpts[6] of two of Radbruch's Post-War articles, which Lon Fuller used is his lectures at Harvard.[7] Hart's dismissive attitude in his famous article referring to Radbruch's theory was certainly not conducive to the reception of this theory in the Anglo-Saxon debate and it is very likely that it has also influenced the international debate in English.

1.4 The Radbruch Formula in Robert Alexy's Works

One might be tempted to say that Radbruch has long been rehabilitated through the works of Robert Alexy (1999, p. 17; 2008, p. 282), who claims to defend the Radbruch formula in the form of—using Alexy's language—the argument from injustice: the slogan of which is 'Extreme injustice is not law'.[8] Alexy does not, however, primarily aim at fully comprehending and explaining Radbruch's legal philosophy as such. He defends his own version of non-positivism, characterised by the argument from correctness (Alexy 2002, pp. 35–39; 2007a, pp. 49–50; 2007b,

[6] It is not clear how long these excerpts were. For example, Hart claims that 'it is clear that the doctrine meant that every lawyer and judge should denounce statutes that transgressed the fundamental principles not as merely immoral or wrong but as having no legal character, and enactments which on this ground lack the quality of law should not be taken into account in working out the legal position of any given individual in particular circumstances.' (Hart 1958, p. 617)

This is not, however, a proper characterisation of Radbruch's Post-War theory. In Paulson's translation into English, a key passage in Radbruch's article from 1946 reads as follows. '[N]ot every judge acting on his own initiative should be allowed to invalidate statutes; rather, this task should be reserved to a higher court or to legislation.' (Paulson 2006, p. 8, footnotes omitted).

This echoes Kelsen's idea of centralised constitutional review. An institutionalization of the Radbruch formula along these lines significantly mitigates the loss of legal certainty, the alleged implication of which is a key argument against this formula (see Borowski 2015, p. 248; 2017, pp. 76–77). If this passage, just one page after the Radbruch formula (Radbruch 2006b, p. 7), was not available to Hart, Fuller's excerpts were very short indeed.

[7] Hart says, 'I have used the translation of part of this essay [Radbruch (1946)] and of Radbruch, Die Erneuerung des Rechts, 2 *Die Wandlung* 8 (Germany 1947), prepared by Professor Lon Fuller of the Harvard Law School as a mimeographed supplement to the readings in jurisprudence used in his course at Harvard.' (1958, p. 617, footnote 42)

This very slim textual basis explains much. For example, according to Hart (1958, p. 617), 'The striking recantation of his previous doctrine is unfortunately omitted from the translation of his works'. There has, however, never been this 'striking recantation'. To be sure, Kurt Wilk's 1950 translation of Radbruch's *Rechtsphilosophie* was available to Hart, and he could have contrasted Radbruch's theory of the validity of law in Chapter 10 of that work with the intolerability formula in Radbruch's 1946 article. Pointing out this ostensible contradiction comes as close to a 'recantation' as possible—although I hasten to add that the contrasting juxtaposition of these two passages from two publications needs to be interpreted in a much broader context.

[8] See also Dyzenhaus (2010, p. 16).

pp. 333–335, 349, and 352–356; 2008, pp. 294–296; 2010, pp. 168–172)[9] and the argument from injustice (Alexy 2002, pp. 40–68), which gives rise to two different kinds of necessary connection between law and morality, a qualifying connection and a classifying connection.[10]

Radbruch's original formula has two parts, the 'intolerability formula'[11] and the 'disavowal formula'.[12] These two parts have different roots in Radbruch's legal philosophy—the 'intolerability formula' in Radbruch's theory of the validity of law, the 'disavowal formula' in his concept of law.[13] What is more, the two parts have different consequences when applied. If the conditions of the intolerability formula are fulfilled, the legal norm in question loses its legal validity. If the conditions of the disavowal formula are fulfilled, the legal norm forfeits its legal character—it does not count as a legal norm from the outset, so that the question whether it is legally valid is meaningless.[14] Whether there is a practical difference or not,[15] Radbruch regards the lack of legal character as more fundamental than the loss of legal validity.[16]

Even though the disavowal formula represents an independent part at the same categorical level as the intolerability formula, there has been a clear tendency to dismiss and neglect the second part of the formula ever since the beginning of the reception of the Radbruch formula. The German Federal Constitutional Court preferred the intolerability formula over the disavowal formula, as does the large majority in the academic literature.[17] Considering the fact that Radbruch employed

---

[9] For criticism, see, for example, Raz (2007, pp. 26–28); MacCormick (2007); Gardner (2012).

[10] In the case of a *classifying connection*, a relevant moral defect of a legal norm deprives this norm of its legal character or its legal validity. By contrast, the *qualifying connection* (resulting from both the argument from correctness (Alexy 2002, pp. 39 and 127) and the argument from principles (Alexy 2002, p. 79) signifies that if the claim to correctness is not satisfied, the relevant norm does not forfeit its legal character or lose its legal validity but is rendered merely legally defective (see ibid.).

Alexy (2002, pp. 68–81) also advances a third argument—the argument from principles—which is based, in the final analysis, on the argument from correctness. However, it is questionable whether the argument from principles is at the same categorical level as the argument from correctness (see Borowski 2011, pp. 592–594).

[11] See Sect. 4.2.

[12] See Sect. 4.1.

[13] See Borowski (2019, pp. 30–33) and Borowski (2021, pp. 631–632). See also Sects. 4.1 and 4.2.

[14] This distinction is clearly expressed in the wording of both parts of the comprehensive formula. (See also Borowski 2015, pp. 245–246 and 72; 2019, p. 33).

[15] From the standpoint of the judge who asks whether he or she is empowered and under an obligation to apply a certain norm of positive law, there is no practical difference. (See Borowski 2017, p. 75).

[16] Expressed in the phrase 'then the statute is not merely "flawed law", it lacks completely the very nature of law' (Radbruch 2006b, p. 7).

[17] BVerfGE 23, 98 (106); 95, 96 (134); Paradigmatic proponents in the literature are Dreier (1993, p. 58); Dreier (1997, p. 423); Alexy (1999, p. 16); Haldemann (2005, p. 166); and Bix (2011, pp. 46–47). By contrast, the *Bundesgerichtshof* (German Federal Court of Justice) placed the aspect of discrimination centre stage (BGHZ 16, 350 [354–355]), which points in the direction of

the disavowal formula to overcome morally outrageous statutes enacted by the National Socialists[18]—not the intolerability formula—this is even more astonishing.

The fundamentally wrong course was set by Hans-Ulrich Evers (1956, pp. 82–83) who introduced the idea of the subjective reading according to which the disavowal formula requires a subjective intent on the part of the lawgiver to disavow or betray justice. Since the phrase 'deliberately betrays' may well be read as requiring subjective intent on the part of the lawgiver,[19] many commentators regarded Evers's subjective reading as convincing.[20] There are, however, weighty arguments on behalf of an objective reading of the disavowal formula. On this reading, cases of extreme discrimination are instances of the second part of the Radbruch formula, according to which '[p]ositive law disavows justice if it represents a case of extreme discrimination, such as discrimination on grounds of sex, birth, class, race or on other comparable grounds' (Borowski 2021, p. 635).[21] The neo-Kantian foundation of Radbruch's legal philosophy points to objective meaning rather than subjective intent[22] and an objective reading of the disavowal formula squares with Radbruch's objective account of legal interpretation.[23] What is more, even though Radbruch repeatedly emphasised relativism in his *Rechtsphilosophie*, close inspection reveals limits to his relativism.[24]

In fact, Alexy does not defend and support both parts of the Radbruch formula, but only the first part, the intolerability formula. He does not defend and support the second part, which Radbruch himself used to overcome morally iniquitous statutes of the National Socialists. What is more, while Alexy's writings on his argument from injustice date back to the 1990s, it was not until recently that he undertook to enquire more comprehensively into key elements of Radbruch's legal philosophy in the essay 'Gustav Radbruch's Concept of Law', an original paper in his most recent collection of articles and chapters, *Law's Ideal Dimension* (Alexy 2021).

an objective reading of the disavowal formula rather than in the direction of the intolerability formula.

[18] See Borowski (2019, pp. 34–37). Regarding the two formulae in Radbruch's 1946 article, Stanley L. Paulson writes: 'Radbruch does not bring either formulation to bear on the cases he discusses in the article of 1946' (2006, 27). To be sure, for Radbruch, individual acts are not part of the law anyway, since they lack 'generality', a necessary condition of positive law (Radbruch 1950, p. 76). However, this is not a convincing reconstruction compared to Hans Kelsen's conception of 'individual norms' (on which see Kelsen 1992, pp. 67–70; 1961, pp. 134–142; 1967, pp. 236–250 and 256–267). Arguably, Radbruch confused 'generalisability' with 'generality' (see Borowski 2015, p. 256).

[19] See Borowski (2019, p. 38) and Borowski (2021, p. 632).

[20] See, for example, Dreier (1993, pp. 57–58); Alexy (1999, p. 16); and Seidel (1999, pp. 174–175) who provides further references.

[21] See also Borowski (2019, p. 45).

[22] See Funke (2003, pp. 3–16); Borowski (2019, pp. 42–43; 2021, p. 633).

[23] Seidel (1999, p. 176); Borowski (2019, p. 41); Borowski (2021, p. 633).

[24] Borowski (2019, pp. 43–45); Borowski (2021, pp. 633–635).

1.5 Radbruch's Complex Non-Positivistic Theory

Radbruch argues that there is a necessary connection between law and morality using no fewer than three elements of his theory[25]—(1) in his key characterisation of the law, according to which it 'is the reality whose meaning is to serve the idea of law', with justice as a key component of the idea of law,[26] (2) in his concept of law, in which equality characterises justice (reflected in the disavowal formula), and (3) in his theory of legal validity, in which extremely unjust positive law can have no legal validity (which is reflected in the intolerability formula). These elements and their relations will be outlined in what follows. Apart from moral correctness, every non-positivistic theory needs to address the issues of authoritative issuance of positive law and its social efficacy. Here Radbruch's formal concept of law,[27] which complements his substantive concept of law, comes into play. On the whole, Radbruch developed an interesting legal philosophy beyond his famous formula and this legal philosophy deserves more attention than it has to date received in the international debate in English language.

2 Legal Obligation as a Normative Entity

A legal obligation is a normative entity. The empirical fact that I am forced by external powers to do something or refrain from doing something does not, as such, give rise to a legal obligation. The same applies to the mere prediction[28] that a certain act—unlawful behaviour—will result in another act—the legal sanction. A legal obligation presupposes an objective *reason* or objective *justification* that a conditioning fact gives rise to a conditioned consequence. In Hans Kelsen's Pure Theory of Law this is 'peripheral imputation', the specific legal ought that must be clearly distinguished from causality. For Kelsen, a legal obligation represents an abstract normative entity that must be distinguished from physical and psychical facts (Kelsen 1992, p. 23 *et passim*; 1961, pp. 45–47). In this sense, the theory of legal obligation is intimately connected to the issue of the normativity of law: 'The concept of legal duty is … nothing but a counterpart to the concept of legal norm' (Kelsen 1961, p. 58). The legal norm is front and centre in analysing the law and 'the principle according to which the science of law describes its object is normativity' (ibid., p. 46). While Kelsen supports the idea of the normativity of law from a positivistic point of view, *non-moral normativity*, non-positivists may assume that

[25] These non-positivistic elements were present in Radbruch's legal philosophy from the outset. Only his theory of legal validity changed to a certain extent between 1932 and 1945 when the non-positivistic dimension became more pronounced. See Sect. 5.3.

[26] See Sect. 3.1.

[27] See Sect. 5.1.

[28] As expressed in Oliver Wendell Holmes's (1921, pp. 167–173) famous prediction theory.

morality lends law a moral dimension, brought about by the necessary connection between law and morality—*moral normativity*.[29]

To be sure, whether or not law boasts a normative dimension and whether or not this is brought about by a necessary connection between law and morality, are both hotly contested. A working definition, according to which a legal obligation merely involves some kind of normative relation, must suffice for now.

3 Key Elements of Radbruch's Legal Philosophy

There are a few passages in which Radbruch directly addresses the issue of legal obligation. However, a proper understanding of these passages requires familiarity with key elements of Radbruch's legal philosophy. With an eye to a reconstruction of the idea of legal obligation, three elements are crucial—a specific relation between reality and value, the separation between 'Is' and 'Ought' and a specific conception of relativism.

3.1 Reality and Value

Radbruch's first fundamental assumption is the neo-Kantian distinction between reality and value. He distinguishes between four points of view:

(i) the 'value-blind point of view' (*wertblinder Standpunkt*) (Radbruch 1950, pp. 49–50, translation altered);
(ii) the 'evaluating point of view' (*bewertender Standpunkt*) (ibid., p. 50, translation altered);[30]
(iii) the 'value-relating point of view' (*wertbeziehender Standpunkt*) (ibid., translation altered); and
(iv) the 'value-transcending point of view' (*wertüberwindender Standpunkt*) (Radbruch 1950, pp. 50–51, translation altered), which characterises, in particular, religion.

Crucially, according to Radbruch, law is not merely an institutionalised form of ethics and, consequently, an instance of the 'evaluating point of view', but an instance of the 'value-relating point of view'. It is a reality that is necessarily connected to a value in the sense that the reality objectively claims to realise this value. Following

[29] Robert Alexy defends a necessary connection between law and morality but includes Kelsen's idea of a basic norm of a dynamic system of norms into his own legal philosophy (see Alexy 2002, pp. 95–116). This raises the question why Alexy combines non-moral and moral normativity and whether such a combination is either necessary, possible, or convincing.

[30] The value-blind point of view is characteristic of the [natural] sciences(*Naturwissenschaften*), the evaluating point of view characteristic of, in modern parlance, ethics.

Windelband, Radbruch uses examples of, first, a piece of art claiming to represent beauty, second, a scientific enquiry claiming to discover the truth and, third, morals (in the sense of positive morality) claiming to instantiate the Good (Radbruch 1950, p. 50, translation altered). Radbruch's genuine contribution to neo-Kantian legal philosophy is his idea of the original and non-derivative value of justice (see Paulson 2006, p. 29), which he claims is characteristic of the law.

> Law is the reality whose meaning (*Sinn*) is to serve the [peculiarly] legal value, the idea of law. The concept of law is therefore oriented toward the idea of law. Now the idea of law can be none other than justice. (Radbruch 1950, p. 73, translation altered, following Paulson 2006, p. 31)

The phrase 'law is the reality whose meaning is to serve the idea of law, justice' expresses Radbruch's substantive concept of law—Stanley L. Paulson (2006, p. 19 *et passim*) aptly calls this Radbruch's 'basal criterion'. It takes centre stage in Radbruch's 1932 treatise (Radbruch 1950, pp. 52, 73, and 110 *et passim*) and is correlative to the law's specific value-relating point of view. This substantive concept of law presupposes a necessary connection between law and morality and transcends a reduction of law to a mere concatenation of physical and psychical facts.

The idea of law is characterised by a triad of antinomies, namely, justice, legal certainty and purposiveness (ibid., pp. 107–112).[31] In this, 'justice' means substantive justice, 'legal certainty' represents a formal dimension of justice (Radbruch 1914, pp. 172 and 183; 1948, p. 33) and 'purposiveness' is brought about by the relativistic limitation of the cognition of substantive justice (Paulson 2006, pp. 31–32).

3.2 *The Separation of 'Is' and 'Ought': Methodendualismus*

Like Kelsen, Radbruch insists on a clear separation of 'Is' and 'Ought', explicitly following Immanuel Kant: 'Kantian philosophy has taught us that it is impossible from what is to derive what is valuable, what is right, what ought to be' (Radbruch 1950, p. 53). Two pages later we read: 'Statements concerning the Ought may be established or proved only by other statements concerning the Ought' (ibid., p. 55).[32] Unlike Kelsen, however, Radbruch makes no attempt to justify the normativity of law by appeal to a basic norm of a dynamic system of norms or to any other elaborated method.[33]

---

[31] On this idea triad, see Alexy (2021, pp. 111–113).

[32] Kant himself was influenced by Hume (2007, p. 302).

[33] For Radbruch (1937/38, p. 57), relativism (and ultimately an individual's conscience) is key. On this issue, see Borowski (2013, pp. 183–184).

3.3 *Radbruch's Version of Relativism*

Radbruch's third fundamental assumption is relativism, according to which the cognition of justice is impossible: '[U]ltimate statements concerning the Ought are incapable of being proved, they are not subject to cognition but only to confession' (Radbruch 1950, p. 55, translation altered).

Radbruch distinguishes three typical ultimate values or purposes, which are: (1) the individualistic value or purpose, 'freedom'; (2) the transindividualistic value or purpose, 'nation'; and (3) the transpersonal value or purpose, 'culture' (ibid., p. 94). So far as the individual is concerned, Radbruch leaves the decision on the ultimate value or purpose of the law to the individual. It is the individual's conscience that needs to be and is indeed empowered to take the decision (ibid., p. 92). At the collective level, the decision on the 'confession' that Radbruch requires is taken by means of the democratic process (ibid., pp. 99–103).

A clear separation of 'Is' and 'Ought' together with relativism leads Kelsen to positivism. So, how can Radbruch escape arriving at a similar result? It is crucial to understand that, while Kelsen's relativism was consequent and without qualification, a closer reading reveals that Radbruch is actually not a strict relativist, even though he repeatedly emphasised relativism. He accepts that there are certain cases in which the cognition of justice is possible.[34] Limits to relativism are relevant for both his concept of law and his theory about the validity of law, which leads to an important distinction in his legal philosophy.

4 The Concept and the Validity of Law

Throughout all periods of his legal philosophy, Radbruch distinguished clearly between the concept of law and the validity of law by presupposing a concept of law that omits validity.[35] The criteria for the identification of a legal norm differ from those for legal validity, the latter being a contingent property of a legal norm. Interestingly, Alexy (2002, p. 24) explicitly argues on behalf of a concept of law that embraces validity, even though he seems to distinguish the two aspects. Just as Radbruch does, Alexy has separate chapters for the concept of law and the validity of law in his main treatise, *The Argument from Injustice* (Alexy (2002, pp. 11–81 on the concept of law and pp. 83–123 on the validity of law.)[36]

[34] See Sect. 1.4.

[35] On the distinction between concepts of the legal embracing legal validity and concepts of the legal norm omitting legal validity, see generally Alexy (2002, pp. 23–24). On Radbruch's concept of law that omits legal validity, see Borowski (2015, pp. 38–40).

[36] For both the concept and the validity of law there are three possible criteria—authoritative issuance, social efficacy and moral correctness. It is not clear which criterion determines to what extent a legal norm exists or whether it is valid.

However, even though the concept of law and the validity of law can be distinguished, they must be integrated in a consistent and coherent fashion in Radbruch's comprehensive legal philosophy, doing which is among the major challenges reconstructing Radbruch's theory faces. I shall confine myself to a very rough outline of the key aspects this involves.

4.1 Radbruch's Concept of Law

The neo-Kantian relation between reality and value, the value-relating point of view, is the key to Radbruch's concept of law because it implies his basal criterion: 'Law is the reality whose meaning is to serve the idea of law'.[37] According to Radbruch, justice is essentially characterised by equality (Radbruch 2004, pp. 37–39; 1924, p. 44; 1950, p. 74 *et passim*). Positive law that cannot legitimately claim to realise justice understood as equality departs in an extreme way from the objective point of view and does not, consequently, exhibit legal character. The wording of the second part of the Radbruch formula, the disavowal formula (sometimes also called 'the betrayal formula'), shows that it has its roots in Radbruch's concept of law:[38]

> Where there is not even an attempt at justice, where equality, the core of justice, is deliberately betrayed in the issuance of positive law, then the statute is not merely 'flawed law', it lacks completely the very nature of law. (Radbruch 2006b, p. 7)[39]

It is on this basis that Radbruch employs the disavowal formula to deny certain Nazi statutes legal character.[40]

4.2 Radbruch's Theory of the Validity of Law

While Radbruch's concept of law has a distinct neo-Kantian character, his theory of legal validity follows Kantian lines in making legal certainty and avoiding anarchy key. The first part of the Radbruch formula, the intolerability formula, has its roots in Radbruch's theory of legal validity:

> The conflict between justice and legal certainty may well be resolved in this way: The positive law, secured by legislation and power, takes precedence even when its content is unjust and fails to benefit the people, unless the conflict between statute and justice reaches such

---

[37] See Sect. 3.1.

[38] See also Alexy (2021, p. 115), who states that the disavowal formula is 'a direct application of' the basal criterion.

[39] See also Borowski (2019, p. 33); Borowski (2021, pp. 633–636).

[40] See Sect. 1.4.

> an intolerable degree that the statute, as 'flawed law', must yield to justice. (Radbruch 2006b, p. 7)

The consequence of conflict caused by applying the intolerability formula is loss of legal validity rather than loss of legal character, in contrast to applying the disavowal formula.

To be sure, Radbruch's theory of legal validity changed over time and the intolerability formula reflects his theory of legal validity after the War. In his *Outlines of Legal Philosophy* (*Grundzüge der Rechtsphilosophie*) of 1914 and his *Rechtsphilosophie* of 1932 he supported a dual theory of legal validity, which will be explained in Sect. 5.3.

5 Radbruch on Legal Obligation

Radbruch's non-positivism is reflected in a moral justification of normativity. The question is whether, and to what extent and how, his theory of legal obligation reflects non-positivism.

5.1 Legal Obligation as an A Priori Concept

In addition to Radbruch's substantive concept of law (providing his basal criterion), Chapter 4 of his 1932 *Rechtsphilosophie* presents a formal concept of law:

> We summarise the essence of the legal prescription as positive, normative, social and general: Law is the epitome of general prescriptions for the living-together of human beings. (Radbruch 1950, p. 76, translation altered)[41]

Radbruch emphasises that this formal concept of law is a deduction from the idea of law and that it implies certain *a priori* legal concepts. The social nature of legal prescriptions is what generates legal obligations:

> From the validity of law for the living-together of men, their mutual relations, there follows that its contents must be to establish legal relations, and as their elements, legal obligations and legal rights. No legal order is conceivable that may not be resolved into legal relations, rights and duties. (Ibid., pp. 77–78, translation altered)

5.2 Morality as the Only Justification for Legal Obligation

Then, in Chapter 5 of the same work, Radbruch contends that the phenomenon of legal obligation presupposes morality. The key passage reads:

[41] See also Radbruch (1948, p. 34).

> Morality alone can justify the obligatory power of the law. It has been shown that from legal rules as imperatives, expressions of a will, we may possibly derive a Must but never an Ought. Of legal norms, legal Ought, legal validity, legal obligations, we may speak only when the legal imperative is endowed with moral obligatory force by the individual conscience. (Ibid., pp. 84–85, translation altered)

Because he considers that there are no objective standards subject to rational cognition, he sees no objective justification for coercion against an individual's conscience. In this, anarchy lurks. Radbruch acknowledges this danger but postpones dealing with it later in his Chapter 10.

> The impression that basing legal validity on morality renders that validity dependent on the correctness of the law, along the lines of natural law or, in an anarchical way, subject to the individual's conscience, remains to be assuaged later, when the problem of validity is discussed. (Ibid., p. 85, translation altered)

Further in Chapter 5, Radbruch speaks of a 'twofold value character' (ibid., p. 85). Moral value is embraced by legal value, for legal obligation is part of the reality whose meaning is to serve justice. Morality, he continues, is the purpose of the law.

> At first, law is just as foreign, just as differentiated from and possibly opposed to morality as the means always is in relation to the end: it is only subsequently that, as the very means for the realization of moral values, the law partakes of the worthiness of its end and is thus incorporated in morals with the reservation that it operates according to its own rules. (Ibid., p. 87, translation altered)

In short: The phenomenon of legal obligation is justified by morality. Legal obligations are means to moral ends and, in this sense, necessarily elements of morality.

5.3 *Radbruch's Dual Theory of Validity*

In his 1914 and 1932 treatises, Radbruch defends a dual theory of validity, in which two standpoints are distinguished, the standpoint of the individual and the standpoint of the judge. This distinction has many consequences.

His exposition of legal validity in Chapter 10 of his *Rechtsphilosophie* of 1932 commences with three fundamentally different approaches to legal validity. According to the first, the juridical doctrine of legal validity, authoritative institutionalisation is key. Radbruch does not have a solution to the problem of the basic norm and discards this juridical doctrine rather quickly (see Radbruch 1950, pp. 112–114). In this context, it should be emphasised that his formal concept of law[42] requires the positivity of law anyway. This is to say that the character of a legal norm as positive law serves as a criterion for the concept of law, to be distinguished from the criteria for legal validity.[43] Thus, for Radbruch positivity cannot be a meaningful criterion for legal validity.

[42] See Sect. 5.1.

[43] On Radbruch's concept of law that omits legal validity, see Sect. 4.

With an eye to the second approach, the sociological doctrine of legal validity, two versions are distinguished, power and recognition.

> [C]ommand and power imply only a Will and a Can, so that they can give rise to a Must at most but not an Ought on the part of the addressee, perhaps obedience but never an obligation to obey. (Ibid., p. 114, translation altered)

Recognition, Radbruch claims, can only be based on a fiction and provides no answer (ibid., p. 116).

Only the third approach, the philosophical doctrine of validity, according to which substantive correctness is key, can provide the answer. In an unmitigated form this doctrine of validity leads to natural law in the form of the strong connection thesis—'[every] injustice is no law'. Radbruch emphasises, however, that we need to avoid a 'relapse into the errors of natural law' (ibid.) and presses relativism, which serves as a justification of legal authority: 'If no one is able to determine what is just, someone must lay down what is to be legal' (ibid. p. 117, translation altered). But he also praises legal certainty: 'Justice is the second great task of the law, while the most immediate one is legal certainty, peace and order' (ibid., p. 118).[44] However, giving absolute precedence to legal certainty over substantive correctness implies a positivistic theory of validity, based on authoritative institutionalisation and social efficacy alone.[45] Radbruch is not, however, prepared to support—in modern parlance—the separability thesis and a positivistic theory.

> [W]ith fatal one-sidedness, the past age of legal positivism saw only the positivity and certainty of the law and caused a long standstill in the systematic examination of the purposiveness, not to mention the justice, of enacted law, for decades nearly silencing legal philosophy and legal policy. (Ibid. p. 111)

5.3.1 Legal Validity from the Standpoint of the Individual

Against the backdrop of his substantive concept of law or, in other words, his basal criterion,[46] it does not come as a surprise that Radbruch is not prepared to simply declare substantive correctness irrelevant.

Having repudiated the other two approaches, he continues his exposition of legal validity, by asserting: 'But such cannot remain the last word of legal philosophy on the question of validity' (Radbruch 1950, p. 118). He then refers to his idea triad, in which 'justice' (in the sense of substantive correctness) and 'legal certainty' are found at the same categorical level and emphasises that 'in case of conflict there is no decision between them but by the individual conscience' (ibid.). The

[44] See also Radbruch (1914, pp. 172 and 183); Radbruch (1948, p. 33).

[45] Positivistic at least with an eye to the criteria for the identification of legally valid law, not necessarily with an eye to the justification of these criteria. On this distinction, see Borowski (2018, pp. 101–107).

[46] See Sect. 3.1.

consequence is obvious. '[T]he absolute validity of all positive law for every individual cannot be demonstrated' (ibid.).

In what follows, Radbruch assumes that most individuals will behave responsibly in a morally mature way.

> The individual conscience usually will, and properly may, deem an offense against positive law more objectionable than the sacrifice of the individual's own conviction ... but there may be iniquitous statutes which conscience refuses to obey. (Ibid., translation altered)

Such 'iniquitous statutes' are generally those statutes that give rise to a 'conflict between statute and justice [that] reaches ... an intolerable degree' (Radbruch 2006b, p. 7) in the sense of the intolerability formula. This means that Radbruch's theory of legal validity from the standpoint of the individual in 1914 and 1932 clearly anticipates the non-positivistic intolerability formula of 1946.

5.3.2 Legal Validity from the Standpoint of the Judge

But things are completely different from the standpoint of the judge.

> The judge, charged with interpreting and serving the positive legal order, ought not to know any but the juridical doctrine of validity ... It is the professional duty of the judge ... to ask only what is legal and not if it is also just. (Radbruch 1950, p. 119)

He continues.

> Even when he ceases to be the servant of justice because that is the will of law, he still remains the servant of legal certainty. We despise the parson who preaches in a sense contrary to his conviction, but we respect the judge who does not permit himself to be diverted from his loyalty to the law by his conflicting sense of justice. (Ibid., translation altered)

5.3.3 Conflicting Results from Different Standpoints

Radbruch is perfectly aware that the two standpoints may come to different conclusions on legal validity.

> Yet the judge, who is in his conscience bound to consider all enacted statutes valid, may be faced by a defendant who is bound by his conscience to regard an unjust [...] statute as invalid although it is enacted. (Radbruch 1950, 119, translation altered)

He admits that there is 'no solution' (ibid.). Nevertheless, he insists that

> [a]gainst the latter, the law may prove its power but can never demonstrate its validity. The case of the 'criminal from conviction' proves a truly tragic case because there is no solution for it. (Ibid.)

5.3.4 Radbruch's Renunciation of the Dual Theory of Legal Validity

After the War, in 1946, Radbruch replaces the dual theory of validity with the intolerability formula, which does not distinguish between the standpoint of the individual and the standpoint of the judge. The theory of legal validity from the standpoint of the individual is extended to the judge. Now, from both standpoints, positive law loses its validity given an intolerable degree of conflict between a positive statute and justice.[47]

6 A Critical Evaluation of Radbruch's Dual Theory of Validity and His Conception of Legal Obligation

Having outlined Radbruch's theory of legal obligation and his dual theory of legal validity, the question arises whether this part of his legal philosophy is consistent and convincing. Considering Radbruch's non-positivistic basal criterion and his non-positivistic concept of law, is his dual theory of legal validity positivistic in nature?

6.1 Is Radbruch's Dual Theory of Legal Validity Positivistic?

To begin with, it might be useful to compare and contrast Radbruch's dual theory of legal validity with a paradigmatically positivistic theory of law.

According to Hart, Radbruch's mistake—with an eye to the Radbruch formula, the first part of which is anticipated by the dual theory of legal validity—is that it constitutes an

> enormous overevaluation of the importance of the bare fact that a rule may be said to be a valid rule of law, as if this, once declared, was conclusive of the final moral question: 'Ought this rule of law to be obeyed?' (Hart 1958, p. 618)

Even if a morally iniquitous statute is valid law, 'Law is not morality; do not let it supplant morality' (ibid.). A morally iniquitous statute can give rise to a legal obligation for it is not to be understood that there is necessarily a moral obligation to obey such a statute. On the contrary, there may actually be a moral obligation to disobey the statute.

The practical consequences of Radbruch's dual theory of validity seem to be no different from Hart's positivistic approach. According to Hart, the judge is under a legal obligation to apply the morally iniquitous statute and the individual is under a

[47] Even though Radbruch makes clear that the legal power to disregard extremely unjust positive law should be vested in judges only or even in judges of a centralised court (see Radbruch 1946, footnote 20).

legal obligation to acquiesce to the legal sanction. Both a judge and an individual, from their respective standpoints, may have no corresponding moral obligation to apply the statute or may even have a moral obligation to disapply or disobey the statute, which does not, however, alter any legal obligation.

For Radbruch, a judge is under a legal obligation to apply the morally iniquitous statute and the individual is subject to the state's factual power to impose the sanction. The sanction is a legal sanction from the standpoint of the judge and a *merely factual sanction* from the standpoint of an individual. The individual is exposed to an external factual power, just like he or she is exposed to a natural disaster. Radbruch is clear that the morally iniquitous statute has no legal validity for the individual. This will not, however, prevent the sanction being imposed and enforced by the officials of the legal system. In practical terms, the lack of legal validity from the standpoint of the individual is superseded by the fact that the judge must assume legal validity from his own viewpoint.

There is, however, a theoretical difference. Radbruch uses moral correctness as a criterion for the legal validity of statutes from the standpoint of the individual. This side of the dual theory of validity up to 1932 anticipates the intolerability formula from 1946, which clearly reflects a non-positivistic theory of legal validity. This, in turn, suggests that the theory of legal validity from the standpoint of the individual also reflects a non-positivistic theory of legal validity—or a non-positivistic part of a theory of legal validity (see Neumann, 2007, pp. 14–15; Dreier 2011, p. 32; Borowski 2015, p. 262; 2019, p. 32; 2021, p. 636). The theory of legal validity from the standpoint of the judge does not permit referring to moral correctness as a criterion for identifying valid law (see Borowski 2021, p. 636). Nevertheless, Radbruch's passages on his theory of legal validity from the standpoint of the judge in 1932 are the cornerstone of the orthodox 'conversion thesis', according to which he was a positivist in 1932 and was converted to natural law by the experience of the atrocities of the National Socialists.[48]

However, Radbruch's non-positivistic theory of legal validity from the standpoint of the individual renders his comprehensive theory of legal validity of 1932 non-positivistic.[49] What is more, Radbruch's basal criterion reflects non-positivism (see Borowski 2021, pp. 642–644) and his concept of law had been non-positivistic at least since 1924, when he introduced his idea of justice as equality using a conception of equality that contains a modest substantive dimension (see Borowski 2015, pp. 249–259). This means that there are already three necessary connections between law and morality in Radbruch's legal philosophy in 1932, so that the 'thesis

[48] In his 1958 article, H.L.A. Hart supports the conversion thesis (see Sect. 1.3). See also von Hippel (1959, pp. 228–229) and Bauer (1968, p. 302). More references from the early German literature can be found in Seidel (1999, pp. 112–115) and, more recently, Haldemann (2005, p. 164) and Hoerster (2006, p. 79). In the original German version of his main treatise on the problem of law and morality, Alexy (1992, p. 114) also supports the conversion thesis. However, in later publications in English (Alexy 2002, p. 4; Alexy 2021, p. 114), he becomes more circumspect.

[49] Every non-positivistic element in a theory of law renders the overall theory non-positivistic. See Borowski (2015, p. 240); Borowski (2021, p. 638).

of non-positivistic continuity',[50] which has been gaining support recently, holds true. Changes between 1932 and 1946—among them the renunciation of the theory of dual validity—may have strengthened or clarified these necessary connections, but they did not give rise to a conversion from positivism to non-positivism.

6.2 *On the Certainty of Cognition of Iniquitous Statutes*

With an eye to legal validity from the standpoint of the individual, the question of the identification of 'iniquitous statutes' arises. According to Radbruch's relativism,[51] there is no objective criterion for a threshold. Even if his relativism has bounding limits, represented by a modicum of substantive equality,[52] this characterises Radbruch's concept of law, which is, for him, more fundamental than the validity of law. In other words, inside the frame of the concept of law, it seems to be left completely to the individual's conscience whether the threshold of an 'iniquitous' statute is crossed or not. It is telling that, even after abandoning the dual theory of legal validity and introducing the intolerability formula in 1946, he remains very sceptical about cognition of—in modern parlance—extremely unjust statutes. Such cognition is, he believes, 'a matter of degree' (*Maßfrage*) (Radbruch 1948, p. 33),[53] while cognition of the requirements of the disavowal is, for him, a matter of principle (see Borowski 2015, p. 246; 2019, p. 39) that can be determined with 'utmost clarity' (Radbruch 2006b, p. 7). This is probably among the reasons, if not a decisive reason, why Radbruch preferred the disavowal formula over the intolerability formula for overcoming atrocious statutes of the National Socialists.

That there is hardly any certainty in the objective cognition of iniquitous statutes does seem to give rise to the danger of anarchy. This danger is, however, averted by the 'positivistic' theory of legal validity from the standpoint of the judge of 1932, which renders the loss of legal validity from the standpoint of the individual insignificant in practical terms.

[50] Early supporters of the thesis of non-positivistic continuity were Engisch (1949–1950, p. 315) and Baratta (1959, p. 505). More recent supporters are Paulson (2006, p. 19), Paulson (2008, p. 106), Paulson (2015); Dreier (2011, pp. 19 and 43), Dreier (2015b, p. 228), Borowski (2015, p. 264), Borowski (2019, p. 265), and Borowski (2021, p. 644).

[51] See Sect. 3.3.

[52] See Sect. 4.1.

[53] See also Radbruch's reference to it being 'impossible to draw a sharper line' (2006b, p. 7).

6.3 *Radbruch's Dual Legal Obligation*

Radbruch's dual theory of validity in his pre-War writings gives rise to a theory of dual legal obligation. There are two kinds of legal obligation, depending on the standpoint. A norm of positive law is valid[54] and gives rise to a legal obligation from the standpoint of the judge, if the statute has been authoritatively issued and is socially efficacious.[55] By contrast, there is only a legal obligation for the individual, if the relevant statute has been authoritatively issued and is socially efficacious[56] and, additionally, proves not to be an 'iniquitous statute', measured by the individual's conscience.[57]

This distinction gives rise to disagreements over legal validity and, consequently, over legal obligation.[58] If the statute is not unjust at all, it is legally valid and gives rise to obligations from both the standpoint of the judge and the individual. If it is unjust below the threshold of an 'iniquitous statute', the same applies—for the judge, moral correctness is not a relevant criterion at all, for the individual, measured by his own conscience, the relevant threshold is not crossed. In the 'truly tragic case' (Radbruch 1950, p. 119), in which the individual considers the threshold of an 'iniquitous statute' crossed and the judge is bound to regard positive law as valid nevertheless, there is valid law from the standpoint of judge, but not valid law from the standpoint of the individual. Since there can be no legal obligation without valid law, there is no legal obligation from the standpoint of the individual. Radbruch is clear that the legal sanction imposed by the judge is merely a matter of

---

[54] See Sect. 5.3.2.

[55] Admittedly, Radbruch is not particularly clear on the requirement of social efficacy. According to his basal criterion, law is a 'reality', and it would be surprising if he were to regard inefficacious statutes—statutes that are not obeyed by the population and not enforced in cases of non-obedience—as a proper 'reality'.

[56] Radbruch does not explicitly discuss the relevance of authoritative issuance and social efficacy from the standpoint of the individual but characterises the 'truly tragic case' as follows. 'Yet the judge, who is in conscience bound to consider all enacted law valid, may be faced by a defendant who is bound in his conscience to regard unjust law or law that is not purposive as invalid *although it is enacted*.' (Radbruch 1950, p. 119. translation altered, my emphasis added)

According to Radbruch's concept of law, without the existence of an authoritatively issued and socially efficacious norm, positive law, there is no law. A conflict between positive law and moral correctness, which is front and centre in Radbruch's characterization of legal validity, can only emerge if there is positive law in the first place. This applies from both standpoints, the standpoint of the judge and the standpoint of the individual.

[57] See Sect. 5.3.1.

[58] There is another source of potential disagreements. In Radbruch's 1932 theory of legal validity, the judge and an individual can disagree whether the requirements for the existence of positive law are met. After Radbruch changed his theory of legal validity via the intolerability formula, this also affects whether there is an intolerable degree of tension between moral correctness and positive law. It is this kind of potential disagreement that led him to call for a centralization of the power to declare positive laws invalid or devoid of legal character. (See Radbruch 1946, footnote 20).

brute force or factual power from the standpoint of the individual so does not count as an expression of law and legal obligation.[59]

In reconstructing the 'split' in Radbruch's dual theory of validity, Ulfrid Neumann (2015, p. 39) has characterised it as a 'relational validity doctrine',[60] according to which validity becomes a two-place predicate—validity or non-validity is not ascribed as such but ascribed to certain persons or officials respectively (Neumann 2015, p. 31; Alexy 2021, p. 14). The same can be said of legal obligation. According to Radbruch's dual theory of legal validity and legal obligation, a norm does not give rise to a legal obligation as such or not, as it may give rise to a legal obligation for the judge, but not for the individual.

There is, however, a reason why this 'relational obligation doctrine'[61] is hardly convincing. If an individual's conscience regards a certain norm of positive law as 'iniquitous' and if this implies that there is no legal obligation on the part of this individual, this individual also has no legal obligation to acquiesce in the legal sanction imposed by the judge. Using the metaphor of the natural disaster again,[62] in so far as the individual is exposed to the danger of a natural disaster, he or she is at liberty to defend him- or herself against this danger. If there is no legal obligation of the individual, there is also no legal obligation of the individual to acquiesce to the imposition and enforcement of the legal sanction by the state. Consequently, imposing and enforcing the legal sanction by the state counts as an unlawful attack by the state and the individual would be entitled to self-defence. The state can hardly tolerate such alleged self-defence because the officials are under an obligation to enforce positive law even against acts of alleged 'self-defence', which implies that the individual has, indeed, a legal obligation to acquiesce to the legal sanction imposed by the judge and enforced by other officials of the legal system. But can we really say that there is *no legal obligation* on the part of the individual to, for example, perform action 'X', if non-performance of 'X' is sanctioned by the state and the individual is under a legal obligation to acquiesce to enforcement actions by state officials because of not having performed action 'X'?

Radbruch is quite unclear whether there is such legal obligation of the individual. The crucial passage reads:

> [The] case of the 'criminal from conviction' proves a truly tragic case precisely because there is no solution for it. Duty demanded the crime of the perpetrator, duty demands the sentence of the judge, and duty may possibly demand that one submit to the penalty incurred for the crime committed out of duty – for the sake of the law's inviolability, of legal certainty. (Radbruch 1950, pp. 119–120).

The word 'duty' appears three times in this quotation without any further qualification, which is a plausible translation of three occurrences of *Pflicht* in the German

---

[59] See Sect. 6.1.

[60] Translation following Alexy (2021, p. 114).

[61] This phrase draws a parallel between Neumann's 'relational validity doctrine' and the corresponding phenomenon regarding legal obligation.

[62] See Sect. 6.1.

original, again without any further qualification. The first 'duty', that in 'Duty demanded the crime of the perpetrator' refers to a *moral obligation*, originating from the individual's moral viewpoint according to the individual's conscience. By contrast, the second 'duty', that in 'duty demands the sentence of the judge' expresses a *legal obligation* of the judge. The third 'duty', that in 'duty may possibly demand that one submit to the penalty incurred for the crime committed', concerns precisely the obligation to acquiesce to the legal sanction imposed by the judge and enforced by other officials of the legal system. Is this third 'duty', however, a moral obligation—like the first 'duty'—or a legal obligation—like the second 'duty'? Things become even more enigmatic because of Radbruch's phrase 'may possibly' (*vielleicht* in the German original). This leaves open whether there is an obligation at all, of whatever nature it might be.

Thus, it is not entirely clear whether Radbruch assumes a legal obligation of the individual to acquiesce to the legal sanction imposed by the judge and enforced by other officials of the legal system. If this is the case, it is hardly plausible to deny that the statute in question gives rise to a legal obligation of the individual. If this obligation is merely a moral obligation, the individual would be legally entitled to self-defence, which results in a hardly plausible solution either.

7 Conclusion

Radbruch's 1932 dual theory of validity and dual theory of legal obligation represents his attempt to preserve as much of—in modern parlance—the ideal dimension of the law[63] without too much loss of legal certainty or even causing anarchy. Fourteen years and a horrible dictatorship later, Radbruch changed his mind and abandoned the 'positivistic'—if viewed in isolation—theory of validity from the standpoint of the judge. On the basis of the intolerability formula, iniquitous statutes lose their legal validity from both the judge's and the individual's standpoint morally and, in turn, do not give rise to any legal obligation. However, Radbruch remained sceptical about this, considering it far more difficult to establish whether the criteria of the intolerability formula are met, compared to the criteria of the disavowal formula, and he employed the disavowal formula to overcome Nazi statutes. Thus, the manifest change in Radbruch's theory of legal validity is without any consequence regarding the morally iniquitous laws of the Third Reich.

Radbruch's dual theory of legal validity and relative legal obligation in his earlier works expresses an attempt to take a middle ground between a position such as Hart's or Kelsen's clearly positivistic approaches and Radbruch's own more pronounced non-positivistic approach from 1946 on. Even though this attempt is hardly convincing, an enquiry into Radbruch's dual theory of legal validity and legal obligation provides the backdrop to a thorough understanding of his 1946 formula with

[63] On the distinction between the ideal and real dimension of law, see, in particular, Alexy (2010).

its two parts, the intolerability formula and the disavowal formula. And it shows how close one can come to a positivistic theory of legal validity and legal obligation from a clearly non-positivistic standpoint.

References

Alexy R (1992) Begriff und Geltung des Rechts, 1st edn. Alber, Freiburg

Alexy R (1999) A defence of Radbruch's formula. In: Dyzenhaus D (ed) Recrafting the rule of law – the limits of legal order. Hart Publishing, Oxford, pp 15–39

Alexy R (2002) The argument from injustice. Oxford University Press, Oxford

Alexy R (2007a) An answer to Joseph Raz. In: Pavlakos G (ed) Law, rights, and discourse. Hart Publishing, Oxford, pp 37–55

Alexy R (2007b) Thirteen replies. In: Pavlakos G (ed) Law, rights, and discourse. Hart Publishing, Oxford, pp 333–366

Alexy R (2008) On the nature and the concept of law. Ratio Juris 21:281–299

Alexy R (2010) The dual nature of law. Ratio Juris 23:167–182

Alexy R (2021) Gustav Radbruch's concept of law. In: Alexy R (ed) Law's ideal dimension. Oxford University Press, Oxford, pp 107–117

Baratta A (1959) Relativismus und Naturrecht im Denken Gustav Radbruchs. Arch Philos Law Soc Philos 45:505–537

Bauer F (1968) 'Das gesetzliche Unrecht' des Nationalsozialismus und die deutsche Strafrechtspflege. In: Kaufmann A (ed) Gedächtnisschrift für Gustav Radbruch. Vandenhoeck & Ruprecht, Göttingen, pp 302–307

Bix B (2011) Radbruch's formula and conceptual analysis. Am J Jur 56:45–57

Borowski M (2011) Discourse, principles, and the problem of law and morality. Jurisprudence 2:575–595

Borowski M (2013) Sein und Sollen am unteren Ende des Stufenbaus der Rechtsordnung. In: Anderheiden M, Keil R, Kirste S, Schaefer JP (eds) Verfassungsvoraussetzungen. Gedächtnisschrift für Winfried Brugger. Mohr-Siebeck, Tübingen, pp 183–201

Borowski M (2015) Begriff und Geltung des Rechts bei Gustav Radbruch. In: Borowski M, Paulson SL (eds) Die Natur des Rechts bei Gustav Radbruch. Mohr Siebeck, Tübingen, pp 229–265

Borowski M (2017) Die Vernichtung von Recht durch Moral. In: Saliger F (ed) Rechtsstaatliches Strafrecht. Festschrift für Ulfrid Neumann zum 70 Geburtstag. C F Müller, Heidelberg, pp 71–83

Borowski M (2018) Grundrechte als Prinzipien, 3rd edn. Nomos, Baden-Baden

Borowski M (2019) Radbruch's formula and human rights. In: La Torre M, Niglia N, Susi N (eds) The quest for rights. Edward Elgar, Cheltenham, pp 27–48

Borowski M (2021) Gustav Radbruch's critique of legal positivism. In: Spaak T, Mindus P (eds) The Cambridge companion to legal positivism. Cambridge University Press, Cambridge, pp 627–650

Dreier R (1993) Gesetzliches Unrecht im SED-Staat? Am Beispiel des DDR-Grenzgesetzes. In: Haft F et al (eds) Strafgerechtigkeit. Festschrift für Arthur Kaufmann. C F Müller, Heidelberg, pp 57–92

Dreier H (1997) Gustav Radbruch und die Mauerschützen. Juristenzeitung 52:421–434

Dreier R (2011) Gustav Radbruchs Rechtsbegriff. In: Mahlmann M (ed) Gesellschaft und Gerechtigkeit. Festschrift für Hubert Rottleuthner. Nomos, Baden-Baden, pp 17–44

Dreier H (2015a) Die Radbruchsche Formel – Erkenntnis oder Bekenntnis? In: Borowski M, Paulson SL (eds) Die Natur des Rechts bei Gustav Radbruch. Mohr Siebeck, Tübingen, pp 1–22

Dreier R (2015b) Kontinuitäten und Diskontinuitäten in der Rechtsphilosophie Radbruchs. In: Borowski M, Paulson SL (eds) Die Natur des Rechts bei Gustav Radbruch. Mohr Siebeck, Tübingen, pp 183–228
Dreier R, Paulson SL (2003) Einführung in die Rechtsphilosophie Radbruchs. In: Dreier R, Paulson SL (eds) Gustav Radbruchs Rechtsphilosophie, 2nd edn. C F Müller, Heidelberg, pp 237–253
Dyzenhaus D (2010) Hard cases in wicked legal systems, 2nd edn. Oxford University Press, Oxford
Engisch K (1949–1950) Gustav Radbruch als Rechtsphilosophie. Arch Philos Law Soc Philos 38:305–316
Evers H-U (1956) Der Richter und das unsittliche Gesetz. De Gruyter, Berlin
Funke A (2003) Überlegungen zu Gustav Radbruchs 'Verleugnungsformel': Ein Beitrag zur Lehre vom Rechtsbegriff. Arch Philos Law Soc Philos 89:1–16
Gardner J (2012) How law claims, what law claims. In: Klatt M (ed) Institutionalized reason. Oxford University Press, Oxford, pp 29–44
Haldemann F (2005) Gustav Radbruch vs. Hans Kelsen: a debate on Nazi law. Ratio Juris 18:162–178
Hart HLA (1958) Positivism and the separation of law and morals. Harv Law Rev 74:593–625
Hoerster N (2006) Was ist Recht? C.H. Beck, Munich
Holmes OW (1921) The path of the law. In: Holmes OW (ed) Collected legal papers. Harcourt & Brace, New York, pp 167–202
Hume D (2007) A treatise of human nature, vol 1. The Clarendon Press, Oxford
Kelsen H (1961) General theory of law and state, 1st edn (trans: Wedberg A). Russell & Russell, New York
Kelsen H (1967) Pure theory of law, 2nd edn (trans: Knight M). University of California Press, Berkeley
Kelsen H (1992) Introduction to the problems of legal theory (trans: Litschewski Paulson B, Paulson SL). The Clarendon Press, Oxford
MacCormick ND (2007) Why law makes no claims. In: Pavlakos G (ed) Law, rights, and discourse. Hart Publishing, Oxford, pp 59–67
Müller I (1991) Hitler s justice. The courts of the Third Reich. Harvard University Press, Cambridge
Neumann U (2007) Naturrecht und Positivismus im Denken Gustav Radbruchs. Kontinuitäten und Diskontinuitäten. In: Härle W, Vogel B (eds) Vom Rechte, das mit uns geboren ist. Aktuelle Probleme des Naturrechts. Herder, Freiburg, pp 11–32
Neumann U (2015) Zum Verhältnis von Rechtsgeltung und Rechtsbegriff. Wandlungen in der Rechtsphilosophie Gustav Radbruchs. In: Borowski M, Paulson SL (eds) Die Natur des Rechts bei Gustav Radbruch. Mohr Siebeck, Tübingen, pp 129–149
Paulson SL (1995) Radbruch on unjust laws. Competing earlier and later views? Oxf J Leg Stud 15:489–500
Paulson SL (2006) On the background and significance of Gustav Radbruch's post-war papers. Oxf J Leg Stud 26:17–40
Paulson SL (2008) Ein ewiger Mythos: Gustav Radbruch als Rechtspositivist. Juristenzeitung 63:105–115
Paulson SL (2015) Zur Kontinuität der nichtpositivistischen Rechtsphilosophie Gustav Radbruchs. In: Borowski M, Paulson SL (eds) Die Natur des Rechts bei Gustav Radbruch. Mohr Siebeck, Tübingen, pp 151–182
Paulson SL (2021) Zur Rechtsphilosophie Gustav Radbruchs. In: Paulson SL, Neumann U (eds) Rechtsphilosophie im Spiegel der Zeit. Mohr Siebeck, Tübingen, pp 1–7
Radbruch G (1914) Grundzüge der Rechtsphilosophie. Quelle & Meyer, Leipzig [Reprinted in Kaufmann A (ed) Rechtsphilosophie II. Vol 2 of Gustav Radbruch, Gesamtausgabe (Collected Works). (RGA 2). C F Müller, Heidelberg, 1993, pp 9–204]
Radbruch G (1924) Die Problematik der Rechtsidee. Die Dioskuren. Jahrbuch für Geisteswissenschaften 3:43–50. Reprinted in RGA 2:460–467
Radbruch G (1932) See Radbruch G (1973)

Radbruch G (1934) Le relativisme dans la philosophie du droit. Archives de Philosophie du Droit et de Sociologie Juridique 4, 105–110. German translation: Der Relativismus in der Rechtsphilosophie. In: Radbruch G, Der Mensch im Recht. Vandenhoeck & Ruprecht, Göttingen 1957, pp 80–87. Reprinted in Kaufmann A, Hassemer W (eds) Rechtsphilosophie III, vol. 3 of Gustav Radbruch, Gesamtausgabe (Collected Works). (RGA 3). C F Müller, Heidelberg 1990, pp 17–22

Radbruch G (1937/38) Le but du droit. In: Annuaire de l'Institut de Philosophie du Droit et de Sociologie, pp 48–59. German translation: Der Zweck des Rechts. In: Gustav Radbruch, Der Mensch im Recht. Vandenhoeck & Ruprecht, Göttingen 1957), pp 88–104. Reprinted in RGA 3:37–50

Radbruch G (1945). Fünf Minuten Rechtsphilosophie. Rhein-Neckar-Zeitung 12 September. Reprinted in RGA 3:78–79

Radbruch G (1946) Gesetzliches Unrecht und übergesetzliches Recht. Süddeutsche Juristenzeitung 1:105–108. Reprinted in RGA 3:83–93

Radbruch G (1947) Gesetz und Recht. Stuttgarter Rundschau, January: 5–6. Reprinted in RGA 3:96–100

Radbruch G (1948) In: Schubert H, Stoltzenburg J (eds) Vorschule der Rechtsphilosophie, 1st edn. Scherer, Heidelberg. Reprinted in RGA 3:121–227

Radbruch G (1950) Legal philosophy. In: Wilk K (trans and ed) The legal philosophies of Lask, Radbruch, and Dabin. Harvard University Press, Cambridge, pp 47–224

Radbruch G (1973) Rechtsphilosophie. 8th edn. (1st edn 1932). Wolf E. Schneider H-P (eds) Koehler, Stuttgart. Reprinted in RGA 2:206–450

Radbruch G (2004) In: Adachi H, Teifke N (eds) Rechtsphilosophische Tagesfragen. Nomos, Baden-Baden

Radbruch G (2006a) Five minutes of legal philosophy (trans: Litschewski Paulson B, Paulson SL). Oxf J Leg Stud 26:13–15

Radbruch G (2006b) Statutory lawlessness and supra-statutory law (trans: Litschewski Paulson B, Paulson SL). Oxf J Leg Stud 26:1–11

Raz J (2007) The argument from justice, or how not to reply to legal positivism. In: Pavlakos G (ed) Law, rights, and discourse. Hart Publishing, Oxford, pp 17–35

Seidel K (1999) Rechtsphilosophische Aspekte der 'Mauerschützen'-Prozesse. Duncker & Humblot, Berlin

Spaak T (2009) Meta-ethics and legal theory: the case of Gustav Radbruch. Law Philos 28:261–290

Von Hippel E (1959) Das Naturrecht in der Rechtsprechung der Bundesrepublik. In: von Hippel E (ed) Mechanisches und moralisches Rechtsdenken. Meisenheim am Glan, pp 224–237

Zhao J (2020) Die Rechtsphilosophie Gustav Radbruchs unter dem Einfluss von Emil Lask. Nomos, Baden

Part III
Forms of Legal Obligation

Is There a Legal Duty Not to Harm in Tort Law?

Diego M. Papayannis

1 Introduction

In this chapter, I address the question of whether there is a legal duty not to harm in tort law (what in the continental tradition is called 'civil responsibility').[1] This is an important question. Without answering it, we cannot assess the different theories of tort law adequately, for we do not know exactly what these theories are supposed to account for.

According to what I take to be the conventional view, tort law comprises two pairs of rights and duties. First, everyone enjoys a right not to be harmed that is correlative to a duty not to harm. If this primary right is violated or infringed (and the correlative duty thereby breached), a secondary right to receive compensation that is correlative to a secondary duty to pay damages is triggered. This is a very well-known picture but not all its elements have been studied in the same depth. In recent years, considerable effort has been expended on elucidating the rationale that links primary rights and duties and their correlative (compensatory) remedies,[2] but no

With the support of Research Projects PID2020-114765GB-I00 and CEX2021-001169-M, financed by the Ministry of Science and Innovation (MCIN, Spain).

[1] On the extent to which tort law and civil responsibility are the same kind of practice, see Papayannis (2024).

[2] The most relevant attempts are MacCormick (1982), Weinrib (1995), Gardner (2011, 2018), and Ripstein (2016).

D. M. Papayannis (✉)
University of Girona, Faculty of Law, Girona, Spain
e-mail: diegomartin.papayannis@udg.edu

D. Beyleveld, S. Bertea (eds.), *Theories of Legal Obligation*, Law and Philosophy Library 146, https://doi.org/10.1007/978-3-031-54067-7_6

effort has been made to show that primary rights and duties are part of the reality of current tort law systems. Because the plausibility of theories that link primary and secondary rights depends on the existence of primary rights and duties in the domain of tort law, these cannot be taken for granted.[3]

Some theories explicitly reject the existence of primary rights and duties altogether.[4] This is the case with economic views.[5] From a purely economic standpoint, any discourse on duties not to harm (and correlative rights not to be harmed) is superfluous implying that accounting for them does not merit any theoretical attention. A directive such as '*You shall not harm another with your negligent conduct*' does not function as an incentive for rational agents. Unmoved, the rational agent will merely respond with a question, '*What happens if I cause harm*?', which is to say, her main concern pertains to the consequences of violating this directive. As such, the directive itself lacks motivational power and therefore needs to be complemented with a secondary duty to compensate, such as, '*If you cause harm, you must compensate the victim*'. The first directive is no longer necessary, since all the motivational work can be performed by the second. In other words, a complex directive like, '*You should not cause harm, and if you cause harm, you must compensate the victim*', does not fulfil any function distinguishable from the simple directive, '*You must compensate for the harm you cause*'. This simple directive provides all the information *homo economicus* is interested in when it comes to decision making. In terms of motivation, what is added in the first more complex directive is irrelevant to rational agents seeking to maximise their own benefit. The language regarding first order rights and duties should be banished from tort law theory because it does not fulfil any significant function.

This said, the importance of determining whether there is a legal duty not to harm in tort law should not be downplayed. If there is a duty not to harm, then economic theories will be discredited, because it will be clear that they are ill equipped to provide a good explanation of legal practice. From the economic perspective, primary rights and duties make no sense in tort law, so *they cannot exist*, at least, not in a meaningful way. At most, they are parts of a vacuous discourse. However, it is important to make clear that my argument is not directed exclusively against economic views. It has a broader target. Economic theory is merely a good example of theorising that rejects the existence of a duty not to harm, so occasional reference to it will be useful for expository purposes.

At this point, the reader might think that establishing the existence of a legal duty should not be too problematic. Of course, any claim about the existence of a legal

---

[3]Among the authors that take for granted the existence of a duty not to harm, see Weinrib (1995, p. 10; 2012, p. 93); Stevens (2007, pp. 4–19); Perry (2009, p. 81); Gardner (2018, p. 182); Goldberg and Zipursky (2012, p. 261; 2020, pp. 13ff).

[4]In the continental tradition, Pantaleón (2000, p. 171) and García Amado (2011, pp. 1268–1269) reject the existence of the duty not to harm. In the Anglo-American literature, Coleman (1992, p. 316) claims that there is a duty not to harm, but the domain of tort law is that of secondary duties of compensation (2001, p. 34).

[5]See Landes and Posner (1987); Shavell (1987).

duty depends on the concept of legal duty that one employs, which determines the conditions under which the existence of a duty can be asserted. But even if one is committed, as I am, to a positivistic approach to this issue, the question of the existence of a duty is not at all trivial.

That legislation does not mention primary rights and duties does not mean that they do not exist in practice, nor does it imply that explicit reference to them (in those legal systems in which they are mentioned) entails that they necessarily exist. It all depends on whether they truly play some role in the conceptual framework that holds the practice of tort law together. If it turns out that tort law systems usually include a duty not to harm that performs no economic function, so much the worse for the economic view. This would show that the economic perspective is unable to account for an essential feature of the legal practice. If tort law were designed merely to achieve efficient results, a duty not to harm would not be a part of it.

In what follows, I will try to show that many aspects of current legal systems and the pattern of inferences that leads to different remedial responses in tort law are puzzling without the assumption of the existence of primary rights not to be harmed and duties not to harm. In Sect. 2, I will discuss three of the most common arguments against the existence of such a duty. As I will show, none of these arguments is sound. There are no good reasons to reject the existence of a duty not to harm in tort law. In Sect. 3, I will make explicit my conception of legal obligation, upon which I will advance four arguments for the existence of a duty not to harm in tort law systems that share some common features.

2 Three Arguments Against the Existence of a Legal Duty Not to Harm

In this section, I will review three arguments against the existence of a legal duty not to harm in tort law. The first and the second are explicitly present in the literature, while the third is not, but I think it addresses a source of legitimate concern. Considering these arguments is important for the discussion that follows in Sect. 3.

2.1 It Is Not Explicitly Recognised in Its Legislation

Some authors have pointed out that legislation does not usually impose a duty not to harm. Instead, most legal systems include provisions like art. 1902 of the Spanish Civil Code, according to which 'The party whose actions or omissions cause harm to another, involving fault or negligence, is under the obligation to repair the harm caused.' On this basis, Salvador Coderch (2000, p. 11) claims that the norm contained in art. 1902 is so generic that it is inconceivable that it expresses a duty not to harm.

However, it is obvious that nothing can be inferred about the interpretive method the relevant legal community finally applies to authoritative texts from the language used in the legislation. Consider article 138.1 of the Spanish Criminal Code: 'A person who causes the death of another will be punished, as guilty of homicide, for a term ranging from ten to fifteen years in prison'. Any capable lawyer knows that homicide is prohibited in Spain, and that the source of that prohibition is art. 138.1. If the focus is set on the literal interpretation of the provision, then the most we can say is that it contains a prophecy, namely, that the person who commits homicide will be punished. This is obviously absurd. A less literal interpretation suggests that art. 138.1 imposes on the judge a duty to punish those who commit homicide. This is true, but it is also true that the Criminal Code is not only addressed to public officials but to the population at large. The legal community ascribes a different interpretation to art. 138.1 than the one based on its literal meaning. The shared understanding is that homicide is prohibited; and from this statement, many other inferences are warranted, such as that all persons have a duty not to cause the death of another, that causing the death of another is wrong, and so on.

Returning to art. 1902 of the Spanish Civil Code, a *literal* interpretation of the text not allowing us to understand that it contains a duty not to harm still does not indicate that the practice does not assign that meaning to it. A careful inquiry into the rules of the system requires delving into other aspects of the practice to determine whether, despite not being explicitly mentioned, a duty not to harm can still be derived from the doctrinal or theoretical theses assumed by legal practitioners;[6] alternatively, whether it can be determined from other social facts, such as the belief and attitudes of the participants, or the inferential pattern that structures legal thought and discourse, which cannot be explained without claiming the existence of a duty not to harm.

2.2 It Makes Social Life Impracticable

The second argument (see Pantaleón 1991, p. 1995) is that an absolute duty not to harm would be incompatible with the way we organise social life. A norm such as this is contrary to an economic system based on competition, which allows, and even encourages, activities that are statistically detrimental to the interests of others. Presented in this way, the argument is quite plausible. However, precisely for this reason, the existence of a duty not to harm was never claimed to be categorical. The duty not to harm requires not harming others *unjustly*. This duty is not absolute or unqualified, in the sense that any harm, inconvenience, or loss that we cause to our neighbours constitutes a breach of duty and, consequently, brings about responsibility. That would certainly make social life unattainable or unbearable, but a subset of

[6] It should be kept in mind that legal reasoning implicitly assumes certain normative premises that are not based on the texts passed by the legislator, but on the conceptual apparatus used to interpret those texts. See Guastini (2010, pp. 130–131, and footnote 24).

the harms that we cause to each other must be considered wrongful. This does not represent a danger to the practicability of social life. Indeed, it is a necessary condition for social life to flourish.[7] A legal system that prohibits the causation of all harm is as troublesome as one that allows for the causation of all harm.

This means that the duty not to harm, properly understood, is a duty not to harm *in certain ways* or *in specific circumstances*. For example, peaceful and productive interaction requires banning negligent or unreasonably risky conduct from the set of admissible social relations. Such prohibition is precisely what defines the scope of the duty not to harm. Under a negligence rule, agents have a duty not to harm by failing to take reasonable precautions. Which harms are wrongful is a contingent matter, depending on what the specific rules of the system require. Thus, provisions such as art. 1902 of the Spanish Civil Code *could be* interpreted as imposing a duty not to harm through negligent conduct, while strict liability rules would establish a duty not to harm through certain well-defined risky (but lawful) activities.

In sum, the existence of an absolute or unqualified duty not to harm others would indeed be senseless, but that thesis is not what I am defending here.

2.3 *The Purported Duty Not to Harm Is Useless*

A final concern relates to the practical relevance of a duty not to harm. What good is it? Does it really play any role in practical reasoning?

Let me expand the challenge a little. Even if the duty not to harm is habitually mentioned in the literature and in judicial decisions, it plays no logical role in the justification of the conclusions of the legal syllogism. Yet the duty to pay damages is essential to reaching decisions in tort law cases. To see this, let us examine a very schematic reconstruction of the legal syllogism that leads to a responsibility judgment, including two normative premises (NP1 and NP2), a factual premise (FP), and the decision (D), which is the sentence.

(NP1): For all X and for all Y, X has a duty not to harm Y
(NP2): For all X and for all Y, if X harms Y, then X has a duty to pay damages to Y
(FP): X harmed Y

(D): X has a duty to pay damages to Y

Briefly put, the problem is that D does not follow from NP1 and FP alone, but it does follow from NP2 and FP, which means that NP1 is irrelevant to a tort law case. Therefore, all the discourse involving first-order duties not to harm is superfluous.

The answer to this challenge is simple. The duty not to harm is obviously superfluous in a case in which the harm has already been caused. It is logically impossible

[7] For an argument about how tort law contributes to social cohesion by encouraging individuals to take into account the interests and well-being of others, see Gerhart (2010, p. 14).

to apply the rule 'Do not cause harm to Y' if Y has already been harmed. As von Wright (1963, p. 75) points out, 'an order to shut the window … applies when a certain window is open'. But this does not warrant inferring that the duty not to harm is completely irrelevant to tort law. As I will argue later, the preventive turn in tort law—that is, the most modern trends regarding prevention, at least in continental legal systems—can be explained as an attempt to enforce the duty not to harm. The same can be said about injunctive relief in common law jurisdictions. How can we make sense of injunctions in general if not by basing the remedy on the right not to be harmed, and the correlative duty not to harm?

This, however, does not explain why the case law includes many references to the duty not to harm in cases where the harm has already occurred. My guess is that the decision-maker takes the opportunity to express her view about the ultimate foundations of the duty to pay damages. Of course, at a superficial level, the duty to pay damages is binding because there is a legal source for it. It satisfies the criteria of validity set out in the rule of recognition (see Hart 1994, p. 110). But at a deeper level, judges might be trying to convey the idea that the duty to pay damages is a normative consequence of breaching the duty not to harm. Although there is no logical connection between the two duties we are analysing, there is a normative connection. The duty to pay damages is, as Gardner (2011, p. 33) says, the rational echo of the duty not to harm that was breached in the first place. While it could be said that this is mostly speculative,[8] it is an interesting possibility.

3 Building the Case for the Existence of a Legal Duty Not to Harm

In the previous section, I tried to show that the arguments usually presented to reject that tort law includes a duty not to harm are rather weak. In this section, I will try to show that, to the contrary, there are good reasons to think that the duty not to harm is at the core of tort law. As I explained in the Introduction, the literature lacks good arguments in this respect. Most of the time, the existence of a duty not to harm is rashly assumed or taken to be a necessity derived from the nature of legal ordering.[9] I share the view that a duty not to harm is completely reasonable, a sensible idea. However, I will try to offer a convincing argument even for those theorists reluctant to rely on natural law premises. In this sense, I am concerned with the existence of

[8] Yet, there are some judicial decisions that explicitly ground the duty to pay damages on the duty not to harm. In Spain, the Navarra Court of Appeal (Audiencia Provincial) claimed that '[t]he tort liability action of art. 1902 CC … is grounded on the legal principle of "alterum non laedere" [do not cause harm to others] as the basis of social coexistence …'. (See SAP NA, 744/2015, July 10th, 2015). In Argentina, the Supreme Court has acknowledged that the duty not to harm has a Constitutional rank. (See CSJN, Santa Coloma, Luis c. Empresa Ferrocarriles Argentinos, Fallos 308:1160).

[9] See, among many others, Mosset Iturraspe (1980, p. 22); Bueres (1991, p. 153).

a duty not to harm as a matter of fact, as a matter of social practice, not as a matter of plausibility or moral theory. My strategy is to show that many of the salient features of our tort law practices become unintelligible or puzzling without assuming that there is a duty not to harm. I will start by saying something about the notion of legal duty or obligation I have in mind.

3.1 What Is a Legal Duty or Obligation?

The view I endorse of legal obligation is based on the work of H. L. A. Hart, but it also includes some insights developed by Joseph Raz. Hart approaches the concept of legal duty or legal obligation (actually, he does not find any theoretical relevance in the distinction) by first analysing those conceptions he deems to be flawed. Pointing out the unsatisfactory aspects of these views will allow us to appreciate which features of the phenomenon have remained unclear.

Let us quickly rule out, then, two different coercive accounts of legal obligation. According to the first, the notion of legal obligation can be explained in terms of an order backed by a threat of sanction. Let us imagine that Axileas approaches Xenophon and says 'Give me all your money, or I'll break your legs'. Because Axileas is able to carry out his threat and Xenophon values his physical integrity much more than the money he carries in his pocket, Xenophon gives Axileas seven drachmas. In one sense, it can be said that after the threat, it is no longer an option for Xenophon to keep the seven drachmas. If obligations are related to actions that are no longer *optional*, then Xenophon is under an obligation.

However, as Hart observes, it is inappropriate to say that Xenophon was under *an obligation* or duty to give the money to Axileas. It seems much more accurate to say that Xenophon felt obligated (was forced) to do so. Xenophon acts motivated by the belief that something bad will happen to him if he does not hand over the money combined with a desire to avoid the suffering threatened. However, these beliefs and motives, which are purely psychological facts, cannot be the building blocks of the notion of obligation, at least insofar as we think that an obvious truth about obligations is that they apply to us regardless of whether we think we have them. That is to say, the beliefs regarding the negative consequences of doing φ are neither necessary nor sufficient conditions for an agent to be under an obligation to do φ. Certainly, a person can be unaware of her obligations, and that is often the case with many of them. But it may also be that she is perfectly aware of her obligation and does not believe that she will suffer any harm in the event of non-compliance. This shows that the content, and hence the truth conditions, of statements about obligations and those about what a person felt obligated to do are not equivalent.[10]

In order to free the coercive theory from this subjective burden, some authors, such as John Austin, define obligations in terms of the likelihood that the obliged

[10] See Hart (1994, pp. 82–83).

person is sanctioned whenever she departs from the required standard of behaviour. Notice that the probabilities of being sanctioned do not depend on the perception of the agent whose conduct is obligatory. According to this view, statements about the obligations we have do not describe psychological facts. Instead, they contain an assessment of the probabilities that the person will be sanctioned.[11] Therefore, the statement 'Axileas is under a legal duty to do φ' *means* that it is highly likely that the authority will sanction Axileas in the event that he fails to do φ. This view, however, is problematic, since in ordinary language it makes perfect sense to claim that Axileas has breached his legal duty when there is practically no chance that he will be punished. If probabilistic judgments were at the core of our notion of obligation, this statement would be logically inconsistent. Equally, it is not redundant to claim that Axileas breached his legal duty and that there is a good chance that he will be punished for doing so (see Hart 1982a, p. 135).

The lesson to be learnt from this analysis is that Austin's theory misrepresents the relationship between breach of duty and sanction. There is no *conceptual relationship*, in the sense that all behaviour linked to a high probability of being sanctioned is wrong and the opposite behaviour mandatory. Nor is there a merely *causal relationship* between breach of duty and high probabilities of being sanctioned. Instead, the relationship is *justificatory*. The breach of duty justifies a critical reaction or sanction. From the participant's point of view, the fact that Axileas fails to perform his obligation to do φ is a *reason* to disapprove of Axileas' behaviour (see Hart 1994, p. 84). By ignoring this relationship, Austin's theory misses the importance of rules in *guiding* and *evaluating* action. The existence of a rule that imposes obligations defines *right* and *wrong*. Participants use duty-imposing rules to assess different states of affairs as ideal or non-ideal. This is not only reflected in the way individuals talk (distinguishing between having an obligation and feeling obliged), but also in what they do when they invoke a rule. Normally, rules are invoked to demand that an action is performed, to criticise or reprehend deviation from the required pattern of conduct, to justify one's actions, to ask for an explanation, to impose sanctions, or to hold the wrongdoer accountable. However, they also provide guidance as to when it is appropriate, for example, to demand or offer an apology, or to express disapproval or resentment (see Hart 1994, p. 90).[12]

Thus, if it is obligatory to do φ, then there is a rule according to which omitting φ is wrong and, in virtue of this fact, criticism for deviation is considered legitimate or justified. In turn, this implies that it would be inappropriate to criticise the critics for criticising (see Hart 1994, pp. 57 and 85). The context in which all these attitudes are appropriate is normative. If we were to reduce the rules of obligation to psychological attitudes or to causal relationships or probabilistic predictions, we would miss an important part of the phenomenon as it is understood by the participants in the legal practice.

---

[11] See Hart (1994, pp. 83–84). Hart explains Austin's theory (Austin 1832 in these terms.

[12] On the link between obligation, wrongdoing, and accountability, see Bertea (2019, p. 38).

However, what has been said so far is not enough to distinguish obligations from other normative requirements, such as those that correspond to the rules of etiquette. Of course, if Axileas shows up without having shaved on his daughter's wedding day, that might draw some criticism since Axileas *should have* shaved for the occasion to express approval for the marriage and, at the end, respect for the bride and the groom. But in these cases, Hart thinks, describing the situation in terms of obligations or duties might be excessive. A rule is usually understood to impose an obligation when the general demand for compliance is persistent and the pressure placed on deviations is substantial (see Hart 1994, p. 86). On the other hand, an action is hardly considered obligatory if it is not believed to be important for the maintenance of community life. For these reasons, Hart assumes that the rules of etiquette do not impose real obligations. They are rather standards of social adequacy or good taste, but not rules that are considered important for the preservation of society. Nor is their breach a matter of concern to public authorities (see Hart 1994, p. 87).

Another essential feature of obligations is that they may conflict with the interests of the addressee, and they often do. Although Axileas has a duty to pay taxes, he has an interest in not paying them (see Hart 1994, p. 87). Unfortunately for Axileas, obligations are something completely different from prudential reasons. When someone is under an obligation to do φ, she cannot justify not doing φ simply on the basis that φ is opposed to her wishes or interests. These kinds of subjective considerations are irrelevant to justify departure from the required conduct. In this sense, obligations purport to exclude prudential reasons from the balance of reasons for action.

Drawing on this argument, it is also possible to distinguish obligations from mere *burdens*. Burdens are usually necessary conditions for obtaining a benefit or realising an interest. Therefore, understanding burdens as a kind of obligation would be misleading. Burdens are a requirement of instrumental rationality that are not independent of the person's interests. If you want to achieve X, you must necessarily do Z. This being the case, Z is a burden, because it is a necessary step for an agent to achieve her goals. However, and this is the key to the argument, omitting Z does not warrant any of the critical attitudes mentioned above. If it is truly a burden, Z remains completely optional for the agent, for she only has prudential reasons in favour of Z; and, as I have just said, obligations make some courses of action non-optional regardless of the addressee's interests (see Himma 2013, p. 21).

Furthermore, obligations do not only exclude prudential reasons. According to Joseph Raz (1990, pp. 49–85; 1979, p. 17), if φ is obligatory, then the reasons for doing φ are protected against other opposing reasons. This means that obligations exclude at least some reasons from the balance of reasons and the addressed agent is not allowed to act on them. Imagine that Axileas needs money to pay his mortgage. If he does not pay the debt, he will lose his house. Axileas asks Xenophon to help him out. As a friend, Xenophon feels that he has a moral duty to help Axileas. However, if he lends Axileas the money, Xenophon will not be able to pay his own taxes. In this situation, Xenophon has a reason to pay his taxes, but also a reason to help Axileas, because friends are supposed to help each other. However, from the legal point of view, this reason is excluded from the balance when it comes to deciding whether to pay the taxes or not.

The core of the conception of obligation I endorse can be summarised as follows.[13] If Axileas is under an obligation to do φ in circumstances C, then in circumstances C there is a rule that imposes on Axileas the obligation to do φ. And, from the point of view of the rule, (1) Axileas has a reason to do φ, which also counts as a reason to exclude at least some other opposing considerations (especially, but not only, his own interests or desires) that might recommend a different course of action; (2) it would be *prima facie* wrong to omit φ;[14] (3) it is justified to demand the performance of φ by Axileas or even, depending on the circumstances, to force him to do it; and (4) criticism, disapproval, resentment, reprehension and punishment, among many others, may be appropriate attitudes against Axileas if he does not do φ.

Some of these statements ground other statements. For example, since obligations depend on the existence of rules and not on any particular state of mind of the addressee, an agent might be unaware that she is under an obligation. The first statement, in turn, explains why civil law denies the validity of purely discretionary obligations, the fulfilment of which depends exclusively on the will of the debtor. An obligation of this kind would be an obligation in name only. Discretionary obligations are obligations that can be ignored by the person under them; and optional obligations seem to be an oxymoron. The third statement, which is quite complex, specifies that if Axileas has an obligation to pay a sum of money to Xenophon and does not do so, Xenophon can demand Axileas to pay the money, without having to justify his request. The obligation offers sufficient justification for the demand.

Some aspects of this conception deserve further analysis. Let us continue with the third statement. What does it mean that Axileas can be *forced* to do φ, in case of non-compliance? Naturally, enforceability depends on the kind of obligation under consideration. If we are concerned with the possibility of enforcing an obligation using the coactive powers of the state, then this is only the case with *legal* obligations. Moreover, what makes an obligation *legal*? According to Hart (1994, p. 94), it is that the rule that imposes the obligation meets the criteria of validity set out in the rule of recognition, which is a social (customary) rule practiced by the officials of the system. Certainly, that the duty-imposing rule meets the criteria of validity is not enough to justify state coercion. An obligation can be legally enforced only if the proper procedures are followed. That is, in order to demand compliance, the 'rules and principles regulating such demands for action' must be respected (see Hart 1982a, p. 160).

Nevertheless, it is important to understand that state coercion is not the only way to enforce a duty-imposing rule. Even if the rule establishes a sanction, the potential plaintiff might prefer to avoid the judicial system and enforce the rule by other means. For example, a creditor might try to increase social pressure to force the

---

[13] Many of these features are part of the concept of obligation, not only part of a particular conception of it. See Bertea (2019, p. 30ff).

[14] See Bertea (2019, p. 36).

debtor to pay her debt. Provided that the creditor avails herself of non-illegal methods to achieve the result, she cannot be subject to criticism for trying to force the other party to fulfil her *legal* duty. Suppose the creditor mentions to other businesspersons that the debtor is behind in her payments and does not pick up the phone. Unless a legal rule prohibits this behaviour, let us say, for being shameful to the debtor, the creditor is justified in increasing the social pressure for compliance since the debtor is under an obligation to pay her debt.

There is much more to say about the idea of a legal obligation, but the aspects explained above are enough for my purposes in this chapter. In the following sections, I will present four arguments to support the claim that there is a legal duty not to harm in tort law. None of the arguments is supposed to be conclusive. However, the four arguments in combination are compelling, because they leave too many loose ends to those who reject that there is a duty not to harm. Put differently, when the existence of a duty not to harm is denied, many familiar aspects of our tort law practices remain without explanation. On the other hand, the existence of a duty not to harm makes sense of all of them.

3.2 Normatively Ideal Worlds in Tort Law

As explained in Sect. 2.2, if there is a duty not to harm, it is not an absolute duty. It is a qualified duty not to harm in some circumstances carefully specified by the rules of the legal system. In tort law, the grounds of liability (the most common being negligence, intention, and strict liability) determine the scope of the duty not to harm.

Now, duty-imposing rules not only guide conduct, they are also criteria according to which different states of the world can be assessed. If a duty not to harm exists, then the legally *ideal world* is one in which no harm occurs in the way specified by the rules (viz., negligence, intention, or risky activities). It is an ideal world because none of the rules forbidding certain types of harms is broken. On the other hand, the world in which the harms in question are caused is a *defective world*. They are not supposed to happen according to the rules of the system. Finally, there is a world in which the specified harm occurs, but it is repaired by the operation of a remedial rule (such as compensatory damages). I will refer to this as a *non-ideal world*. After compensation, the world ceases to be defective altogether, but it does not become ideal because conventional wisdom tells us that the remedy is a second best when compared to respecting the duty-imposing rule in the first place (see Gardner 2018, p. 127).

However, if the existence of a duty not to harm does not exist, then the only duty would be to compensate for the harm done. The primary legal wrong would be not paying compensation to the victim once she was harmed in the relevant way or circumstances.[15] Hence, if immediately after harming the victim, the person (not the wrongdoer yet!) takes out her checkbook and generously compensates the victim, from the point of view of tort law the world is as perfect or ideal as the one in which the harm never takes place. In short, the rejection of a duty not to harm commits us to deny that the world in which no harm occurs is, from the legal point of view, normatively better than, or preferable to, one in which all harms are compensated. In effect, the rejection thesis denies proposition (1) below, and asserts (2):

1. *Duty not to harm*: No harm $\succ$ compensated harm $\succ$ uncompensated harm
2. *No duty not to harm*: No harm $\equiv$ compensated harm $\succ$ uncompensated harm

According to the rejection thesis, the harm is not completely irrelevant because it is the condition that triggers the remedy. However, in terms of how the different worlds are to be assessed from the legal perspective, the no-harm world is equivalent to the compensated-harm world. This, I think, is highly problematic, for it does not fit well with our shared scheme of legal thought.

To test our intuitions, let us compare two situations.

Case 1: Axileas walks into Xenophon's restaurant, orders a meal, eats, asks for the bill, pays, and leaves.
Case 2: Axileas is driving his car; he gets distracted and crashes into Xenophon's restaurant. Axileas immediately approaches Xenophon, makes a generous estimate of the damages to avoid any controversy, takes out his checkbook and pays for the harm caused. Assume that the sum of money written in the check is in fact compensatory for all the harm suffered by Xenophon.

I suspect that most people would say that both cases are normatively different. But why? It is obvious that while Axileas eats the meal he is not doing anything wrong. The first wrong thing would be to sneak out of the restaurant without paying the bill. On the other hand, wouldn't we think that if, in Case 2, Axileas ran away from the restaurant after causing the harm, he would be committing *a second* wrong? The first was to crash the car into Xenophon's restaurant; the second, to run away from the scene of the accident without paying compensation for the harm done. The fact that most people would share this intuition, of course, does not prove the existence of a duty not to harm. The point is whether we can accommodate this intuition with the rejection of such a duty, and I think we cannot. Unless the existence of a duty not to harm is assumed, we cannot make sense of the judgment that Axileas commits two wrongs when he crashes the car and then flees from the restaurant. Moreover, if there were no duty not to harm, why would the world in which the crash does not occur be *normatively* better than the one in which Axileas pays for the damages caused to the restaurant?

On the other hand, would it make sense in Case 1 that Axileas, after finishing the meal and paying the bill, offered an apology to Xenophon? That would be odd. In

[15] From a more realist perspective, the legal wrong could be defined as not paying compensation to the victim who files a valid claim, meeting all the procedural requirements. See Smith (2019, p. 3). I find this reconstruction unconvincing, but I cannot offer a full reply in this chapter.

sharp contrast, in Case 2, it makes perfect sense for Axileas to pay for the damage he caused with his car and *also* to apologise to Xenophon for damaging his property. Why does the apology make sense? Because paying damages, remedying one's wrong, is not the same as not causing it. Even in cases in which the remedy is close to undoing the wrong, the wrong is not eliminated from the picture. If I take something that belongs to you without your permission and then, 5 min later I give it back with no harm, even if my restitution in a way makes you whole, taking and giving back is not the same, in normative terms, as not taking. In Case 2, by imposing on Axileas the duty to pay damages, the law does not eliminate the wrong to Xenophon. It only provides a remedy for the wrong. That means that we move from the defective world of uncompensated harm to the non-ideal world of compensated harm. On some occasions, compensation might bring us quite close to the ideal world, but never to a point of indifference between paying damages and not harming.

The asymmetry between the two examples shows that the harm is something that, ideally, *should have never happened*. Whereas in a restaurant, customers are expected not to abstain from eating the meal that is served to them, everyone is expected to abstain from causing negligent harm with their cars. This is so because paying compensation has a different meaning from that of payment of the bill at the restaurant. Compare the two triggering facts: eating the meal and crashing the car into the wall of the restaurant. Axileas has a reason not to crash his car into the wall of the restaurant, and this reason does not depend on his interests and desires. By contrast, the only reasons Axileas might have for not eating the meal depend exclusively on his current purposes and tastes. There is no duty not to eat the meal. At most, it is a burden. If he does not wish to incur the obligation to pay the bill, he should abstain from eating the meal. Asserting the same thing regarding Case 2 would be inappropriate. Usually, not harming others is not seen as a burden to avoid liability.

Finally, note that the analysis does not appeal to our purported personal preference for a world without accidents, a preference that, to some extent, should be shared by all rational persons. Instead, I am pointing out the way in which we frame a case, the inferences that we make, and the assumptions underlying our judgments. All this reflects the norms we apply when we evaluate factual situations from the legal point of view; and, as a matter of positive law, tort law is in large part made up of the rules that we actually use to analyze and decide legal cases. If we feel that Axileas, after he runs away, commits two wrongs, we are in fact evaluating his behaviour based on a rule according to which the harm that Axileas caused to Xenophon was wrong, hence he must have had the duty not to harm him in that way. At this point, either we revise the assumptions of our reasoning and change the conclusion that he committed two wrongs, or we accept that our legal reasoning incorporates a duty not to harm.

As I mentioned, this argument is not meant to be conclusive. It is just a starting point because, as we will see, there are more features of our legal systems that address the existence of a duty not to harm in tort law.

3.3 *The Role of Criminal Law in Strengthening Tort Law's Normative Structure*

Delving a little deeper, and closely related to the above, we should note that the domains of tort law and criminal law overlap to a considerable extent. Not all torts constitute a criminal offence, of course, but many do. The subject matter of regulations is basically the same: the protection of life, bodily and psychological integrity, property, and reputation.[16] From this fact, I shall argue that, without assuming a duty not to harm in tort law, criminal law regulation is hard to explain. In contrast, the presence of a duty not to harm in tort law makes the criminal law regulation intelligible. Additionally, I will suggest that there are powerful reasons why not all torts are made criminal offenses.

Let us begin with the idea that, without the existence of a duty not to harm in tort law, criminal law regulation would be puzzling. In effect, if harming others—say negligently—is not prohibited, and the only possible wrong against the victim is committed once the responsible agent does not pay damages, what is the point of establishing criminal sanctions for much of the conduct that is subject to tort liability? Adding criminal consequences to some core torts seems to contradict the scheme according to which causing a loss to the victim constitutes no wrong, provided she receives adequate compensation. The thesis that denies the existence of a duty not to harm is incompatible with imposing sanctions because, *ex hypothesi,* this harmful conduct is not prohibited. Even if compensation were offered to the victim, the criminal charges would hold in most cases. (I will come back to this later.) The message conveyed to the addressees would be incoherent: there is no duty not to harm, only a duty to pay damages, but if you harm you might face criminal consequences (that often are considerably more severe than tort liability).

It could be argued that harming others is not a civil offence, but *sometimes* constitutes a criminal offense. Still, I think that the idea of conceiving the justification of criminal law and tort law as separate domains is implausible. Ideally, no harm to others should be made a criminal offence if it is not serious enough to count as a civil wrong first. Denying the civil wrong in these cases while asserting the criminal wrong would be tantamount to claiming that the (policy) reasons to punish the wrongdoer have nothing to do with the fact that she harmed the victim. However, the justification of criminal law would then be called into question, because it should focus only on 'wrongfully harmful conduct' (see Duff 2007, pp. 83–84). The thesis I am analysing claims that the harm that Axileas caused to Xenophon is a public wrong but not a private wrong, and this makes us wonder how the harm that Xenophon suffers can be a wrong committed to the community at large without being, first and foremost, a wrong committed *to him* personally (see Duff 2007, pp. 55–56).

[16]According to Ripstein (2016, p. 8), tort law gives effect to a certain 'morality of interaction', which is based on the idea that 'others must not interfere with your body, property, or reputation'. In the following paragraphs I will extend the argument to criminal law.

On the other hand, if causing harm is not a civil wrong, why does the responsible agent face both civil and criminal consequences in certain cases? The only way to escape the problem would be to deny that paying damages is a legal response aimed at correcting a wrong (see Weinrib 2012, p. 16). Instead, the payment of damages would be an obligation that emerges once the agent causes the harm to the victim. But what could be the justification of such an obligation if it is not related to undoing the consequences of the interaction? If the point of the remedy is merely to provide a benefit to the victim, a kind of subsidy, why is the defendant responsible for this and not the whole community, or the richest person in town? In addition, if the point is indeed undoing the consequences of the interaction in which the *defendant took part*, why is it justified to undo those consequences if they are not wrongful? The rejection thesis leaves too many questions unanswered.

Compare the picture above with the one in which the duty not to harm is present. In this picture, the role of criminal law is fully consistent with tort liability. The reason criminal law punishes certain tortious actions is to prevent agents from treating the potential victim's right not to be harmed as if it were merely a right to receive compensation in certain circumstances. If not for the support of criminal law, tort liability might be understood by some agents as a 'pay as you go system' in which, whenever it is beneficial to cause harm, it is allowed provided the victim is compensated for the harm she has suffered. To preclude this type of maximising behaviour, which is inconsistent with the rights of the victim and the duty not to harm that the agent ought to obey, criminal law intervenes by imposing additional sanctions when the agent breaches her duty not to harm. In this way, criminal law attempts to alter the rational agent's preferences, making it more attractive to respect the victim's rights than to harm and face the legal consequences (paying damages, plus the criminal sanctions).

This point was originally made by Calabresi and Melamed (1972, p. 1126). They distinguished between the protection of rights with property rules and those with liability rules. Property rules require whoever wishes to acquire the right of another person to obtain their consent. Liability rules, on the other hand, allow the agent to appropriate the resources of another, provided she is willing to pay a price collectively established by market mechanisms. Legal systems include both types of rules because the former work well in contexts of low transaction costs and the latter favour the optimal allocation of resources when transaction costs are very high or prohibitive. However, in the absence of criminal law, even in contexts of low transaction costs, individuals may be tempted to treat property rules as if they were liability rules. After all, the sanction for failing to obtain the victim's consent is none other than civil liability. Why waste time bargaining with the potential victim? The agent could find it convenient to cause the harm and compensate later, rather than investing time and money negotiating *ex ante* with the victim. To avoid this result, criminal law establishes sanctions other than pecuniary ones, hopefully sufficient to motivate individuals to respect the rights of their potential victims.

In the end, what is at stake is whether or not the norms of tort law are a set of prices for performing harmful actions. Without a duty not to harm, the agent is at liberty to choose between *not harming* and *harming and paying compensation*. As in the case of the restaurant, Axileas can choose between not eating the meal or eating it and paying the bill. Can Axileas also choose between not crashing his car into Xenophon's restaurant and crashing it and paying damages to Xenophon? A tort system like this would be very similar to a *price system.*[17]

The problem with this view is that our current tort law practices are not organised in the same way as our markets. Tort law's pattern of reasoning is articulated around a series of normative concepts such as obligations, rights, responsibility, precaution, fault, lawful risk, justification, and many more. At the same time, the rules of the practice are the criterion according to which the participants guide their conduct, evaluate deviations from the required pattern of behaviour and, consequently, justify their critical attitudes towards the wrongdoer. A violation of a rule justifies criticism, reprehension, and sometimes even outrage or resentment. But none of these attitudes, nor the concepts mentioned above, find a place in a system of prices. As Coleman (2011, pp. 121–122) points out, whoever breaks a rule owes an explanation and, in some cases, compensation or redress. Not all these features of legal systems cohere with a price system. First, the decision to pay or not to pay a price is immune to interpersonal criticism, so in this area no one owes another an explanation for what they have done. Secondly, the lack of adequate sensibility to prices (following the usual inverse relationship between price and quantity) does not justify criticism, outrage, or resentment.

At this point, a possible response could try to undermine the general scope of my argument. It could be argued that, at best, I have shown only that there might be a duty not to harm *intentionally*, since criminal law only tries to deter injurers who view tort liability as a price for pursuing their interests. But this is not the case. Criminal law also punishes some negligent conduct. It is true that most individuals do not decide to cause harm because they choose to pay a price. Nevertheless, it is possible that some agents get used to paying for damages instead of preventing harm, especially when an activity is beneficial, and the precautions are deemed to be expensive. The message conveyed by criminal law is that reasonable precautions are required in any case. Compensation will not eliminate the wrongful nature of the harm caused, placing the agent on safe ground, granting him the typical immunity the agent enjoys when the world is normatively ideal. On the contrary, as I have said, compensation improves the world by providing a remedy that will take us out of the defective world. However, after the wrongful harm is inflicted, the ideal world is unattainable. Remedies are still part of a non-ideal world. This reasoning seems to be implicit in some legal systems, such as the Spanish, in which repairing the loss suffered by the victim only serves to ease criminal liability (see article 21 of the Spanish Criminal Code). Therefore, offering compensation to the victim might reduce the severity of the sanction instead of excluding it (except in the case of minor harms), because the wrong is not fully corrected by this remedy. Some punishment may still be required as a proper response to the harm done.

[17] On the idea that the law functions as a system of implicit prices, see Ogus (2006, pp. 102–103).

Even so, my argument does not seem to reach cases regulated under strict liability. In the case of lawful activities, the purported duty not to harm is not backed by criminal sanctions. Two considerations are relevant here. First, as I previously said, none of the arguments is conclusive by itself. They should be evaluated together. The only point I am making here is that without assuming a duty not to harm, the role of criminal law—when it does intervene—remains puzzling. Second, there is a good explanation why criminal law does not usually intervene in strict liability cases. Criminal law cannot impose sanctions in these cases without violating *the principle of culpability*, which is essential in a liberal legal system. For reasons of policy, the criminal law response focuses on the most serious offences, those that are intentional or negligent; and, in this sense, the absence of strict criminal liability offers no support whatsoever to the rejection thesis, according to which a *duty not to harm does not exist in this area of tort law*. Nevertheless, this fact only shows that there are duties whose breach is more serious than the breach of others. The breach of the duty not to harm is much more serious when the harm is intentional than when it is negligent. In turn, it is more serious to harm with fault than to harm in the course of a risky (but lawful) activity. Social life requires tolerating certain annoyances from others, but not all of them. At a given point, the legislator must draw a line to mark that certain harms are unjustified. That is when tort law, administrative law, criminal law, etc., enter the game. In this sense, the distinction between right and wrong is categorical, not a matter of degrees. But within the category of wrongful actions, graduations can certainly be established: from the legal point of view, some obligations are more important than others (see MacCormick 2008, pp. 83–84). Consequently, some breaches are more serious than others. It would be excessive to back up with criminal sanctions the duty not to harm in the course of risky (but lawful) activities. Since that kind of harm is not the worst kind of breach of the duty not to harm, and the culpability principle would be compromised if strict liability cases received criminal punishment, the law leaves strict liability torts without the protection of criminal law.

3.4 Making Sense of Prevention Trends in Current Tort Law

The importance of the preventive aspect of tort law and the new trends, especially in continental legal systems, must be taken seriously. These characteristics of current legal practices reaffirm, in my view, that the normatively ideal world is one in which harms do not occur and not one in which they are systematically compensated. Within the framework of tort liability, the idea that potential victims can ask courts to act beforehand to neutralise certain risks that threaten to cause severe harm is gaining attention. In continental law systems, there are many examples, including court orders to: (1) stop the publication of photographs that violate the right to privacy; (2) adopt measures when it is clear that a neighbouring dilapidated building might cause serious and imminent harm to the claimant's property; (3) end any kind of nuisance (all disturbance due to sounds, smoke, vibrations, lights, smells, and so on, that exceed the normal tolerance between neighbours); or (4) suppress the broadcasting of advertisements that *prima facie* are denigratory to the competition. Amongst many others, these are examples in which the courts enforce the duty not to harm, instead of waiting for its production to enable an *ex-post* remedy.[18]

Orders of this type comprise what in the literature is called 'inhibitory protection' or, in common law systems, 'injunctive relief', and they are not difficult to find in comparative law (see Llamas Pombo 2008, pp. 464–469). Different legal systems admit a series of typical, or well-defined, cases, such as the ones mentioned in the previous paragraph, but there is a doctrine that militates for the incorporation of a general clause of inhibitory protection, one for all kinds of cases, even if they are not specifically provided for in the regulation. On the basis of a general clause of inhibitory protection, courts may issue orders to refrain from acting in a certain way or that require the defendant to take positive steps to prevent harm. In turn, these orders can have a definitive or only a temporary character (see Lorenzetti 1995, pp. 1223–1224). Since systematic characterisation is not possible, the admissibility of any given request must be left to judicial discretion. These decisions imply a judgment on the compatibility of two values that modern societies try to balance: freedom of action and personal safety. Thus, when wrongful harm is imminent or, because of its nature, is irreparable, freedom of action is less undermined by inhibitory protection since most of the time the agent has no right to endanger the victim in that way. Therefore, in those situations, court orders can be issued more easily.

Certainly, the way in which the practice has developed in some countries—which sometimes refuse to grant the preventive request based on the solvency of the defendant to face the reparation of any harm that could be caused[19]—can lead us to think that, in the end, judges are more concerned with guaranteeing the enforcement of the eventual compensatory duty than with the prevention of harm. In other words, if upon the request of a protective measure, judges only make sure that the defendant has sufficient funds to assume the eventual compensation, this seems to indicate that they interpret the victim's claim in a purely compensatory and not preventive sense. Properly understood, the objection concludes, the interest that the victim can secure by applying for an injunctive relief is her eventual claim for compensation.

Contrary to this interpretation, I think that the cases in which injunctive relief or the inhibitory protection is denied offer no support for the thesis that rejects the existence of a duty not to harm. As I said, finding the right balance between freedom of action and personal safety is not an easy task. Courts do not intend to confer absolute or unconditional protection on potential victims, since neutralising all risk would also mean the extinction of our freedom of action. This is consistent with my earlier claim that the duty not to harm is confined to some specific circumstances, and some concrete ways of causing harm, such as acting unreasonably or performing an activity marked as 'risky' by the rules of the system. Given that the

---

[18] For a good explanation of a preventive trend, see Vargas Tinoco (2022, Chapter 8).

[19] Argentinian courts have been clear in stating that 'given the solvency of the defendant highlighted by the plaintiff … the negative effects that might result [from the advertisement] could, eventually, be adequately compensated by suing for damages' (C. Nac. Civ. y Com. Fed., Sala 3ª, 09/27/2000, 'Clorox Argentina SA').

admissibility of an inhibitory protection is always evaluated before the agent violates her duty not to harm, in some cases it is difficult to justify granting it without unduly curtailing freedom of action.

Easy cases are those in which it is clear that the conduct of the defendant is *per se* illegal. In these cases, since the defendant is breaching her duty of care, this fact already provides grounds to suppress the risk, and these grounds are independent of the imminence of the harm. Remember that if Axileas is under an obligation to take precautions, then it is appropriate to demand that he takes them. But in hard cases, it might not be clear whether the defendant breached her duty of care. In analysing whether it is justified to issue an order to neutralise a risk, judges are normally bound by verifying the legal plausibility of the request (the existence of a right that deserves protection) and the urgency of the request (that there is an actual danger to the rights of the claimant if the request is denied). Therefore, judges need to make their decisions before examining all the relevant facts regarding the unlawfulness of the defendant's behaviour, which explains why injunctions are sometimes rejected. Think, for example, of comparative advertisement cases. It is surely hasty to claim categorically that an advertisement is denigratory, thus unlawful, before considering all the merits of the case. In such an event, the decision must be taken by weighing, among other things, the gravity, or the irreparable nature of the potential harm, if it occurs, and the gravity or irreparable nature of the potential harm to the defendant if the claimant's request is, after all, not justified.[20] All this is just a consequence of the dilemma faced by judges: how to provide an effective protection to the victim before she suffers any harm, without incurring a high rate of judicial error that unjustifiably restricts the freedom of action of potential defendants. Within an analytical framework, the denial of an injunction remains compatible with the existence of a duty not to harm. On the contrary, granting an injunction is unintelligible if a duty not to harm is not assumed. If there is only a duty to pay damages once the victim suffers a loss, why is the defendant's freedom curtailed before she causes harm?

Put differently, if no duty not to harm exists, the mere fact that the injurer has the means to pay damages would be a decisive factor to allow her to continue the harmful activity (which she has no obligation to cease). Imagine that a magazine is going to publish without the required consent a photograph of the sick daughter of a celebrity inside the hospital when she is about to receive treatment. Suppose the celebrity finds this out before the magazine is published and requests, as a preventive measure, that the publication be cancelled. Could the magazine reply 'Look, we are more than happy to pay damages, so there is no need to stop the publication since the only right the victim has is to be compensated!'? This kind of argument will certainly fail in most legal systems. So, the preventive aspect of tort law cannot be fully understood without grasping the role of the duty not to harm in its normative structure.

Additionally, there are other normative manifestations of the preventive aspect of tort law that cannot be understood without assuming the existence of a duty not to harm. Take, for example, preventive expenses. Art. 2:104 of the Principles of

[20] For further details, see Papayannis (2010).

European Tort Law establishes that 'Expenses incurred to prevent threatened damage amount to recoverable damage in so far as reasonably incurred'.[21] The justification for this provision in the framework of tort law is complex, since it admits of several possible theoretical reconstructions (see Martín Casals 2011, pp. 23–24). However, one thing is clear: preventive expenses empower the potential victim to take, at the expense of the party who creates the risk, reasonable precautions in order to avoid suffering harm. Obviously, these are precautions that the victim is not under obligation to take because otherwise their omission would make the victim contributorily negligent. If the victim is not under an obligation to take such precautions, then she is allowed to take them or to ignore them. This discretionary power conferred *upon the victim* shows that it is not up to the agent to choose between *not harming* and *harming and paying compensation*. Instead, it is the victim who has the final say in the matter. Her decision to be free of harm prevails and is institutionally recognised with the right to recover the expenses she had to incur not to suffer the harm. If part of the meaning of having a right is to have a legally respected choice (Hart 1982b, pp. 188–189), it can be said that the victim has a right not to be harmed, correlative to a duty of the agent not to harm her.

True, it could be argued that preventive expenses only reflect the existence of a right not to be exposed to unreasonable risks, not a right not to be harmed. But this is not all that clear. In many cases the victim faces certain harm, and she takes precautions (that she has no duty to take) to avoid it. In other cases, she merely diminishes the risk of harm. In both cases she can recover her expenses unless they are unreasonably high. We should wonder why it is important to make available to the victim a means to neutralize risks. It seems that the point of this rule is to offer the victim an additional chance of preventing harm. And this is consistent with the idea that the victim enjoys two rights: a right not to be harmed, *and* a right not to be exposed to unreasonable risks.

3.5 The Obligation Not to Harm, Duties of Care, and Reasons for Action

In this last section, I will suggest that a system that includes a general duty of care but denies a duty not to harm is in an important way incoherent.[22] I am not claiming that the system incurs a logical contradiction. A system that imposes a duty to take reasonable precautions, but not a duty not to harm, is logically consistent. It imposes a duty to take the reasonable steps to achieve a certain result, not a duty to achieve it. However, as I will try to show, in terms of practical reason, it makes much more

[21] The Argentinian Civil and Commercial Code (2015) also includes preventive expenses in its art. 1710, subsection b.

[22] For the notion of incoherence, see MacCormick (1978, p. 152).

sense to require the addressees to take reasonable precautions not to harm *because* they have a duty not to harm. Let us look at the argument.

As I explained before, according to Joseph Raz, that Axileas has a duty to do φ means that Axileas has both (1) a primary reason for φing, which does not depend on his own desires, interests or goals, and (2) a second-order reason for not acting on the basis of *at least some other reasons* that recommend omitting φ. In Raz's words, the duty to do φ implies that there is a protected reason for doing φ. Let us look at another example to grasp the idea better. Imagine that Axileas is the security guard of a warehouse and that Xenophon, his boss, ordered him not to let anyone in after 8 pm. This fact gives Axileas a first-order reason not to let anyone in and a second-order reason not to act on the basis of at least some other conflicting reasons. Suppose that Telemachus, one of the usual truck drivers, arrives a little later than 8 pm. He tells Axileas that if he fails to make the delivery, as a sanction, he will be paid much less. The fact that Telemachus will be sanctioned if Axileas does not let him in is a reason that is excluded from the balance of reasons by the duty not to let anyone in after 8 pm. However, if the police showed up at the warehouse with a search warrant, things would be different. We can assume that the fact that not letting the police in would constitute obstruction of justice is a reason that *is not excluded* by his duty as a security guard. Duties are not absolutely protected reasons, though they are usually protected against a good range of opposing considerations.[23]

Let us focus on the duty of care now. A duty of care is a first-order reason (that does not depend on the agent's desires, interests, or goals) to take reasonable precautions[24] in order to avoid the accident, and a second-order reason not to act for at least some other conflicting reasons. Hence, a duty of care is a protected reason to take reasonable precautions to avoid harming others. The duty urges the agent to try not to harm, that is, to act in a way that she causes no harm to another person. This, in turn, means *acting in order for* the agent's actions to *contribute* to the avoidance of harm. As Gardner (2001, pp. 134ff) observes, the action's contribution to the avoidance of harm is a reason for that action if there are independent reasons not to harm. In a similar way, we cannot understand that Axileas has a reason for taking

[23] Of course, there are no facts that by their nature are included or excluded from the agent's consideration. In this sense, I assume that the example is intuitive enough to make the point.

[24] The meaning of 'reasonable precautions' might be debatable. However, there is some consensus about the core elements of a reasonableness judgment in this area. Among other things, the agent must consider 'the nature and value of the protected interest involved, the dangerousness of the activity, the expertise to be expected of a person carrying it on, the foreseeability of the damage, the relationship of proximity or special reliance between those involved, as well as the availability and the costs of precautionary or alternative methods' (Principles of European Tort Law, art. 4:102). Even with these guidelines in hand, the agent might fail to identify what the reasonable precautions are in the circumstances. The duty of care does not relieve the agent from all deliberation, only the deliberation regarding whether to take precautions or not. The duty of care is a protected reason to take precautions only up to the point at which it would be unreasonable to demand more.

the train to Girona if we do not assume that he has a reason for arriving in Girona; reasons to try to do something are intelligible in light of the reasons to achieve it.

Obviously, fulfilling the duty of care does not guarantee that no harm will result from the agent's conduct. The victim can be harmed even if the agent takes reasonable precautions. Suppose that Axileas leaves the supermarket with his shopping and the bag containing a bottle of olive oil breaks. Consequently, the sidewalk is covered with a litre of extra-virgin olive oil. The fact that this imperils other persons is a reason for Axileas to clean the sidewalk and throw some sand on top of the remaining oil. If Axileas left the oil on the sidewalk, he would be at fault. However, cleaning the sidewalk does not preclude the possibility that Xenophon will slip anyway. If this happens, the duty of care would not have been infringed, despite the production of harm.

According to the duty of care, the fact that cleaning the sidewalk and throwing sand on it contributes to Xenophon not being harmed by Axileas is a reason for Axileas to clean the sidewalk and to throw sand on it.[25] Moreover, this reason is protected against many of the reasons that might be given for leaving the oil on the sidewalk. For example, the fact that the match between Panathinaikos and Olympiakos is about to start is *a* reason to sit in front of the TV right away and for leaving the oil on the sidewalk, but it is *excluded* by the duty of care. That is what the duty of care is all about. Now, if this analysis is correct, reasons to take precautions are only intelligible through independent reasons not to harm. If *reasons to try* make sense only when the agent also has *reasons to succeed*, then reasons to try not to harm make sense only if there are reasons not to harm. Why try to achieve something you do not have reasons to achieve? The crucial question is whether to make sense of a protected reason to take precautions, we need to assume a *protected* reason not to harm. Only if this is the case, can we claim that the duty of care implies a duty not to harm. But it would be incorrect to derive the existence of a duty not to harm from a duty of care.[26] The fact that a duty of care is intelligible in light of a *reason* not to harm does not entail that it is only intelligible in light of a *duty* not to harm. Reasons alone are not duties; protected reasons are.

Nevertheless, the analysis shows something interesting. Those who reject the existence of a duty not to harm think that, at least, one (if not both) of the following statements is true: (1) that there are no reasons not to harm; and (2) that reasons not to harm are not also reasons to exclude some other reasons that recommend the harmful course of conduct. That is, if there is no duty not to harm, then, either the primary reason not to harm is absent or, if present, it is not protected against countervailing reasons. According to the previous analysis, the existence of a duty of

[25] As I understand the duty of care, the fact that cleaning the sidewalk contributes to Xenophon not being harmed *by* Axileas is, for Axileas, a protected reason for cleaning the sidewalk. Of course, the fact that Axileas can prevent harm to Xenophon is always a reason for action, but not necessarily a protected one. The law only imposes on us the duty to avoid certain harms—normally harms in which we are causally involved—not all possible harms that could be avoided.

[26] Gardner (2001, pp. 137–141) points out a series of asymmetries between obligations to try and obligations succeed that make it impossible to derive the latter from the former.

care rules out the possibility that there are no reasons not to harm. Remember that the duty of care makes sense only if there are reasons (though not necessarily duties) not to harm. Therefore, those who reject the existence of a duty not to harm must believe that these reasons not to harm are not protected. If this is the case, the rational person must weigh her reasons not to harm against other countervailing reasons. That means that reasons not to harm enter into the agent's balance of reasons and compete with all other reasons for action that are applicable and that recommend harming another person. The fact that choosing not to harm undermines some other important personal goals of the agent certainly counts as a reason to harm; at least this fact has some weight that cannot be ignored in the balance. Personal goals or interests are not excluded by the reasons not to harm, because *ex hypothesis* there is no duty not to harm. Consequently, the law does not require the addressee to act on the basis on any concrete kind of reason. In this way, if after considering all the relevant facts in a given situation, the reason to harm another is not defeated by other considerations, then it would be rational to harm, since it is rational to act on undefeated reasons (see Raz 1990, p. 40).

The odd thing about this picture is that, if there is no duty not to harm, then the agent has the liberty to cause harm, for harming would be facultative.[27] She can decide to harm or not to harm, and the rational thing to do would be to choose the path that is supported by undefeated reasons. However, in the event the reasons to harm defeat all other countervailing reasons, the agent would not be truly free to pursue the harmful course of action because the duty of care drives her away from

---

[27] As Giovanni Ratti pointed out to me, the rejection thesis is ambiguous. It could be a normative proposition according to which the norm O~h (obligatory not to harm) is not a member of a particular legal system or, alternatively, it could be the formulation or issuance of the norm ~O~h (not obligatory not to harm). The first interpretation is compatible with the existence of a normative gap regarding not harming, so it would be weakly permitted not to harm. This is incompatible with membership in the same system of a prohibition not to harm and, since this thesis rejects the existence (viz. membership in the same system) of an obligation not to harm, we must conclude that harming is also weakly permitted. Because harming is permitted in the weak sense, and also not harming is so permitted, causing harm is not solved by the normative system at hand (it is, so to speak, optional in a weak sense). On the other hand, the second interpretation requires a more complex analysis. As I understand it, the rejection thesis on this interpretation is committed to the idea that it would be *wrong* to require the agent not to cause harm, not because there is no legal basis for this requirement, but because judges apply the implicit norm according to which it is not obligatory to refrain from causing harm (~O~h). This gives rise to some important consequences in standard deontic logic: an obligation not to harm (O~h) can be defined as permitted not to harm and not permitted to harm (P~h ∧ ~Ph). The negation of the obligation not to harm (~O~h) is equivalent to ~(P~h ∧ ~Ph). By distributing the negation according to De Morgan's laws, we obtain ~P~h ∨ Ph (not permitted not to harm or permitted to harm). Since ~P~h is equivalent to Oh (it is obligatory to cause harm), and this is absurd from the participant's point of view, we can negate ~P~h and conclude Ph. Moreover, we have said that Oh is rejected by the participants. Therefore, they assume the norm ~Oh (it is not obligatory to harm); now, with the conjunction of the norm that it is not obligatory to harm and the norm that it is not obligatory to refrain from causing harm (~Oh ∧ ~O~h), we can conclude that it is both permitted to harm and not to harm: Ph ∧ P~h. Again, to cause harm is optional or facultative in the legal system at hand. For the definition of the deontic operators I use in this argument, see Alchourrón and Bulygin (1971, pp. 37ff).

it: the duty of care requires that the agent take all reasonable precautions to prevent the harm. This shows that a system that does not include a duty not to harm among its norms conflicts with the duty to take reasonable precautions. The duty of care undermines the purported liberty to cause harm that the inexistence of a duty not to harm grants to all individuals. This might indicate that at least one of the reasons not to harm that was outweighed in the balance of reasons is reinforced by the duty of care, and this diminishes the guiding capacity of the purported *undefeated* reasons to harm. In sum, the guidance provided by the duty of care always prioritises safe courses of action, ones incompatible with harmful behaviour. In this way, the duty of care is fully coherent with the existence of a duty not to harm. All persons are under a duty to take precautions to avoid harming others *because* they have a duty not to harm them.

4 Final Remarks

The existence of a duty not to harm in tort law is a controversial issue in the literature. In this paper, I have tried to show that the arguments normally offered to reject that such a duty exists are not compelling. I have also presented four arguments to show that there is a duty not to harm in tort law systems that share some features. In particular, I focused on the rules that legal practitioners apply in their reasoning when they assess a state of affairs as ideal, non-ideal or defective. I tried to show that the role of criminal law in supporting private law's normative structure becomes puzzling if a duty not to harm is not assumed as part of tort law's rules. I suggested that the preventive aspect of tort law, and its vigorous expansion, is inexplicable. Finally, I argued that duties of care do not cohere with the absence of a duty not to harm. These four arguments are not claimed to be individually conclusive. However, when combined, they present an image of tort law much more familiar and transparent to the participants of the practice than the one that results from the rejection of a duty not to harm. In sum, the existence of the duty not to harm is established in the same way we know that some planet or star exists, even if we cannot see it, because of the way all the other spatial bodies move around it. The same happens with the duty not to harm. Its existence is shown by the way in which the practice operates around it.

References

Alchourrón C, Bulygin E (1971) Normative systems. Springer, New York
Austin J (1832) The province of jurisprudence determined. John Murray, London
Bertea S (2019) A theory of legal obligation. Cambridge University Press, Cambridge
Bueres A (1991) El daño injusto y la licitud e ilicitud de la conducta. In: Trigo Represas F, Stiglitz RS (eds) Derecho de daños. Primera Parte. Ediciones La Rocca, Buenos Aires

Calabresi G, Melamed AD (1972) Property rules, liability rules, and inalienability: one view of the cathedral. Harv Law Rev 85(6):1089–1128
Coleman JL (1992) Risks and wrongs. Oxford University Press, Oxford
Coleman JL (2001) The practice of principle. Oxford University Press, Oxford
Coleman JL (2011) The architecture of jurisprudence. Yale Law J 121(1):2–80. Cited by the Spanish translation in Ferrer Beltrán J, Moreso JJ, Papayannis DM (2012) Neutrality and legal theory. Marcial Pons, Madrid-Barcelona
Duff A (2007) Answering for crime: responsibility and liability in the criminal law. Hart Publishing, Oxford
García Amado JA (2011) Razones para una teoría normativista de la responsabilidad civil extracontractual. In: Aramburo Calle M (ed) Responsabilidad civil, derecho de seguros y filosofía del derecho – Estudios en homenaje a Javier Tamayo Jaramillo, vol 2. Biblioteca Jurídica Diké, Medellín, pp 1247–1279
Gardner J (2001) Obligations and outcomes in the law of torts. In: Cane P, Gardner J (eds) Relating to responsibility. Essays for Tony Honoré on his eightieth birthday. Hart Publishing, Oxford
Gardner J (2011) What is tort law for? Part I. The place of corrective justice. Law Philos 30(1):1–50
Gardner J (2018) From personal life to private law. Oxford University Press, Oxford
Gerhart P (2010) Tort law and social morality. Cambridge University Press, Cambridge
Goldberg JCP, Zipursky BC (2012) Rights and responsibility in the law of torts. In: Nolan D, Robertson A (eds) Rights and private law. Hart Publishing, Oxford, pp 251–274
Goldberg JCP, Zipursky BC (2020) Recognizing wrongs. Harvard University Press, Cambridge
Guastini R (2010) Nuovi studi sull'interpretazione. Aracne, Roma. Cited from Moreno Cruz D (trans) Nuevos estudios sobre la interpretación. Universidad Externado de Colombia, Bogotá
Hart HLA (1982a) Legal duty and obligation. In: Hart HLA (ed) Essays on Bentham. Studies in jurisprudence and political theory. Clarendon Press, Oxford
Hart HLA (1982b) Legal rights. In: Hart HLA (ed) Essays on Bentham. Studies in jurisprudence and political theory. Clarendon Press, Oxford
Hart HLA (1994) The concept of law, 2nd edn. Clarendon Press, Oxford
Himma K (2013) The ties that bind: an analysis of the concept of obligation. Ratio Juris 26(1):16–46
Landes W, Posner RA (1987) The economic structure of tort law. Harvard University Press, Cambridge
Llamas Pombo E (2008) Prevención y reparación, las dos caras del derecho de daños. En Moreno Martínez, JA (ed) La responsabilidad civil y su problemática actual. Dykinson, Madrid, pp. 445–478.
Lorenzetti RL (1995) La tutela civil inhibitoria. La Ley 1995-C:1217–1226
MacCormick N (1978) Legal reasoning and legal theory. The Clarendon Press, Oxford
MacCormick N (1982) The obligation of reparation. In: MacCormick N (ed) Legal right and social democracy. Essays in legal and political philosophy. Oxford University Press, Oxford, pp 212–231
MacCormick N (2008) H L A Hart, 2nd edn. Stanford University Press, Stanford
Martín Casals M (2011) La 'modernización' del derecho de la responsabilidad extracontractual. Cuestiones actuales en materia de responsabilidad civil. XV Jornadas de la Asociación de Profesores de Derecho Civil. Servicio de Publicaciones de la Universidad de Murcia, A Coruña, pp 11–111
Mosset Iturraspe J (1980) Estudios sobre responsabilidad por daños. Rubinzal-Culzoni, Santa Fe
Ogus A (2006) Costs and cautionary tales. Economic insights for the law. Hart Publishing, Oxford
Pantaleón F (1991) Comentario al art. 1902 del Código Civil. In Comentario del Código Civil, Vol II. Ministerio de Justicia, Madrid, pp 1971–2003
Pantaleón F (2000) Cómo repensar la responsabilidad civil extracontractual (también la de Administraciones públicas). Anuario de la Facultad de Derecho de la Universidad Autónoma de Madrid 4:167–191
Papayannis DM (2010) Daño injusto y compensación en la publicidad comparativa. Jurisprudencia Argentina 2010-II, issue 12:3–18

Papayannis DM (2024) Civil responsibility. In IVR Encyclopedia. The science of law and the social sciences (forthcoming)
Perry S (2009) The role of duty of care in a rights-based theory of negligence law. In: Robertson A, Wu TH (eds) The goals of private law. Hart Publishing, Oxford, pp 79–112
Raz J (1979) The authority of law. Essays on law and morality. Oxford University Press, Oxford
Raz J (1990) Practical reasons and norms. Oxford University Press, Oxford
Ripstein A (2016) Private wrongs. Harvard University Press, Cambridge
Salvador Coderch P (2000) Recensión a 'Derecho de daños', de Luis Díez-Picazo. InDret 1(2/2000):1–15
Shavell S (1987) Economic analysis of accident law. Harvard University Press, Cambridge
Smith SA (2019) Rights, wrongs, and injustices. The structure of remedial law. Oxford University Press, Oxford
Stevens R (2007) Torts and rights. Oxford University Press, Oxford
Vargas Tinoco A (2022) La prevención en la responsabilidad civil extracontractual. Función, estructura normativa y protección de los derechos. In Papayannis DM (coord) Manual de derecho de daños extracontractuales. Suprema Corte de Justicia de la Nación, México
Weinrib E (1995) The idea of private law. Harvard University Press, Cambridge
Weinrib E (2012) Corrective justice. Oxford University Press, Oxford
von Wright GH (1963) Norm and action: a logical enquiry. Routledge & Kegan Paul, London

Reflections on the Justifiability of Authority: Raz vs. Wolff

Noam Gur

1 Introduction

Authorities are ubiquitous in our social world. Whether instantiated in managers within occupational settings, executive officers in social organisations and associations, or public officials exercising legal powers, authorities are virtually everywhere, placing demands on us and directing our actions. However, surprising as it might be to those unfamiliar with political philosophy discourse, justifying this widespread social phenomenon is difficult or even, according to one respected school of political thought, impossible. This school, as readers of this volume may well know, is philosophical anarchism, whose most notable living protagonist is Robert Paul Wolff (1970, esp. pp. 3–19). Wolff's challenge to authority will be central to the discussion in this chapter, and a prominent attempt to meet Wolff's challenge, that made by Joseph Raz (2009, Chap. 1, esp. pp. 26–27), will be similarly pivotal.[1]

Preliminarily, let me situate my discussion in the context of this volume. Legal obligation, the focus of this volume, is widely thought to be bound up with the idea of authority. When regulators, judges, magistrates, and other relevant state officials generate legal obligations through their official pronouncements, they do so, it is commonly thought, in virtue of the fact that they exercise legal authority. For the moment I skirt around the exact relation between legal and *moral* obligations. But it is worth noting that the view that there is, or that there can be, a *moral* obligation to

[1] It is not my aim here to consider all the existing or possible responses to Wolff. Thus, for example, I will not consider another notable type of response, which denies the supposed correlativity between authority and a duty to obey. Along this line, see Ladenson (1980, pp. 134–159); Sartorius (1981, pp. 3–17); Reiman (1972, pp. xxv, 18, 23, 42–44). Cf. Edmundson (1998).

N. Gur (✉)
Queen Mary University of London, School of Law, London, UK
e-mail: n.gur@qmul.ac.uk

D. Beyleveld, S. Bertea (eds.), *Theories of Legal Obligation*, Law and Philosophy Library 146, https://doi.org/10.1007/978-3-031-54067-7_7

obey the law standardly presupposes the a priori possibility of (morally) *justified* authority,[2] or what is also sometimes referred to as (morally) *legitimate* authority.[3] From this perspective, if the law cannot have justified authority, it also cannot morally obligate us to perform or avoid a given action by means of its say-so.[4] This supposition will sometimes be referred to as 'the no-obligation-without-authority supposition'.[5] Now, since I mentioned the view that there is a moral obligation to obey the law, it is worth keeping in mind that this view has also come up against a posteriori challenges posed by multiple scholars.[6] Such challenges, however, will not be discussed here.[7] The question I will focus on is framed in a priori terms—namely, it is whether justified authority is an a priori possibility.

To forestall potential confusion, I should also add that, by the wording 'justified authority', I do not mean to convey that the content of any given directive is justified.[8] Instead, justified authority is an attribute attached to the *issuer* of the relevant directives (namely, the officials or institution involved, or the system to which they belong) and, if justified authority is attainable at all, it will be attained in virtue of some qualities of the issuer, or of the issuer's mode of constitution or appointment, or of the issuer's characteristic method of decision-making, or the like.[9]

Another comment should be made regarding what I have called the no-obligation-without-authority supposition. Is this supposition strictly tied to a specific view of the *directionality* of the said obligation, that is, to the view that the obligation is ultimately owed to the legal system (or, for that matter, to the state)? Not necessarily. While the no-obligation-without-authority supposition coheres with the above view of directionality, it seems to me to be also compatible with an alternative view of directionality according to which the obligation is ultimately owned to our fellow citizens (i.e., to members of the public on whose behalf the legal system, or the state, operates). This is because the crucial factor in this regard is not the directionality of the obligation, but the question (to put it informally) of 'who calls the shots'.

---

[2] I have added 'morally' to distinguish the authority referred to from authority justified in a sense that is merely-legal-but-not-moral (if there is such a sense).

[3] I have again added 'morally' to indicate that I am not referring to legitimacy in the sense of social perception. The relevant sense of legitimacy is grounded in actual qualities (e.g., substantive, procedural, or structural) of the directive-issuer.

[4] This, of course, does not deny that the content of some laws may (or may not) coincide with what we are anyway under a moral duty to do regardless of the law, which is the case, for example, when the law requires us to avoid mala in se conduct such as murder, theft, or physical assault.

[5] Recall that, notwithstanding this generic label, the reference here is to an obligation to obey the law, not to all obligations.

[6] On the distinction between a priori anarchism and a posteriori anarchism, see Simmons (2001, Chap. 6).

[7] I have expressed some of my thoughts in this regard in Gur (2013). The relevant literature is vast. For an overview, see, e.g., Edmundson (2004); Klosko (2019); Dagger and Lefkowitz (2021).

[8] Relatedly, see Gardner (2012, pp. 139–144), where he elucidates the difference between a claim to moral *authority* and a claim to moral *correctness* or to justice.

[9] Such qualities may have the *tendency* to result in substantively just legal requirements and/or may embody justice.

So long as the moral obligation to obey the law presumes that the entitlement to determine what actions we are obligated to perform or avoid is held by legal institutions or officials, it implicates the notion of justified legal authority, even if these institutions or officials act, not on behalf of themselves, but on the public's behalf, and even if, in some ultimate sense, our obligation is owed to the public.

Above I referred to the notions of a legal obligation and a moral obligation separately. But the relation between them is relevant for situating my question in its wider context. How exactly these two notions interrelate is a contentious matter.[10] For example, some legal philosophers maintain that legal obligations are a subset of moral obligations,[11] or that there is a focal sense of legality in which being under a legal obligation to φ implies being under a moral obligation to φ[12] (call these beliefs, jointly, 'the moral view of legal obligation'). Others, by contrast, regard legal obligation and moral obligation as distinct species (of the same genus) matched with different criteria for determining what acts are obligatory.[13] They believe that being legally obligated to φ does not entail being morally obligated to φ (call this the 'the non-moral view of legal obligation'). Those holding the moral view of legal obligation are likely to regard the justifiability of authority as a precondition for legal obligation. For they are likely to derive this relation directly from the notion that the *moral* obligation to obey the law hinges on the justifiability of authority. But even from the perspective of the non-moral view of legal obligation, the justifiability of authority seems to have important bearings on the notion of legal obligation. I will mention one possible bearing. Suppose that it is part of the concept of law that every legal system necessarily *claims* to have justified authority.[14] If so, there is a conceptual sense in which legal obligations depend on the fact that the relevant system claims justified authority.[15] From such a perspective, it is pertinent to consider whether authority is a priori justifiable because if the answer is 'No' that would (inter alia) place the notion of a legal obligation under significant strain. To wit, a negative answer would imply that legal obligations depend on the systemic assertion of something that is not only false but is also an a priori impossibility.

So much for preliminaries. My analysis will proceed as follow. In Sect. 2, a short exposition of Wolff's argument will be provided. I will then turn to the Razian response, which is centred on his 'service conception of authority' (often referred to

[10] For relevant discussion, see, e.g., Hart (1982, Chap. VI); Köpcke Tinturé (2013); Pavlakos (2015); Wodak (2018); Bertea (2019); Monti (2022).

[11] Greenberg (2014).

[12] This view is inferable, e.g., from Finnis (2011, pp. 14–15 and 314–320). Cf. Lon Fuller's comments on the relation between his eight principles of legal form and what he calls the 'obligation of fidelity to law' or the 'duty to observe the rules' (Fuller 1969, pp. 39–41).

[13] H.L.A. Hart can be read as a proponent of this view (see Hart 1982, pp. 127–128).

[14] The view that law, wherever it may be found, makes such a claim is most notably associated with Joseph Raz (2009, p. 30; 1995, p. 215). However, by drawing on this view, I do not mean to impute to Raz what I am calling the non-moral view of legal obligation.

[15] And, according to this line of thought, whenever the system asserts a legal obligation it (impliedly) reasserts its claim to justified authority.

here as 'the service conception' or 'Raz's service conception'). I will start with a brief description of this response (Sect. 3), will proceed to consider the implications of Raz's service conception for the relation between authority and autonomy (Sect. 4), and will finally point out certain problems or uncertainties concerning the service conception (Sect. 5).

2 Wolff's Anarchist Argument: A Brief Exposition

I will provide a brief outline, rather than a full description, of Wolff's argument against authority. First, clarity will be served by highlighting a distinction, mentioned by Wolff (1970, p. 5), between two types of statement in which the term 'authority' can feature. Although authority is a normative concept, normative concepts can feature in statements that are merely descriptive. Thus, for example, we sometimes descriptively report that a person or body ('A') is *acknowledged* to have authority by a group of people over whom A asserts authority. Such statements convey that A has what Wolff refers to as *de facto* authority (ibid.). In other statements, reference to authority is made with an evaluative or prescriptive signification, as, for example, when one asserts that (or invites us to consider whether) ascription of authority to A is morally warranted, or that A ought to be treated as an authority, or the like. To avoid ambiguity, in evaluative or prescriptive statements about authority, Wolff sometimes uses the term *de jure* or *legitimate* authority (1970, pp. 5 and 9),[16] and I will do the same. Wolff readily accepts the descriptive observation that people often accede to what they consider to be an authority (ibid., p. 8). What he questions, and ultimately denies, is the possibility of justifying authority, namely the assumption that there can be legitimate authority.

Wolff's objection to authority can be distilled into a three-step argument. This three-step structure is not so much a structure adhered to by Wolff as my own way of arranging the argument for the purpose of my exposition.

The first step is a conceptual observation regarding authority. Authority, Wolff points out, is distinguishable from the mere ability to compel compliance through the use or threat of coercive force (ibid., p. 4). Authority is a normative concept; those who have it (if anyone does) possess a certain right by virtue of having it. A right to what? According to Wolff, a right to *command*, which implies a right of the person or body that issues the command ('A') to be *obeyed*,[17] and an obligation of some other persons to *obey* A (ibid., pp. 4 and 9).

---

[16] In Sect. 1 above, I used the phrase 'justified authority' with the same meaning.

[17] The reader may notice that Wolff argues here in terms consonant with one of the two alternative views of directionality that I mentioned in Sect. 1 above. But this does not change the point, made in Sect. 1, that the no-obligation-without-authority supposition is compatible with an alternative view of directionality. Moreover, I believe Wolff's argument could be retained with a limited adaptation to the alternative view of directionality.

In the second step, the meaning of obedience is clarified. To obey is not simply to do what someone tells us to do. Rather, it is to do what someone tells us to do *because he or she tells us to do it* (ibid., p. 9). So, if John Doe performs an action required by the law because he judges it to be a right or desirable action on its merits, and not because it is legally required[18]—say, he offers his employees an insurance scheme consistent with the Affordable Care Act (ACA)'s requirements[19] because he believes that the ACA reflects a sensible and desirable policy—he is not, strictly speaking, *obeying* the legal requirement (ibid., p. 5).[20] The better way of describing what John is doing in this instance (and the following is my own paraphrasing, not Wolff's terminology) is to say that he is *conforming to* the requirement.[21]

In the third step, moral autonomy comes to the fore. Wolff argues that subjecting oneself to the will of another in the way described above—namely, acting simply because another person has 'said so'—contravenes a fundamental principle incumbent on us as moral agents: the principle of moral autonomy. There are some basic attributes that are requisite for the exercise of autonomy, such as a basic capacity to choose and to reason (ibid., pp. 12–13). But when such attributes are present, autonomy is not merely a condition available to the agent, but also, in an important sense, a duty. Drawing on Kantian ethics,[22] Wolff explains this notion and highlights its foundational status. 'The fundamental assumption of moral philosophy', he notes, 'is that men are responsible for their actions' (ibid., p. 12). People sometimes refuse to engage in moral deliberation, but by so doing they cannot simply give up or divest themselves from the ultimate responsibility for their actions (ibid., p. 14). Indeed, it is incumbent on them to take responsibility by acting to the greatest extent possible through the exercise of their judgement on the moral merits of what they do (ibid., pp. 15 and 17). As Wolff puts it, '[t]he moral condition demands that we acknowledge responsibility and achieve autonomy wherever and whenever possible' (ibid., p. 17).[23]

What emerges from these three steps is that the notion of legitimate authority prescribes a mode of action incompatible with moral autonomy.[24] Now, for Wolff, autonomy is not a value on a par with other 'substantive' moral values or goods. It is, in a sense, prior to, and more foundational than, other values or goods. Since the

[18] Or simply and only to escape punishment.

[19] In its full name, the Patient Protection and Affordable Care Act.

[20] In similar vein, Wolff notes that '[a]uthority resides in persons; they possess it – if indeed they do at all – by virtue of who they are and not by virtue of what they command' (Wolff 1970, p. 6); and that '[a]n authoritative command must also be distinguished from a persuasive argument' (ibid.). Cf. Regan (1990); Sevel (2018). See also Shapiro (2002, pp. 382–391).

[21] Wolff (1970, p. 18) uses the term 'complying' in the same sense.

[22] See further Wolff (1973).

[23] Against this, see Reiman (1972). Cf. Smith (2013) who advances, as an alternative to Wolff's autonomy-centred argument, the claim that 'if there were an obligation to obey the law, such an obligation would uniquely threaten *the moral status of the subject's self*' (ibid., p. 348, emphasis added).

[24] For further analysis of this conflict see, e.g., Iosa (2014).

capacity for autonomous action is constitutive of moral agency, it provides the very link between a human actor and the realm of morality and moral responsibility. [25] If the capacity for autonomous action and the duty to exercise moral autonomy hold the foundational status just pointed out, it becomes easier to appreciate why Wolff is not willing to place them on a single plane in a trade-off relationship with other 'substantive' values or goods. This stance leads Wolff to conclude that moral autonomy should prevail over authority; and (because, as noted above, he considers the conflict between them to be inevitable) that there is no such thing as legitimate authority (ibid., p. 72). With specific reference to state authority, Wolff remarks:

> If all men have a continuing obligation to achieve the highest degree of autonomy possible, then there would appear to be no state whose subjects have a moral obligation to obey. (Ibid., p. 19)

Moreover, because he holds that authority is a defining mark of the state, he concludes that 'the concept of a *de jure* legitimate state would appear to be vacuous' (ibid.).

Three clarifications are worth making regarding Wolff's argument.

(1) Wolff does not level his criticism against an act of compliance performed out of fear of suffering a sanction.[26] The mode of action he rejects is, once more, submission to a requirement on account of the very fact that it emanates from an authoritative source.
(2) He acknowledges that we cannot realistically hope to be fully autonomous all of the time (ibid., pp. 16–17). There is too much information—including information that cannot be easily grasped without technical expertise—which we would have to master if we were to decide everything entirely on our own, and there is not enough time. So, it is inevitable that we sometimes act on what other people with relevant knowledge prescribe. This is allowed for, to a certain extent, by Wolff's conception of the duty of autonomy, in that the duty he envisions is, as said above, a duty to be autonomous *to the greatest extent possible*.
(3) One exception that Wolff makes to his claim concerns a *unanimous direct democracy*. This method of collective decision-making, he accepts, can in theory have a morally legitimate binding force. Thus, if everyone agrees to the passage of a law, he suggests, there is no loss of autonomy if a participant is later required to conform to it despite his/her contrary inclinations at that point in time. However, given the rarity of consensus on political matters, Wolff notes that the conditions for reaching valid decisions through this method are 'impossibly restrictive conditions which make it applicable only to a rather bizarre variety of actual situations' (ibid., pp. 22–23). This method, he adds, is so

[25] It forms, if you like, a gateway to the moral realm. Thus, for example, it is part of what distinguishes human agents, as bearers of moral responsibility, from, say, an automaton, internet bot, or the like, which, even if capable of bringing about harm, would not be treated as a bearer of moral responsibility.

[26] Which is, I take it, what he means when referring to compliance done 'for reasons of prudence' (Wolff 1970, p. 9).

limited in its application that 'it offers no serious hope of ever being embodied in an actual state' (ibid., p. 69). Indeed, since unanimous direct democracy could attain its success only by ruling out the very disagreements that politics is designed to resolve, 'it may be viewed as the limiting case of a solution rather than as itself a true example of a legitimate state' (ibid.).

3 The Razian Response: A Brief Exposition

Raz, in a sense, accepts Wolff's assumption that individuals with the capacity for autonomous action should never simply abdicate their autonomy. Expressing this in a characteristic Razian terminology—namely, that of 'practical reason'—we may say that agents should always act on the basis of their judgement about the reasons that apply to them (Raz 2009, p. 27; 1990, p. 40).[27] But Raz seeks to reconcile this principle with the notion of obedience to authority. How? He does so through a set of claims known as 'the service conception of authority'.

Authorities, according to this conception, are meant to serve the governed and to do so in a particular way, namely by guiding the governed to better conform to reasons for action that apply to them. Raz correspondingly tailors his definition of the key condition for qualifying as a morally legitimate authority. The key condition, encapsulated in a thesis known as *the normal justification thesis* (hereafter: 'the NJT'), is that for an ostensible authority ('A') to gain legitimate authority over a person ('P'), it must be the case that P would be more likely to conform to reasons that apply to him/her (hereafter: 'background reasons') by following A's directives than by trying to follow those reasons directly (Raz 1986, p. 53).[28] For this to be the case, A must be in possession of certain attributes that render A's decisions likelier than P's to successfully track relevant reasons for action. Institutions or individuals who claim authority but lack those attributes (and this, in Raz's view, is by no means a rare occurrence) have no legitimate authority; namely, their directives should *not* be treated as having an authoritative normative force. But when P is faced with an A that recognisably meets the NJT condition, the normative inference is different. Because A's directives are likely to track background reasons better than P's independent judgement on those reasons, it becomes warranted (from a perspective of practical reason) for P to follow A's directives, rather than to rely on his/her own (less reliable) judgement on the background reasons.

The latter notion is more formally encapsulated by Raz in a thesis entitled *the pre-emption thesis*, which reads as follows:

---

[27] See also Hurd (1991, p. 1613).

[28] The wording 'reasons that apply to him/her' in my above formulation is intended to mean reasons other than the very fact that A has issued a directive (a fact that, according to Raz, would itself be a reason if A is a legitimate authority).

> [T]he fact that an authority [i.e., a *legitimate* authority; normally, one that has met, inter alia, the NJT condition – N.G.] requires performance of an action is a reason for its performance which is not to be added to all other relevant reasons when assessing what to do, but should exclude and take the place of some of them. (Raz 1986, p. 46)

Raz calls the authority-given reason described in this passage a *pre-emptive reason* (ibid., p. 42).[29] A 'pre-emptive reason', according to him, is a combination of two reasons: (1) a reason for action (i.e., for performing the authority-required act); and (2) a reason that excludes some other reasons. The second of these two types Raz calls an *exclusionary reason* (Raz 1990, p. 39), which he more specifically defines as a reason to refrain from acting for certain other reasons (ibid.). He characterises exclusionary reasons as reasons that belong to a second order of reasons (ibid). They are second-order reasons because their primary and direct object is not our actions, but some other reasons that, in turn, bear on our actions (first-order reasons, in Razian terminology).[30] Now, the idea of pre-emptive reasons in Raz's service conception explains how agents can follow a legitimate authority, rather than their ordinary (first-order) reasons for action, without abdicating their responsibility to act upon reasons. They are acting on reasons, just reasons of a special type: pre-emptive reasons.

For illustration, consider the following scenario. Nick lives in the countryside, in a house adjacent to a large national park. When driving to work and certain other destinations, Nick could use a dirt trail that goes through the national park, instead of the road encircling the park. This is a shortcut that would save Nick a fair amount of time, which is a reason to do so. There are also some reasons against doing so, such as the fact that it would disturb, or might even put at risk, hikers, joggers, and other park users, and that it could also affect wildlife inhabiting the park. Overall, Nick thinks that, given his house location, the benefit of him using the dirt trail in terms of time saving, etc., outweighs the limited expected negative effect of his doing so. But now suppose that the relevant National Park Authority has issued a by-law that prohibits driving on dirt trails in the park. Nick believes that the National Park Authority is better placed than he is to weigh correctly relevant reasons on such matters because it has more information and expertise and a better overview of the broader range of policy considerations involved, and because it is likely to be more impartial than he is. From this, he concludes that he should follow the National Park Authority's requirements on such matters and refrain from trying to act directly on background reasons, or at least on background reasons against the prescribed conduct, such as the time-saving consideration in this example. In other words, Nick regards the fact that the National Park Authority has issued the above by-law as a

[29] In some places Raz uses the term 'protected reason' for the same idea (e.g., Raz 2009, p. 18; 1990, p. 191). I will use the term 'pre-emptive reason' throughout.

[30] Exclusionary reasons do not operate at the normative level of ordinary reasons and do not compete with them in weight. Rather, in the case of a conflict between an exclusionary reason and an ordinary reason that falls within the exclusionary reason's scope of application, the exclusionary reason prevails regardless of the ordinary reason's weight (Raz 1990, pp. 36, 40, 189, and 190; 2009, pp. 22–23).

(first-order) reason not to drive on the dirt trail and a (second-order) reason that excludes from the balance the time-saving reason to drive on the dirt trail. This twofold reason, to reiterate, is what Raz calls a pre-emptive reason.

Importantly, Raz stresses that an agent who treats an authority in the way just described is not engaged in *blind* obedience:

> No blind obedience to authority is here implied. Acceptance of authority has to be justified, and this normally means meeting the conditions set in the justification thesis. This brings into play the dependent reasons, for only if the authority's compliance with them is likely to be better than that of its subjects is its claim to legitimacy justified. (Raz 1995, p. 215)

Thus, an agent such as Nick in the above example recognises that, since the authority is better placed to decide on the matter, his best and most rational course of action is to entrust the authority with the decision. The agent's belief that he should accede to the authority, then, is based on a *reasoned* inference. Thus, in contrast to Wolff, Raz maintains that it does not involve an unwarranted abdication of autonomy. Does Raz think that the agent's autonomy has been compromised *at all*? From at least some of his comments, one can infer a negative answer, as he can be understood to imply that autonomy and authority are in fact entirely compatible with one another. For example, he remarks:

> [Wolff] tacitly and correctly assumes that reason never justifies abandoning one's autonomy, that is, one's right and duty to act on one's judgment of what ought to be done, *all things considered*. I shall call this the principle of autonomy.
>
> He also tacitly and wrongly assumes that this is identical with the false principle that there are no valid exclusionary reasons, that is, that one is never justified in not doing what ought to be done on the balance of first-order reasons. I shall call this the denial of authority.
>
> This confusion is natural if one conceives of all reasons as essentially first-order reasons and overlooks the possibility of the existence of second-order reasons. If all valid reasons are first-order reasons then it is a necessary truth that the principle of autonomy entails the denial of authority, for then what ought to be done all things considered is identical with what ought to be done on the balance of first-order reasons. But since there could in principle be valid second-order reasons, *there is nothing in the principle of autonomy that requires the rejection of all authority*. (Raz 2009, p. 27, emphasis added)[31]

Thus, since Raz envisions a two-tier hierarchy of reasons, he is able to say that when an agent refrains from acting on a first-order reason that has been excluded by a second-order reason (but allows for all other relevant reasons), the agent has fully fulfilled his/her duty to act on his/her judgement *all things considered*, which is what Raz calls the principle of autonomy. This leads Raz to say that *there is nothing* in the principle of autonomy that requires the rejection of all authority—which, read in context, implies that the principle of autonomy is entirely compatible with what Raz defines as legitimate authority.

---

[31] Elsewhere he makes the following comment, which seems to point in a similar direction: '[T]he primary value of our general ability to act by our own judgment derives from the concern to conform to reasons, and that concern can be met in a variety of ways' (Raz 2006, p. 1017). This 'variety of ways', as I understand Raz, includes compliance with authority.

4 What Implications Follow from the Service Conception for the Relation Between Authority and Autonomy?

Turning to an appraisal of Raz's response, the first question worth considering is the following. Assuming all else in Raz's account is correct, does his response really show that authority and autonomy are perfectly compatible, that there is no tension between them? Or does his account actually substantiate a somewhat different and more qualified conclusion? Without doubting the significance of Raz's arguments, it appears to me that they do not go as far as showing complete compatibility between the two. This may be easier to appreciate when one bears in mind that autonomy itself is not a monolithic notion, but rather one that consists of different dimensions that may be in tension with one another. Along these lines, it seems helpful to distinguish between two different dimensions of autonomy: the first dimension consists in exercising one's judgement on the merits of one's action here and now, whereas the second dimension concerns a forward-looking choice as to what mode of deliberation (or, if you like, decision-making strategy) one should adopt in order to optimise one's performance over the long run. For ease of reference, we might call the first dimension 'action-specific exercises of autonomy' and the second dimension 'choice-of-deliberation-mode exercises of autonomy'. Against this background, the upshot of Raz's arguments seems to be appropriately interpretable as follows. While Raz may have shown that deference to legitimate authority is compatible with the second dimension, it remains the case that deference to legitimate authority compromises the first dimension of our autonomy. This accommodation, if Raz's service conception is correct, is reasonable and justified, but it remains a compromise nonetheless.

A possible way of pushing back against my above claim is the following. There is, in fact, correspondence between, on the one hand, the two dimensions of autonomy I described above, and, on the other hand, the two orders of reasons identified by Raz. In other words, what I labelled *action-specific exercises of autonomy* corresponds with what Raz calls the balance of first-order reasons for action, whereas what I labelled *choice-of-deliberation-mode exercises of autonomy* can be associated with Razian second-order reasons. And precisely because second-order reasons have a superior standing in relation to first-order reasons, acting on a second-order reason does not diminish one's autonomy even if it means refraining from acting on a first-order reason. To do so is simply to be responsive to the hierarchy between reasons. It is to act for the higher of two reasons, which is exactly what reason (all things considered) requires us to do, and which is therefore fully consistent with an autonomous exercise of judgement.

However, I do not find this latter rejoinder particularly persuasive. For one thing, it should be borne in mind that second-order exclusionary reasons do not simply *eliminate* the reasons they exclude. As Raz puts it: 'Exclusionary reasons are reasons for not acting for certain valid reasons. They do not nullify or cancel those reasons' (1990, p. 184); and elsewhere: '[T]he reasons which are to disregard are not canceled' (1989, p. 1158).[32] Since the excluded first-order reasons remain valid, they also retain at least some sort of normative significance. What is more, it seems sensible to say that if an agent can act correctly on the balance of first-order reasons without needing the guidance of authority, this is normatively preferable to an (otherwise identical) situation in which the agent can only conform to the balance of first-order reasons through the mediation of, and reliance on, authoritative directives. In light of this, to say that submission to a legitimate authority involves a justified trade-off between different aspects of our autonomy seems more intuitively plausible than to say that it does not involve a compromise of our autonomy at all.

5 The Service Conception: Two Problems and an Open Question

In the previous section I considered the implication of Raz's service conception for the relation between authority and autonomy. I will now focus on the service conception itself. I will make three main points. The first highlights what I consider to be an unresolved issue arising from the dispute between Raz and Wolff, whereas the second and third points are what I consider to be weaknesses in the service conception.

5.1 *Positive Second-Order Reasons and the Case for Authority*

Raz defines a second-order reason as any reason to act for a reason or to refrain from acting for a reason (Raz 1990, p. 39). Enfolded in this definition are two subcategories: (1) a reason to act for a reason, which is what Raz calls a *positive second-order reason* (ibid., p. 189); and (2) a reason to refrain from acting for a reason, which is what Raz calls an *exclusionary reason* or a *negative second-order reason* (ibid., p. 17). Upon introducing the idea of second-order reasons in his *Practical Reason and Norms*, Raz states: 'Exclusionary reasons are the only type of second-order reasons with which we will be concerned here' (ibid., p. 40). Thus, not much is said about the notion of a positive second-order reason in the rest of the book. He does, however, clarify that when two second-order reasons conflict with one another, the resolution of this conflict will turn on the relative weight of these competing second-order reasons (ibid., p. 40). One inference that can be drawn from this is that authority-given exclusionary reasons can be defeated by positive second-order reasons (namely, by reasons to act for first-order background reasons). This ramification is not discussed by Raz, at least not explicitly and directly. But it could have significant implications for his account.

[32] See further Raz (1989, pp. 1156–1164).

How significant? This depends, in part, on whether conflicts between exclusionary reasons and positive second-order reasons are merely occasional or a prevalent phenomenon. And this, in turn, depends on how general, and widely applicable, positive second-order reasons are. One moral notion that can arguably be seen as a general positive second-order reason is moral autonomy itself. In other words, moral autonomy, as Wolff understands it, can be seen as a reason for the agent to act directly on (i.e., by recourse to his/her assessment of) the content-based reasons that bear on the merits of his/her action (rather than obeying authoritative directives).[33] When commenting on Wolff's argument, Raz (2009, p. 27) describes autonomy as 'one's right and duty to act on one's judgment of what ought to be done, *all things considered*'. But it is pertinent to note here that Wolff seems to accord specific and independent moral significance to the exercise of judgement by the agent on the (content-based) merits of his/her action, i.e., on what Raz calls first-order reasons and I sometimes refer to as background reasons. Hence the above suggestion that the moral significance, or value, consisting in this aspect of autonomy might be conceived of as a positive second-order reason.

As far as I am aware, there is no explicit mention of the above possibility in Raz's texts. However, some comments of his can be read as an implicit reference to it, or at least seem relevant to it. I have in mind, *inter alia,* the following comments. Immediately after Raz notes that the NJT accounts for the (normal) 'reasons there can be *for* accepting authorities' (Raz 1986, p. 56, emphasis added), he remarks:

> But a complete justification of authority has to do more than to provide valid reasons *for* its acceptance. It has also to establish that there are no reasons *against* its acceptance which defeat the reasons for the authority. Because the reasons against the acceptance of authority vary it is not possible to discover in advance how strong the reasons for acceptance of the authority need be to be sufficient.
>
> Some reasons against the acceptance of authority pertain, with varying force, to many situations. (Raz 1986, pp. 56–57)

He adds:

> The case for the validity of a claim to authority must include justificatory considerations sufficient to outweigh such counter-reasons. That is one reason why the case is hard to make. But if anarchists are right to think that it can never be made, this is for contingent reasons and not because of any inconsistency in the notion of a rational justification for authority, nor in the notion of authority over moral agents. (Ibid., p. 57)

In this connection Raz cites two examples of 'recurring' reasons against the acceptance of authority. The first example is not material to the present discussion.[34] The second example is described as follows.

---

[33] Cf. Edmundson's comment that '[a] reason to do one's duty for duty's sake exemplifies a positive second-order reason' (Edmundson 1993, p. 329).

[34] 'One recurring kind of reason against accepting the authority of one person or institution is that there is another person or institution with a better claim to be recognized as an authority' (Raz 1986, p. 57).

> Another cluster of recurring considerations concerns the intrinsic desirability of people conducting their own life by their own lights. This obviously applies to some areas of life more than to others, to choice of friends more than to the choice of legal argument in a court case. (Ibid.)

Such considerations are elsewhere encapsulated in one of the conditions for legitimate authority under Raz's service conception—namely, what Raz calls 'the independence condition'—which requires that the regulated matter be one regarding which it is more important to act in conformity with reason than to decide for oneself what to do (Raz 2006, p. 1014).

I wish to make two points regarding Raz's above quoted remarks. First, the intrinsic moral value of autonomously exercising our judgement on the first-order reasons is seen quite differently by Raz and by Wolff. While Wolff regards it as generally overriding, Raz accords to it a context-sensitive variable significance that is amenable to being outweighed by the desideratum of attaining greater conformity with reasons. On the face of it, Raz's view on this matter seems to accord more readily with the realities of our moral lives and practical reasoning, and particularly with the extent to which these realities generate and involve practices such as reliance on experts and recourse to technological means that substitute aspects of our autonomous operation.[35] It also offers a framework better geared to avoid some unpalatable spectres—such as widespread social disorder, rampant mutually harmful behaviour, or the like—which are arguably liable to occur if everyone were to decide for themselves on all or nearly all matters.[36]

Secondly, as quoted above, Raz points out that since the reasons against the acceptance of authority are variable, the requisite strength of reasons for acceptance of the authority is not discoverable in advance. This suggests that an agent over whom authority is claimed should make (with a degree of frequency that I am not entirely certain about) weight comparisons of these two sets of reasons. How particularistic are these comparative weight assessments? To what extent do they require recourse to (and identification of) the relevant first-order reasons, and what type of recourse? Relevant inferences can be made from various comments of Raz (see, e.g., 2006, pp. 1014–1018), but one would have welcomed more direct answers, including an explanation of their compatibility with the exclusionary character he ascribes to authority-given reasons. (Note that the weight comparisons just mentioned are distinct from assessments of whether the NJT is satisfied—assessments which Raz discusses at a greater length, and which I have analysed elsewhere [Gur 2018, pp. 31–42]).

---

[35] My above statement takes into account Wolff's qualification that our duty is to be autonomous *to the greatest extent possible*. This feasibility rider seems less readily able to accommodate the aforementioned practices (i.e., their extent, role, etc.) in comparison with Raz's context-sensitive variable evaluation of the intrinsic significance of autonomy.

[36] See related discussion in Gur (2018, Chap. 6).

5.2 The Challenge from Justified Disobedience Situations

The second issue I wish to highlight has featured in a previous work of mine, namely *Legal Directives and Practical Reasons* (ibid.). In Chapters 2–4 of this book, I claimed that the *modus operandi* of pre-emptive reasons, with their exclusionary character, involves too strong a type of bindingness by authority, such that it fails to adequately accommodate some situations where (notwithstanding the authority's compliance with Raz's conditions of authority) it is justified to disobey in order to avoid a directive-specific or situation-specific serious and manifest immorality. Below is a thumbnail sketch of the main considerations underpinning this claim.

(1) The fallibility of even competent and informed authorities[37] means that even such authorities may, on occasion, direct their subjects to morally wrong actions. Moreover, the generality of rules means that even good rules may, under certain contingencies, point their subjects to morally objectionable actions.
(2) In some of these cases, the gravity and the manifest nature of the immorality involved will be such that, as moral agents, we should refuse to go along with it—such that it must compel disobedience.
(3) Such cases do not lend themselves to exhaustive specification in advance through detailed descriptions of all the circumstances in which they arise.
(4) The pre-emption thesis can go some distance towards accommodating those cases of justified disobedience, through an attempt to mark them out, either as emanations of illegitimate authority or as situations where disobedience is justified by first-order reasons outside the scope of exclusionary reasons. But this attempt, I have argued, falls short of the mark (Gur 2018, Chaps. 3–4). For no criterion of legitimate authority or of the exclusionary scope can demarcate and screen out *all instances* of those justified disobedience cases—except for criteria that involve weight comparison of the first-order reasons for and against compliance. But the latter criteria are ineligible for purposes of defending exclusionary reasons because the whole point of exclusionary reasons is their ability to defeat first-order reasons regardless of their weight. In other words, the above demarcation task faces the following predicament. Either it invokes some specifically and sharply defined criteria that can be applied without weighing of first-order reasons, but that have limited elasticity and reach—and, thus, cannot screen out all instances of justified disobedience. Or it invokes open-ended and elastic demarcation criteria that can perhaps reach, and screen out, all instances of justified disobedience, but whose application depends on weight comparison of the first-order reasons—what, once again, renders such criteria ineligible for the pre-emption thesis defender on pain of inconsistency.

[37] Including those whose comparative competence and information render them generally apt to direct the relevant subjects to better conform to reasons in the domain in question.

I have expounded and demonstrated these arguments at length in the above-cited book and will therefore refrain from doing so here. If I was right, the problem revealed by these arguments should hold us back from accepting the notion of authority-given pre-emptive or exclusionary reasons.

5.3 *Does the NJT Contain a False Dichotomy?*

Finally, I will highlight what I consider to be a deficiency in the NJT. I described the NJT in Sect. 3, and for convenience I now quote it.

> [T]he normal and primary way to establish that a person should be acknowledged to have authority over another person involves showing that the alleged subject is likely better to comply with reasons which apply to him (other than the alleged authoritative directives) if he accepts the directives of the alleged authority as authoritatively binding and tries to follow them, rather than by trying to follow the reasons which apply to him directly. (Raz 1995, p. 214)

As can be seen from this quote, the legitimacy condition stated in the NJT is a *binary* condition. It is binary in the sense that it refers to two alternative modes of reasoning: (1) the agent 'accepts the directives of the alleged authority as authoritatively binding and tries to follow them' (an alternative which, by Raz's understanding, means acceptance of the directives as pre-emptive reasons); or (2) the agent tries 'to follow the reasons which apply to him directly' (a mode of reasoning consistent with what I have elsewhere [Gur 2018, pp. 14–17 and 73–74] referred to as 'the weighing model'). The normal and primary way to establish (legitimate) authority, according to the thesis, is to show that the person over whom authority is supposed to be exercised is likely better to conform with reasons that apply to him/her by recourse to alternative 1 than by recourse to alternative 2.

However, I suggest that the binary character of the NJT condition is unwarranted, as it is predicated on an erroneous dichotomy. There are other possible modalities apart from action on the balance of first-order reasons (alternative 1 above) and action on pre-emptive reasons (alternative 2 above).[38] In the aforementioned book, I highlighted one such possibility, which I called the dispositional model (Gur 2018, pp. 135–219).[39] It consists in a relatively stable, but overridable, law-abiding disposition—so that an agent with such a disposition shows a commitment to law-abidance that is, on the one hand, more steadfast than that of an agent who merely

[38] This argument chimes with a point made by Shapiro (2002, p. 409) (though he understands Raz's second alternative as involving a subject who 'completely ignores' an authoritative directive and 'deliberates in its absence' [ibid.], whereas Raz may mean here a more inclusive weighing process that takes account of reasons for action that the directive brings into play). To a similar effect, see Durning (2003, pp. 606–607).

[39] It has been suggested that the dispositional model is reconcilable with the pre-emption thesis and with the weighing model. I will reply to these suggestions elsewhere and will explain why I disagree with them.

follows the balance of reasons for and against acting as the law requires, but is, on the other hand, less conclusive than that of an agent who lets authoritative laws pre-empt his/her judgement within their scope of application. This is not to suggest that the dispositional model is the only other possibility. There are additional possibilities.[40] My purpose at this point is not to offer an exhaustive list thereof, but merely to draw attention to what I consider to be a problem in the NJT.

6 Conclusion

Raz's service conception of authority yields an attractive response to Wolff's philosophical anarchism—one that engages with Wolff's on his own, autonomy-centred, terms. In this chapter, however, I sought to highlight not only the appealing features of this Razian response, but also some of its limitations and vulnerabilities.

Following an exposition of Wolff's argument and the Razian response, I considered what implications follow from Raz's service conception for the relation between authority and moral autonomy. I argued that, even if correct, the service conception does not fully harmonise the notions of authority and moral autonomy. Instead, I suggested, the normative resolution reflected in the service conception is best seen as a trade-off in which one aspect of our autonomy (i.e. that which consists in exercising our judgement on the merits of our action here and now) is compromised by another aspect of our autonomy (i.e. that which consists in a forward-looking selection of a decision-making strategy designed to optimise one's performance over the long haul). If the service conception is correct, this compromise is justified, but it is a compromise nonetheless, not a complete congruence between authority and moral autonomy.

I then offered three main observations regarding the service conception itself. First, I highlighted the (barely discussed) possibility of positive second-order reasons that conflict with authority-given exclusionary reasons. This issue, I suggested, has not received the amount of attention it deserves in Raz's writings, considering that several connected questions may have implications for Raz's central claims—for example, the questions of what ambit those positive second-order reasons have, how particularistic the assessments of their comparative weight need be, whether such assessments require recourse to (and the identification of) relevant first-order reasons, and, if so, what type of recourse. Secondly, I pointed out what I consider to be a crucial deficiency of Raz's pre-emption thesis: there are cases of justified disobedience that the thesis, I suggested, is unable to adequately account for. Having discussed this claim elsewhere at length, I only briefly sketched out here the line of

[40] For example, Frederick Schauer's notion of presumptive normative force exercised by rules (Schauer 1991a, pp. 196–206; 1991b, pp. 674–677) and Stephen Perry's notions of reweighing reasons and epistemically-bounded reasons (Perry 1989, pp. 933–945). On these notions, see Gur (2018, pp. 193–197 in the body text and footnotes).

reasoning underpinning it. Thirdly and finally, I claimed that the condition encapsulated in the NJT refers to an incomplete set of alternatives. That is, while the thesis contains a binary comparison between two alternative modes of practical reasoning, the spectrum of alternative modes of practical reasoning that can be used in response to authority-issued directives is richer. Thus, the justificatory inference associated with the NJT can only be validly derived from a more inclusive condition that compares additional modes of practical reasoning.

References

Bertea S (2019) A theory of legal obligation. Cambridge University Press, Cambridge
Dagger R, Lefkowitz D (2021) Political obligation. In: Zalta EN (ed) The Stanford encyclopedia of philosophy. https://plato.stanford.edu/entries/political-obligation/
Durning P (2003) Joseph Raz and the instrumental justification of a duty to obey the law. Law & Philos 22:597–620
Edmundson WA (1993) Rethinking exclusionary reasons: a second edition of Joseph Raz's Practical Reason and Norms. Law & Philos 12:329–343
Edmundson WA (1998) Three anarchical fallacies: an essay on political authority. Cambridge University Press, Cambridge
Edmundson WA (2004) State of the art: the duty to obey the law. Leg Theory 10:215–259
Finnis JM (2011) Natural law and natural rights, 2nd edn. The Clarendon Press, Oxford
Fuller LL (1969) The morality of law, 2nd edn. Yale University Press, New Haven
Gardner J (2012) Law as a leap of faith. Oxford University Press, Oxford
Greenberg M (2014) The moral impact theory of law. Yale Law J 123:1118–1625
Gur N (2013) Actions, attitudes, and the obligation to obey the law. J Polit Philos 25:326–346
Gur N (2018) Legal directives and practical reasons. Oxford University Press, Oxford
Hart HLA (1982) Essays on Bentham: jurisprudence and political theory. Oxford University Press, Oxford
Hurd HM (1991) Challenging authority. Yale Law J 100:1611–1677
Iosa J (2014) The structure of the conflict between authority and autonomy. Can J Law Jurisprud 27:415–438
Klosko G (2019) Why should we obey the law? Polity Press, Cambridge
Köpcke Tinturé M (2013) Finnis on legal and moral obligation. In: Keown J, George RP (eds) Reason, morality, and law. Oxford University Press, Oxford, pp 379–395
Ladenson R (1980) In defense of a Hobbesian conception of law. Philos Public Aff 9:134–159
Monti E (2022) Could legal obligations possibly be moral obligations? In: Bertea S (ed) Contemporary perspectives on legal obligation. Routledge, Abingdon, pp 133–152
Pavlakos G (2015) The relation between moral and legal obligation: an alternative Kantian reading. In: Pavlakos G, Rodriguez-Blanco V (eds) Reasons and intentions in law and practical agency. Cambridge University Press, Cambridge, pp 228–244
Perry SR (1989) Second-order reasons, uncertainty and legal theory. South Calif Law Rev 62:913–994
Raz J (1986) The morality of freedom. The Clarendon Press, Oxford
Raz J (1989) Facing up: a reply. South Calif Law Rev 62:1153–1235
Raz J (1990) Practical reason and norms, 2nd edn. Princeton University Press, Princeton
Raz J (1995) Ethics in the public domain: essays in the morality of law and politics. Revised paperback edn. The Clarendon Press, Oxford
Raz J (2006) The problem of authority: revisiting the service conception. Minn Law Rev 90:1003–1044

Raz J (2009) The authority of law: essays on law and morality, 2nd edn. Oxford University Press, Oxford
Regan DH (1990) Reasons, authority, and the meaning of 'obey': further thoughts on Raz and obedience to law. Can J Law Jurisprud 30:3–28
Reiman JH (1972) In defense of political philosophy. Harper & Row, New York
Sartorius R (1981) Political authority and political obligation. Virginia Law Rev 67:3–17
Schauer F (1991a) Playing by the rules: a philosophical examination of rule-based decision-making in law and in life. The Clarendon Press, Oxford
Schauer F (1991b) Rules and the rule of law. Harv J Law Public Policy 14:645–694
Sevel M (2018) Obeying the law. Leg Theory 24:191–215
Shapiro SJ (2002) Authority. In: Coleman JL, Shapiro SJ (eds) The Oxford handbook of jurisprudence and philosophy of law. Oxford University Press, Oxford, pp 382–439
Simmons JA (2001) Justification and legitimacy. Cambridge University Press, Cambridge
Smith MN (2013) Political obligation and the self. Philos Phenomenol Res 86:347–375
Wodak D (2018) What does 'legal obligation' mean? Pacif Philos Q 99:790–816
Wolff RP (1970) In defense of anarchism. Harper & Row, New York
Wolff RP (1973) The autonomy of reason: a commentary on Kant's Groundwork of the Metaphysics of Morals. Harper & Row, New York

GPSR Compliance
The European Union's (EU) General Product Safety Regulation (GPSR) is a set of rules that requires consumer products to be safe and our obligations to ensure this.

If you have any concerns about our products, you can contact us on

ProductSafety@springernature.com

In case Publisher is established outside the EU, the EU authorized representative is:

Springer Nature Customer Service Center GmbH
Europaplatz 3
69115 Heidelberg, Germany

www.ingramcontent.com/pod-product-compliance
Ingram Content Group UK Ltd.
Pitfield, Milton Keynes, MK11 3LW, UK
UKHW020821290926
15470UKWH00003B/1286
* 9 7 8 3 0 3 1 5 4 0 6 6 0 *